BRITAIN'S
AIRLINES

VOLUME ONE: 1946-1951

BRITAIN'S AIRLINES

VOLUME ONE: 1946-1951

GUY HALFORD-MacLEOD

TEMPUS

First published 2006

Tempus Publishing Limited
The Mill, Brimscombe Port,
Stroud, Gloucestershire, GL5 2QG
www.tempus-publishing.com

British Library Cataloguing in Publication Data.
A catalogue record for this book is available from the British Library.

ISBN 0 7524 3696 1

Typesetting and origination by Tempus Publishing Limited
Printed in Great Britain

CONTENTS

PREFACE

When Ron Davies inscribed my copy of his definitive work *A History of the World's Airlines*, he wrote after my name that I was the man 'who is currently expanding the historical record that is all-too-briefly summarised on page 316' – a fitting allusion to my much narrower field of interest. Nevertheless, *Britain's Airlines*, of which this is the first volume, goes beyond just recording the activities of Britain's independent airlines after the Second World War. At an early stage I realised I had to write about the state-owned airline corporations, and the book turned into a wider study of the consequences of nationalising the major British airlines, the challenges that the new air corporations faced, and the relationship that evolved between them, the privately owned airlines, and the government, which now had to reconcile its conflicting roles of industry regulator and airline owner.

It is appropriate to start by recording my thanks to Ron Davies, author, curator, mentor, for his continuing support and encouragement while I researched and wrote this book. He also drew the maps.

I want to pay tribute to those who have gone before: the late John Longhurst; Tony Merton Jones; John Stroud; Ron Cuskelly in Australia; and to the many other historians, biographers and recorders, especially those cited in the book. I have tried to contact all possible copyright holders; where I have failed, please accept my apologies in advance and contact me.

I could not have researched and written the book if I had not had access to the magnificent library of the National Air and Space Museum in Washington, DC, where I work as a volunteer, and I appreciate the help of Phil Edwards, who pointed me towards new sources of material and introduced me to the library of the Federal Aviation Administration. My thanks go to The National Archives at Kew for efficiently copying and posting to me innumerable files and documents; I acknowledge the rights of the Crown and the waiver of copyright.

The publishers of *Flight International* generously and unhesitatingly gave me permission to quote from the magazine and its predecessors. I would also like to thank Macmillan for permission to use the extract from Hammond Innes's *Air Bridge*, and Sunflower Press for permission to quote from Peter Brooks's *The Modern Airliner*.

Brian Pickering at MAP kindly allowed me to reproduce many of his photographs, and it is a pleasure to record my thanks to Richard Riding and the late Roger Jackson, both of whom supplied me with invaluable early photographs; Martin Senn helped prepare them for publication. Karl-Heinz Morawietz supplied the beautiful line drawings for the back cover design.

Finally, there are two very special people without whom this book would never have been written: Errol Cossey and my wife, Johanna.

ONE

WHAT IS PAST IS PROLOGUE
BRITISH AIRLINES BEFORE AND DURING THE SECOND WORLD WAR

NATIONALISATION

'Public ownership shall be the overruling principle in air transport.' This is how Lord Winster, Britain's Minister of Civil Aviation, described on 1 November 1945 the Labour Government's plans for the future development of civil aviation: overbearing would have been more apt. The Labour Party was the outright winner in the first post-war election, gaining a majority of 146 seats over all other parties by the time the votes had been counted on 26 July, and it could look forward to imposing its socialist framework on the country from a position of some parliamentary strength. That framework included, 'securing by suitable control or by an extension of public ownership that our industries and services shall make their maximum contribution to the national well-being'.[1] Nationalisation, sometimes referred to misleadingly as 'public ownership', means the acquisition by the state, or government, of assets that previously were privately owned; those assets can be land, mineral resources, manufacturing industries, industrial capacity or individual companies. Nationalisation has a secondary, related meaning, namely the take over of foreign-owned assets. Governments can also launch state-owned enterprises; the Post Office was of long standing, the British Broadcasting Corporation a more recent addition.

Fifty years later much of the industrial structure that the Labour Government then took into state ownership has in turn been de-nationalised, or privatised as the modern idiom has it. But in the early post-war years the British took for granted that a large proportion of their country's industry, around 20 per cent, was owned and operated by the state, even though up until the war most industrial development had been in the hands of private enterprise. The war had changed people's perceptions, and the Labour Party played to them in its manifesto entitled *Let us Face the Future*: 'The People deserve and must be assured a happier future than faced so many of them after the last war [First World War]'. That happiness was to be assured in part by state control and state ownership, in order that the excesses of private enterprise should be avoided. Lord Winster was quite clear in his mind as to what those excesses were. Civil aviation was going to be different, as he recalled in his speech, 'Railways the World over developed amid a wild frenzy of speculation which has handicapped them ever since', and 'Mercantile Marine services… built up amid a scramble for profits which inflicted inhuman misery and cruelty upon fine seamen who were treated like beasts'. There were other arguments that the socialists put forward in favour of state ownership. Some industrial companies, they claimed, would benefit from being consolidated into bigger, more efficient units and, being under state control, would be less likely to abuse their monopoly position. The government would be able to direct activities for the greater good, rather than mere profit. Wasteful competition, a concept much derided by government regulators, would be controlled, if not eliminated. Also, the government would be able to provide the necessary investment, an important consideration after the war had depleted the nation's resources and battered its transport infrastructure.[2]

The government had already taken over the London General Omnibus Co. and the Underground companies in 1933, creating the London Passenger Transport Board and, as we shall see, Britain's two international airlines were merged and nationalised just before the outbreak of war. Now the new government nationalised the Bank of England, the Cable and Wireless Co., the coal industry, the electricity and gas companies, the coal and steel industry, road hauliers and the four big railway companies, paying out over £2,500 million in compensation to the former owners, funded through Treasury-guaranteed stock. Of interest is the omission of British shipping from the list, despite Lord Winster's strictures. The government never felt able to tackle this particular sector, which lead to an anomaly in Britain's international communications; privately owned shipping continued in a relatively unrestricted regulatory environment, whilst the state-owned international airlines operated within a rigid structure and very much at the behest of government.

When it came to aviation, the government had to look hard to see what there was to take-over; the two main international airlines had already been nationalised and amalgamated to form the British Overseas Airways Corporation (BOAC), which had been responsible for all international services during the war. But domestic routes were still flown by privately owned companies, and it was these smaller companies that were to be rounded up and brought into the pen.

BOAC

BOAC had been created by a Conservative Government which bought out the shareholders of Imperial Airways and British Airways just before the war – doubtless with longer-term military and imperial objectives in mind, but also in response to growing unease over the status of Imperial Airways as a publicly quoted company that received government subsidy – and amalgamated the two airlines, under the chairmanship of Sir John Reith. Effectively merged at the outbreak of war, the corporation was formally created on 1 April 1940. BOAC had an unfortunate start to life: 1940 was not a good year to take over the operations of its two predecessors. Services to points within Europe diminished as more and more countries came under the domination of the Axis powers, and in order to avoid the risk of its long-haul operations being annihilated by enemy attack, bases were transferred overseas. The airline operated under government direction as a quasi-military transport service, with whatever aircraft were available and could be spared, and with little attention paid to costs. This latter tendency had started even before the war, and was to continue long after the war had ended. By contrast, Imperial Airways had been positively parsimonious, paying its staff meagre wages, eschewing lavish office accommodation, but regularly paying its shareholders a dividend. BOAC lost that hard cutting edge and increasingly assumed the role of prestige flag-carrier. One of Reith's first acts was to raise salaries; his reaction to his arrival at the Imperial Airways headquarters is amusingly recounted in his autobiography:[3]

I was brought to the door of an old furniture depository behind Victoria Station. It was Imperial Airways; a plate on the wall said so. Inside were some counters, luggage on the floor, a few people standing about – a booking office evidently. I enquired of a young man behind one of the counters where the head office was. He pointed to a dark and narrow staircase; up there, he said. The managing-director's office? Second floor, he thought. Having ascended thither I went along a passage, also dark and narrow, between wooden partitions, peering at the doors and wondering which to try first. Here it was – a bit of paper with 'managing-Director' written thereon. From Broadcasting House to this.

And the first decision demanded of me was an indication of what had happened to me otherwise. Would I approve the expenditure of £238 on passengers' lavatories at Croydon?

REITH

Lord Reith, as he became, had been the first managing director of the BBC and was then appointed chairman of Imperial Airways in June 1938, following the publication of Lord Cadman's Report. This report, which came out in February 1938, had been critical of the management of Imperial Airways as well as of the Air Ministry. Heads had to roll, and George Woods Humphery, managing director to Imperial Airways for many years, was duly sacrificed, criticised for having 'taken a commercial view of his responsibilities that was too narrow.' After some searching around, the government appointed Reith to be the full-time chairman, in line with the Cadman Report's recommendations that the chairman of the company should give his whole time to the direction of the business. Reith had strong views on state ownership and its responsibilities, and his influence may have been decisive in persuading the Conservatives in government to nationalise Imperial Airways and British Airways. In his view, nationalisation would offer a solution to the problems that had led to the inquiries of the Cadman Committee in the first place; the inquiry had been instigated in large part by a Member of Parliament[4] who had launched a wide-ranging attack on Imperial Airways, ranging from its treatment of pilots to its dominant position in British civil aviation. However, while Reith was able to neutralise the consequences of state ownership on the management of the BBC, his tenure at Imperial Airways, and subsequently BOAC, was so short that he was not able to leave his mark on the new corporation. 'The chief characteristic of the public corporation system is that it is established and owned by the State but not – repeat not – managed by the State', Reith later said in the House of Lords.[5] A laudable view and, had he stayed longer at BOAC, its subsequent post-war history would surely have been different. Instead, the nationalisation of the two airlines, Imperial Airways and British Airways, set a precedent for government interference that was to become pervasive during and after the war.

IMPERIAL AIRWAYS AND BRITISH AIRWAYS

Imperial Airways, the 'chosen instrument', had enjoyed a monopoly of government routes and subsidies from 1924 to 1936. A virile airline in those early days, the main thrust of its development from 1928 had been the Imperial routes to Africa, India, the Far East and on to Australia. Some European services were operated, notably the luxury service between London and Paris, but the tenor of its operations was, as its name implies, long-haul. The obligations of being the chosen instrument included a perceived commitment to buying British built aircraft, an understanding that remained with its successor airlines during the ensuing years. The company continued to receive a subsidy after 1936, but was joined by British Airways in the shared bounty. In 1937 Imperial inaugurated the Empire Air Mail Scheme, mainly using Short 'Empire' flying boats, which provided for the carriage by air of all first-class mail to the countries within the Commonwealth. Neither the government nor Imperial Airways could afford the investment in runways that would have allowed use of larger landplanes on the Imperial air routes. Flying boats, despite their economic penalties, were a cheaper alternative; but the Second World War expedited the building of new, stronger runways throughout the world, leading to the early obsolescence of the flying boat. By 1939 the airline was pioneering transatlantic services, also using flying boats, via Foynes in Ireland and Newfoundland, at that time still a British dependency.

British Airways was formed in 1935 as a result of the amalgamation of the various airlines owned by Lord Cowdray's aviation holding company, Whitehall Securities,[6] and took over their services on 1 January 1936. British Airways concentrated on European routes, flying mainly to destinations in northern Europe, although it also evaluated a possible service to South America via Lisbon. Unlike Imperial Airways, British Airways was not bound to operate British built aircraft, and had re-equipped with modern Lockheed 10s and 14s – twin engine, all-metal monoplanes with a greater turn of speed than Imperial Airways' stately biplane transports. Chamberlain,

Short C Class Empire flying boat G-ADVD *Challenger* at Habbaniya in Iraq, about 25 miles west of Baghdad, an important British air base. (MAP)

Two of British Airways' Lockheed 10s share the Croydon apron with a KLM Douglas DC-2 and a Short Scylla of Imperial Airways, clearly showing why British Airways had to buy American aircraft to remain competitive. (Flight International)

the British Prime Minister, flew to Germany for his meetings with Hitler in 1938 on chartered British Airways Lockheeds; it was considered a blow to British prestige that he should have had to use American built machines for his travels, an attitude that continued to colour British aviation policy for many years after the war.

THE RAILWAYS AND AIR TRANSPORT

The first British railway company to engage in air transport was, perhaps not surprisingly, the Great Western Railway (GWR), always an innovator. GWR officially inaugurated the Cardiff–Plymouth service on 11 April 1933, when Captain Gordon Olley flew a chocolate-and-cream-painted Westland Wessex, chartered from Imperial Airways, over the route; the four-passenger interior was decorated in the style of a first-class railway compartment. The service ceased on 30 September 1933, but the experiment led to the formation of Railway Air Services (RAS) in 1934, in which all the four mainline railway companies participated, along with Imperial Airways. RAS developed a number of trunk-line services from London, to Manchester, Glasgow and Belfast. These were suspended during the war, but the company later resumed their operation and continued to work them until they were nationalised in 1947.

Aside from RAS, the railway companies had financial interests in a significant number of other domestic airlines, and even though at first they did not control them outright, their influence was pervasive; they participated in Great Western & Southern Airlines, Isle of Man Air Services, Channel Islands Airways (parent company of Jersey Airways and Guernsey Airways), and Blackpool-based West Coast Air Services, and Scottish Airways. They were also shareholders in Imperial Airways, and continued to use Imperial crews even after they had acquired their own aircraft.

Although they invested in modern equipment and brought a certain order to the industry, the railway companies' influence on British domestic air transport was not altogether benign: 'The railways were far more interested in acquiring a controlling interest in the airline companies to restrict competition than they were in promoting an orderly expansion of the industry'.[7] Professor Aldcroft's opinion is borne out by the treatment handed out to those few independent airlines that fell outside the embrace of the railway owners and were thus perceived as offering competition; they were subjected to a booking boycott by travel agents for most of the decade. Travel agencies depended on the railways for the bulk of their business, and were easily intimidated by them. Imperial Airways and foreign airlines escaped the boycott but it affected British Airways at the very start of its existence. Matters eased, however, when its chairman, the Hon. Clive Pearson, joined the Board of the Southern Railway. The boycott was not in itself fatal to other domestic airlines, but it made life harder and showed a certain ruthlessness which can be exercised all too easily by large incumbent companies against new upstart competitors. After strong complaints in the House of Commons, the boycott was finally lifted in 1938.

INDEPENDENT AIRLINES

Some airlines managed to stay outside the railway companies' net. By 1939, there remained five independent operators of scheduled services. These were: Lundy & Atlantic Coast Air Lines, flying between Barnstaple and Lundy Island in the Bristol Channel; Portsmouth, Southsea & Isle of Wight Aviation (PSIOWA), operating an intensive shuttle service between Portsmouth and Ryde on the Isle of Wight; Western Airways, operating a similar intensive air shuttle across the Severn between Weston-super-Mare and Cardiff, as well as other services in the West Country; Allied Airways (Gandar Dower), reflecting the name and personality of its doughty owner, Eric Gandar Dower, and flying out of Aberdeen to the northern Scottish isles and North Eastern Airways, which suffered more than most from the booking boycott in its attempt to develop a network of services between Croydon, the North East and Scotland. The first three airlines were niche carriers, with a limited route structure, specialising in high-frequency services that involved a short water crossing, and offering considerable time savings over conventional surface transport. Moreover, they did not offer much obvious competition to the railway companies; indeed RAS even co-operated with Western and PSIOWA over timetable co-ordination. Allied Airways (Gandar Dower) was a pioneer of air services in Scotland, and in so doing competed with the railway companies' Scottish Airways. North Eastern Airways tried to develop trunk services.

THE DIFFERENCES BETWEEN SCHEDULED AND CHARTER AIRLINES

Just as independent were the charter airlines, a number of which had started operations before the war. First, some definitions are needed which are as valid now as they were then. The airlines that have been discussed so far were all operators of scheduled services, some international, others domestic (also called internal). On these flights a would-be traveller can book a ticket to fly on a particular service, either directly with the airline or through a travel agent. The airline runs the service according to a published timetable, or schedule, and flies the service regardless of load. The airline takes the risk on whether the service will operate with enough passengers on it to make a profit, and calculates the fare to be charged accordingly. The scheduled service is in response to demand for a continuously available service; the passenger expects the service to be available to suit his or her travel needs, and to be able to buy a ticket even at relatively short notice. But not all potential passengers will require this level of accessibility, for example those with more narrowly defined travel goals such as an annual holiday or a long-planned visit to relatives overseas, in which case they may prefer to trade it for lower fares.

Charter airlines operate on a different economic basis, and in response to these different demand criteria.[8] The whole capacity of the aircraft is chartered for a specific journey or series of journeys by a third party, which can be an individual, a commercial organisation, a club, a freight forwarder, a government body or a travel agency. The charterer pays the airline to operate the flight, but chooses where the flight is to go, and when. The charterer is also responsible for deciding the load, be it passengers or freight, or even a combination of both. The charterer may choose to retail the seats to the public, perhaps as part of a package that includes holiday hotel accommodation or entry to a sporting event in connection with the flight, for example an away football match or motor race. The charterer may retain the seats on the flight for his or her own use, as in a company taking its employees on a trip for business purposes. Likewise with freight: the charterer may sell on the freight space to another freight forwarder, or retain the entire aircraft for his specific use, for example a motor manufacturer supplying its assembly lines. The charterer takes the risk on loading the flight, and any profit will come from the difference between the charter price that will be charged by the airline and the revenue that the charterer will derive from selling on the seats or cargo space. In the case of an own-use charter, the charterer will benefit from the economics of a bulk purchase; the profit derives from the difference between buying all the space at a discount and the equivalent price in scheduled service fares.

Charter operations need not be the exclusive preserve of charter airlines. Regular scheduled airlines can derive extra income from charter services, and their aircraft utilisation will benefit if those extra services can be flown outside the normal scheduled pattern of operations, for example at weekends or at night. Imperial Airways promoted charter flying vigorously, operating on behalf of oil companies in the Middle East, and even carrying the first inclusive tour passengers by air in the 1930s.

CHARTER AIRLINES

But most charter airlines were more modest affairs. The aircraft they used were relatively small, so that charter operations more closely resembled air taxi flights, with aircraft chartered by individuals in much the same way that taxis, rather than buses, are hired for personal transport; the de Havilland (DH) Rapide seated six to eight passengers, and single-engine aircraft were even smaller. Business opportunities varied, from carrying businessmen and wealthy passengers in a hurry to flying newsreel around the country. The press was an early user of aircraft, not just to obtain more spectacular aerial shots but also to speed the news to the breakfast table. Flying had moved on from its early barnstorming days but for most people flying was still a novelty; many charter companies offered joyrides at holiday resorts, or more sophisticated pleasure flights such as sightseeing trips or day-trips, and some of these developed into regular operations to France and Belgium. But as the 1930s progressed, more and more flying was for the military; much of the army co-operation flying was at night, training searchlight operators.

Some charter flights had far-reaching results. Chamberlain's flights to Germany have already been noted and, on 18 July 1936, Captain Bebb, a pilot with Olley Air

Olley Air Service's famous de Havilland Rapide G-ACYR, used by General Franco in 1936 and now preserved at Madrid's Museo del Aire.

Service, flew General Franco from Las Palmas in the Canaries to Tetuan in Spanish Morocco. There, General Franco raised the Spanish Army against the Republican Government in Spain, leading to the Spanish Civil War.[9] *The Aeroplane* magazine noted laconically, 'Mr Bebb of Olley Air Service made a good trip to Las Palmas last week in a Dragon Rapide carrying three passengers, a W/T operator and an engineer'. Not all such flights were operated as smoothly; Air Taxis obviously had some problems, as the following account shows:

> International flying presents other obstacles to these charter concerns. The other day Mr Crundall, of Air Taxis Ltd, had to go at short notice to Spain. The delay in getting permission to fly over the country caused him to put down his passenger at Biarritz, to continue thence angrily by train.[10]

The Aeroplane listed twenty-seven charter companies in operation in 1935, not including many of the small flying clubs which also chartered out light aircraft. Their names reflect their business: Air Commerce, Air Dispatch, Air Services, Air Taxis, British Air Transport, Olley Air Service, Personal Airways, Surrey Flying Services and Wrightways, all based at Croydon in Surrey, and Air Hire, Airwork, Birkett Air Service, British-American Air

Services and Warden Aviation (R.O. Shuttleworth), all of which flew from Heston in Middlesex. Most charter companies operated in or around London – there were sixty aircraft based at Croydon by 1938 – but a number were also to be found elsewhere in the country, for example at Cardiff and in Yorkshire. A note of caution: the dividing line between scheduled and charter services can be very fine sometimes, even nowadays. Some of the operations listed below resemble scheduled services in their regularity of operation, although in the case of freight services, most of the capacity would have been chartered by a third party:

Air Dispatch
Air Dispatch was formed 9 July 1934 by the Hon. Mrs Victor Bruce, a rather splendid lady much given to breaking endurance records in the air and on land. She subsequently took over Commercial Air Hire, an operator of early-morning newspaper charter flights to Paris. These were like scheduled services, as were the passenger flights she inaugurated linking Croydon and Heston, and later Gatwick, under the 'Inner Circle Air Lines' name. She later operated a large fleet of de Havilland Dragons, Rapides and Dragonflies for army co-operation night-flying and other charter work.

Airwork
Established in 1928 by Nigel Norman and Alan Muntz, Airwork built, developed and operated Heston Airport in north London. Heston rapidly became the social flying centre of the 1930s; Airwork maintained and overhauled aircraft, both its own and for private owners, and ran the flying school there. In 1929 the company became associated, through Lord Cowdray, with Whitehall Securities, already noted as a significant backer of aviation enterprises in Britain. Although Airwork did perform some limited charter flying, this aspect of the business was not developed until after the war. Instead, Airwork participated in a number of overseas ventures: Misr-Airwork in Egypt, a joint venture with the Banque Misr which later became the national Egyptian airline Misrair; and Indian National Airways. In the late 1930s Airwork began operating air services out of Abadan for Anglo–Iranian Oil, and early in the war took over the operation of Iraq Petroleum's aircraft fleet, which had previously been operated for the oil company by Imperial Airways. In 1938 Heston was sold to the government, but the company took hangar space at Gatwick and became a major aircraft service and repair centre during the war.

Birkett Air Service
Formed during October 1932 by Flight Lieutenant Birkett, Birkett Air Service was based at Heston and specialised in flying for the press and newsreel companies, but also undertook other work such as private charters for race meetings.

Cambrian Air Services
First registered on 25 April 1935, Cambrian Air Services started operations with DH Gipsy Moth G–ABOA[11] from Pengam Moors at Cardiff. Most of its activities consisted

Executive flying in the late 1930s from London's fashionable Heston Airport. Passengers board Birkett Air Service's de Havilland Dragonfly G-AEDV, assisted by a smart commissionaire. (MAP)

of private and military charters, especially army co-operation flying. The airline did not have a full-time pilot, relying on freelance pilots, usually instructors from the Cardiff Aeroplane Club. During the war the company made parts for parachutes.

International Air Freight

International Air Freight inaugurated twice-daily freight services between Croydon and Amsterdam in 1937, using a small fleet of red-painted Curtiss Wright Condors with around 3 tons of capacity. They carried mixed cargoes, mostly flowers inbound from Amsterdam; some mail and parcel post was also carried. Services to Brussels were added later, but the airline ceased operations at the end of 1938.

Olley Air Service

Founded in January 1934 at Croydon by Captain Gordon Olley, an Imperial Airways pilot with a great deal of charter flying experience, Olley quickly established itself as a major charter operator. Its first charter was a two-month trip to Central Africa flown by a DH Dragon with extra fuel tanks. Air Commerce, another charter operator based at Heston, was bought out by Olley's parent company, British & Foreign Aviation. Olley also operated some scheduled services in his own right, and took over Cobham Air Routes which had flown between Croydon, Bournemouth and Guernsey. Another of Olley's airlines, Channel Air Ferries, flew the first services between Penzance and the Scillies in 1937, at first using the golfcourse at St Mary's. Golfers soon learned to flatten themselves when an aircraft came into land; a local rule allowed golfers to lift a ball if it had been run over by an

Surrey Flying Services' Avro 504K G-EBDP. Over 300 of these famous wooden trainers were converted at the end of the First World War to carry two passengers, and proved popular for joyriding. (MAP)

aircraft. Olley also participated in a number of other scheduled service airlines with the railway companies: Blackpool & West Coast Air Services (later just West Coast Air services), Isle of Man Air Services and Great Western & Southern Air Lines. By 1939 Olley's companies owned thirty-eight aircraft and were confidently ordering the new all-metal DH 95 Flamingo.

Surrey Flying Services
Formed in 1920, Surrey Flying Services specialised in pleasure flying from Croydon, using developed versions of the Avro 504 K, and also operated a training school. It must surely lay claim to being one of the first, if not *the* first, charter operator. By the end of the 1930s the company had acquired a DH Dragon as well as a small fleet of single-engine types. Operations were suspended during the war.

Wrightways
Originally Wrightson and Pearce, it began flying newspapers to Paris with DH Dragons on 14 May 1934. It was reformed as Wrightways in 1935 and expanded the operation, buying four-engine DH 86 Expressliners which could carry up to 1,700lb of newspapers, and earned a formidable reputation for getting the papers through, whatever the weather. As was the case with Air Dispatch, these flights resembled a scheduled service; passengers could book seats, provided they did not mind rising early (the first departure from Croydon was at 05.25). In 1936 the company launched air tours to the chateâu country in France, offering eight-day trips at £27 10s, inclusive of air fare, accommodation, meals and transfers.

AIR TRANSPORT LICENSING AUTHORITY

In 1938, following recommendations from the Maybury Committee, yet another committee set up to investigate the state of civil aviation in the United Kingdom, the government introduced a system of route licensing, and agreed to pay subsidies for certain internal services. Airlines now had to apply to the Air Transport Licensing Authority (ATLA) for licences to operate scheduled services on specific routes within the United Kingdom, and to the Channel Islands and the Isle of Man; international services were still exempt, as were charter flights, with the exception of special flights for race meetings (*The Aeroplane* was against this: 'Licensing private charter aeroplanes strikes us as a distinct interference with the liberty of the subject. If we want to fly to Doncaster and do not like Mr Olley (actually we like and admire him immensely) why should we be barred from hiring from our other friend Mr Jimmy Edmunds?'). The Maybury Committee set the tone for much of the subsequent argument over competition between airlines:

> Air Transport will hardly pay while wasteful competition continues and frequency, regularity and convenience remain lacking. If the conditions of time-saving, convenience and punctuality are met, success seems not only possible but probable. A pre-requisite is that cut-throat competition must be eliminated. The Committee recommends a provisional regulation of selected routes.

Provisional route licences from 1 November 1938 were issued to the incumbent airlines, and hearings for contested routes were held in late 1938 and early 1939. The chairman of the ATLA was Malcolm Trustram Eve, KC, who was assisted by a small panel. Full licences were finally awarded in July 1939, only to be suspended in September at the outbreak of war. Around £70,000 was paid out in subsidies in the first year. In all, forty-seven licences were granted to fourteen operators:[12] Allied Airways (Gandar Dower), British-American Air Services (Heston to race meetings), Great Western & Southern Air Lines, Guernsey Airways, Isle of Man Air Services, Jersey Airways, Lundy & Atlantic Coast Air Lines, North Eastern Airways, Olley Air Service (London to race meetings), Portsmouth Southsea & Isle of Wight Aviation, Railway Air Services, Scottish Airways, Western Airways and Western Isles Airways. There was unhappiness over some of the route awards, especially in Scotland, but the move to establish the ATLA was, in retrospect, far-sighted. The underlying principle, that an applicant should present a case for a route licence which was decided by an impartial panel, was sound; it gave new airlines a chance to enter the market, but afforded some security of tenure for established airlines. The experiment was short-lived, cut short by the war, otherwise doubtless the system would have been refined, to allow for decisions to be challenged on appeal, and so that licences could be varied. Not until 1960 was a similar licensing authority reintroduced without, however, the benefit of a distinguished lawyer as its chairman. During the intervening post-war years the state-owned airline held a monopoly of all the major and most minor domestic air routes, but it hardly made them pay, even though wasteful competition was eliminated.

AIR SERVICES DURING THE SECOND WORLD WAR:
THE INDEPENDENTS

At midnight on 1 September 1939, just before the outbreak of war, the whole of the eastern half of England became a prohibited area for flying, as did other large areas of England and Scotland. There was a total ban on private and charter flying. Internal scheduled services were withdrawn immediately, although after a brief interval most of the cross-water services were resumed; the Weston-super-Mare to Cardiff services subsequently ceased on 30 March 1940, and services to the Channel Islands stopped just prior to their occupation by German forces in June 1940. For the first year of the war government air communication services were provided under the auspices of the 'National Air Communications Scheme', through which seventeen airlines, both scheduled and charter, voluntarily put their entire aircraft fleets at the disposal of the Air Ministry and operated at its direction and cost. But in practice the aircraft were under-utilised, and the government felt it was paying too much for the privilege of keeping all the airlines in business.

So, from 26 June 1940 the process was changed. The government had already revoked the short-lived air licensing system as an emergency measure, without telling anyone about it until a month after it had gone through. The government record offers a feeble excuse: 'It became not only inconvenient but also embarrassing that the licensing system should continue in war'.[13] The next step was to purchase compulsorily all remaining aircraft from the privately owned airlines, for further use by the Royal Air Force (RAF). Many companies – those with which the railways had no involvement, like Air Dispatch, Air Taxis, Birkett Air Service, North Eastern Airways, Personal Airways and Wrightways – ceased flying. For some of them that was to be the end of their airline operations, although most continued to provide invaluable assistance to the war effort by maintaining and repairing military aircraft as Civilian Repair Organisations, as did airlines like PSIOWA which had stopped flying on the outbreak of war. The railway companies fared better; they retained their aircraft fleets and were allowed to operate the remaining internal services under the auspices of the newly created Associated Airways Joint Committee (AAJC),[14] based at Liverpool. There was one exception; Allied Airways (Gandar Dower) had no railway involvement and still continued to operate services from Aberdeen to the northern Scottish isles. The government agreed to pay these airlines a fixed annual sum, with an additional payment related to mileage flown and capacity provided. Services were provided to the Scottish islands, Belfast, Dublin and between Land's End and the Scillies, using a fleet of four DH 86s, fourteen DH Rapides and two DH Dragons; flights from Croydon resumed in 1944. On 3 June 1941, one of Olley's Dragons was lost operating the Land's End–Scillies service, presumed shot down by a German raider known to be in the area at that time. There were some ownership changes. In 1942 the railway companies bought out Olley's parent company, British & Foreign Aviation, giving them control of West Coast Air Services, Isle of Man Air Services, Great Western & Southern Air Lines, Olley Air Service and Air Commerce; the last named organisation, a charter carrier now based at Liverpool, supplied its aircraft to the other airlines and carried out maintenance and overhaul work for the group. Then in 1943 Whitehall Securities sold its 50 per cent shareholding in Channel Islands Airways to the Great Western Railway and Southern Railway, giving the railway companies full control of the holding company for Jersey and Guernsey Airways. Apart from some residual shipping interests – and Allied Airways (Gandar Dower) – the railway companies now owned all the airlines operating internal services. Although convenient in terms of administration, having the railway companies in charge of internal air services during the war was not popular with some passengers:

> There will be no inducement [to travel] on the internal routes if they are left to the railways. Those who don't travel by the railways' air services will have to travel by the railways anyway, so what is lost on the swings will be gained on the roundabouts.
>
> The excuse 'There's a war on' has, of necessity sometimes, covered a multitude of sins. That excuse still holds good to a certain extent. But it should not have justified some of the comments heard recently about air travel within the United Kingdom. The DH 86s and Rapides of Railway Air Services are old, but there seems no reason why they should be unheated. Rugs are provided, but the report of one traveller who flew from Croydon to Belfast during an unexpected cold spell was not good hearing. All the passengers save one were sick – it was not only cold but bumpy – and all nearly succumbed from being chilled through. Fortunately Speke [Liverpool's airport] was reached in time. But at Speke passengers for Belfast have to alight for security and censorship formalities. For this they are given only 15 minutes. There was a buffet of sorts, but passengers were told they would have to hurry. When they reached the buffet – which seemed to be in the most inaccessible part of the aerodrome buildings – they had to wait while what appeared to be regular inhabitants of the aerodrome were served first. There have been passengers who have never found out that there is a buffet. The London office of RAS is small, shabby and uninviting. London railway stations have never been known for their inviting qualities, but is their dinginess to be accepted for the airline offices?[15]

AIR SERVICES DURING THE SECOND WORLD WAR: THE CORPORATION

Imperial Airways and British Airways were already operating as one unit prior to their full merger on 1 April 1940 to form BOAC. Foreign airlines continued to operate into the United Kingdom, until one by one their respective countries came under German domination. After the fall of France in June 1940 BOAC began running the main Imperial route to Australia from South Africa, the so-called 'Horseshoe' route which operated from Durban via Cairo to Sydney. In 1941 BOAC started operation of the Return Ferry Service between Prestwick in Scotland and Montreal (Dorval) in Canada, using converted Liberator bombers to carry aircrew to North America, who then ferried Lend-Lease aircraft to the UK. Flying-boat services to Newfoundland and on to the United States were operated from Foynes in Ireland. BOAC also maintained regular links between England and the Mediterranean, Africa and the Middle East. BOAC based its aircraft overseas, in Cairo, Montreal, Durban and Baltimore; flights into England were turned round quickly and sent on their way again, to avoid the possibility of loss through enemy attack. Due recognition should be given to the role that BOAC played during the war, which included help given during the evacuation of Crete, the transport of supplies to the armies in the Western Desert and North African campaigns, services to and from Malta at the height of the siege, and the Swedish 'ball bearings' flights.

Given the difficult circumstances surrounding the birth of BOAC, it is not surprising that its development during the war years was chequered. In the early stages of the war when the defence of the nation was so critical, the government was simply not interested in the development of civil aviation – nor in civil aircraft manufacturing, for that matter. There were frequent changes at the top, reorganisations, and an absence of financial controls. Lord Reith left the corporation almost immediately to join the War Cabinet as Minister of Information, and was succeeded by the Hon. Clive Pearson as chairman and the Hon. Leslie (later Lord) Runciman as director-general. Then in March 1943 BOAC was informed by the government of the decision to establish the Transport Command of the RAF. BOAC feared it would become subservient to the new organisation at a time when its board was beginning to plan for the post-war years; these fears were not without some justification, for civil aviation still came under the auspices of the Air Ministry, which also controlled the RAF. The chairman, the director-general and two other board members resigned; only Gerard d'Erlanger, inherited from the board of British Airways, stayed on. The government eventually appointed a new board under the chairmanship of Lord Knollys, formerly Governor of Bermuda, with Brigadier General Critchley as director-general. The latter appointment was seen by many as a mistake: 'There followed a reorganisation chiefly notable for the fact that, in almost every top position in the Corporation's main departments, men from outside the business, most of them picked by [General] Critchley, were brought in and put in authority.'[16] Who were these people? Longhurst quotes from a letter written in 1944 by a senior member of staff: 'Today we are bitter and bewildered. We watch with amazement and envy, the steady flow into BOAC of Marquesses, Group-Captains and Wing Commanders and first-class golfers, commencing in the highest grades and at salaries that we, after 15 years of hard work, mainly overseas, still dream about. We find ourselves unwanted, often unknown to our new masters, and our wide and varied experience apparently rated as of little or no value.'[17]

In any event, after a short two and a half years General Critchley was also out, unable to cope with the impending nationalisation of British civil aviation, although he reappears later in the story.

POST-WAR PLANS (1)

There was a certain amount of hopeful speculation as to what should happen once the war was over. Recognising BOAC's earlier fears, the government gave air transport its own Ministry and appointed Lord Swinton to be the first Minister of Civil Aviation, in October 1944. In a lecture given to the Royal Aeronautical Society on 25 September 1946, Sir Henry Self, the Permanent Secretary at the new Ministry, explained the government's reasons for establishing what was to prove a short-lived Ministry:

> Military and civil aviation were jointly controlled by the Air Ministry, following the establishment of that department in 1918, but there had always been continuous pressure from many quarters for the separation of the two. During the War the Air Ministry was perforce preoccupied with the military side of its duties. Yet, as the War progressed it became increasingly clear that civil aviation would occupy a place in world affairs of far greater importance than that which it had occupied at the outbreak of war. Similarly, although civil aviation in Britain had become submerged beneath military pressure, it was abundantly evident that, if Britain was to take her rightful place in the air transport world after the War, much careful planning and preparation would be necessary. This planning work could not be faithfully overtaken by an already over-burdened Secretary of State for Air.
>
> The government decided, therefore, in October 1944, to appoint a Minister of Civil Aviation, of Cabinet rank, who would 'devote his whole time to carrying forward the work of planning in the field of civil aviation, particularly in its international and imperial aspects'. The Minister would be responsible for formulating the whole policy, both short and long term, of civil aviation at home and overseas and of ensuring that that policy was carried into effect. It was decided, also, that while responsibility for the design and production of civil aircraft, equally with that for military aircraft, would remain with the Minister of Aircraft Production, the Minister of Civil Aviation would have direct access to him on equal terms with the Secretary of State for Air and the First Lord of the Admiralty, in order to ensure a fair share of available resources for civil aviation.[18]

There was concern that BOAC would take over all air services; interested parties began to publish blueprints for the future. Over seventy shipping lines changed their Articles of Association to give themselves the necessary powers to establish air services; five of them combined to form British-Latin American Air Lines (BLAIR).[19] Sir Alan Cobham, a noted record-breaker and entrepreneur in pre-war times, warned against the evils of government monopoly:

> We owe a great debt to the initiative of individuals who have gone ahead on their own account without the direction of a government organisation. We are a nation of individualists; that is our greatest trade asset. Against government monopoly the citizen is virtually powerless. We do not want British Air Transport to be under bureaucratic control. We want it placed in the care of men with determination, initiative and the spirit of adventure.[20]

Many of the pre-war airlines that had survived were also anxious to prepare for a resumption of peace-time operations. Scottish Airways put forward proposals for a fourteen- to sixteen-seat four-engine monoplane with good airfield performance, recognising that war-surplus Douglas DC-3 Dakotas would be too large for most of the island routes. Channel Islands Airways ordered the thirty-four-seat Bristol

Wayfarer to add much needed capacity to its fleet of Rapides, as it correctly foresaw a boom in travel to the Channel Islands. Another airline interested in the Wayfarer was PSIOWA, which at the beginning of March 1945 formed Isle of Wight Airways in partnership with the Southern Railway to resume the pre-war ferry services from the Isle of Wight to the mainland.

POST-WAR PLANS (2): THE RAILWAY COMPANIES

By the end of the war the British railway companies either owned outright, or had controlling interests in, sixteen air companies, three of which were holding companies.[21] In October 1944 the railways announced their own plans for post-war air services; not just domestic services but international services to Europe were envisaged. Although they expected to use British built equipment when it became available, services would start with Dakota aircraft. There would be no need for subsidies, and partnerships would be offered to cross-Channel shipping companies. Services would range as far as Istanbul, Moscow, Athens and Lisbon, but would also include such short sectors as the Orkney inter-island and the Land's End to Scillies routes.

POST-WAR PLANS (3): THE GOVERNMENT

Lord Swinton announced his own plans for the future development of civil aviation in a White Paper on 13 March 1945. Rather than have one single 'chosen instrument', he proposed three air transport corporations, each with exclusive rights within their different areas of responsibility. The first would operate the Commonwealth air routes, transatlantic services, and services to China and the Far East. This corporation would be built around BOAC, in association with British shipping lines.

The second corporation would cover European air routes and the internal services of the United Kingdom. Here the railway companies would dominate, but just about anybody with an interest in transport would also be allowed to participate, including BOAC, the short sea-shipping lines, cross-Channel ferry companies, travel agencies and even those British airline operators which had remained outside the railway net. Profitable routes would cross-subsidise those routes which ran at a loss.

The third corporation would develop the South American route. The subject of some preliminary route-proving by British Airways before the war, the South American route was at last to be exploited by a dedicated company, BLAIR, backed by the shipping lines, but even here there was to be some BOAC involvement. Britain had extensive business and trading interests in South America, but the development of its air services had always been secondary to the Imperial routes.

Lord Swinton did not favour a single corporation holding a monopoly, arguing that it would be too large and far-flung to fulfil the requirement of individual supervision of all the routes: 'Moreover, while it is clearly desirable to eliminate wasteful competition between British operators on the same route, it is none the less desirable both to avoid a sealed pattern of management and operation and to encourage different managements to try out their own ideas.'[22] Competition is still seen as wasteful; worse, it prevented cross-subsidisation. The government fully expected revenues from the more profitable services to support unremunerative services as part of the 'general transport system'. All this – 'at once recognised as the most peculiar hotchpotch of public and private control and finance'[23] – was to be done on the cheap. The government, in buying out existing operators, did not intend to make any allowance for goodwill or development expense, as these same operators would be able to participate financially in the new corporations, and so paying for goodwill would merely inflate the value that they paid themselves. The minister would appoint the board of BOAC and would also approve the appointments to the other two boards. He could also tell any of the companies to operate new routes if necessary. Finally, it was the intention of the government that all the corporations would use British aircraft. The White Paper was subsequently modified to allow for Scottish enterprises to operate from Scotland to Scandinavia, rather than BOAC; in addition, a licensing tribunal would be given powers to allocate routes that had not already been assigned.

POST-WAR PLANS (4): THE AIRCRAFT MANUFACTURERS

Churchill had said after the First World War that civil aviation must fly by itself, but this time round he concluded that some effort should be made to ensure that civil aviation had at least the wherewithal to fly. The British had lost the great lead they had in aircraft production after the First World War; the government hoped to learn from that experience and not squander the production and design expertise which had grown and flourished during this war. It says much for Churchill's buoyancy and spirit that as early as 1942 he could take active steps to promote post-war industrial development; he established a War Cabinet Committee on Post-War Civil Air Transport, chaired by Lord Beaverbrook, to encourage development of British and Imperial air services after the war. An important element would be the manufacture of airliners that would lessen, and hopefully eliminate, dependence on American transport aircraft. The Air Minister, Sir Archibald Sinclair, and the Minister for Aircraft Production, Colonel Llewellin, were asked to make recommendations for future civil aircraft designs. Llewellin in turn asked his predecessor, Lord Brabazon, to set up a committee to study and report back to the Cabinet. Lord Brabazon's committee comprised members from the Air Ministry and the Ministry of Aircraft Production, but nobody from BOAC was invited. After forty-eight days of investigationthe committee made its first recommendations to the Cabinet on

9 February 1943. These were divided into two phases. First, they recommended as an interim measure the adaptation of certain military designs for civil use. These included the Avro York, the Short Sunderland and Shetland, and the Handley Page Halifax. For the next phase the committee proposed five categories of totally new aircraft designs:

Type 1 Multi-engine landplane for North American routes
Type 2 Medium-size twin-engine DC-3 replacement for European routes
Type 3 Four-engine landplane for Empire routes
Type 4 Jet-propelled mailplane for the North Atlantic
Type 5 Fourteen-seat landplane for UK and colonial feeder services

Churchill and the Cabinet agreed these aims and asked for more detailed recommendations, leading to the establishment of the second Brabazon Committee which had a wider membership, this time including BOAC and the aircraft manufacturers. The committee met on a regular basis between November 1943 and January 1945, modifying the proposals as necessary, drawing up more detailed specifications and selecting leading British aircraft design teams; it also took into account international developments such as the Commonwealth Conference of 1943, which was similarly planning for post-war requirements. The committee's work is considered in more detail in Chapter Five.

POST-WAR PLANS (5): BRITAIN, USA, AND THE REST OF THE WORLD

The government found itself at odds with its ally, the United States, when it came to planning for peacetime air travel. The United States was in a strong position, having developed a range of larger, faster landplanes which could fly further, most importantly across the Atlantic; it wanted its airlines to use these aircraft to develop international services, without too many restrictions. 'Open Skies' had not been coined, but 'liberalization' and 'internationalization' were used instead, and with much the same subtext: the skies should be open for US carriers to develop their international air routes, allowing the Americans to benefit from their advantages in equipment and a huge home market. The British did not have the superior equipment, of course – they still relied on flying boats for many of their long-haul services – but together with the members of the Commonwealth they controlled access to large areas of the globe, and were quite determined not to be squeezed out of these markets by the dominant American carriers. The British favoured an international organisation that would control routes, capacity and fares. These opposing policies were laid out at the Chicago Conference of 1944. The British wanted everything to be put on hold until they were ready, but were alternately threatened by the Americans and coaxed by the dominions into making a limited number of concessions so that a framework for international air services could be agreed. The Chicago Convention established the

International Civil Aviation Organisation, at that time only provisional, but later under the auspices of the United Nations, and confirmed the first and second Freedoms of the Air, the right to overfly and transit. But in the matter of traffic rights, that is the right to pick up and set down passengers and cargo, there was no multilateral accord; instead, states would have to continue to agree air services bilaterally. Britain and the US would be among the first to negotiate such an agreement, as recounted in the next chapter.

AFTER THE WAR

Following the end of the Second World War on 8 May 1945, restrictions on private flying continued, but immediate steps were taken to reopen air services to those countries and islands which had been occupied. Jersey & Guernsey Airways[24] operated their first flight to the Channel Islands on 26 May, using a Rapide hired from Railway Air Services, and resumed regular services from 21 June. Domestic services were initially restricted to British built aircraft, because Dakotas supplied under Lend-Lease could not be used on internal routes, so Railway Air Services introduced seven-seater Avro 19s to supplement the ubiquitous Rapide. BOAC was still widely dispersed around the globe, and the job of opening up air communications with Europe was given to No.110 Wing, 46 Group, RAF Transport Command, operating out of Croydon. By September 1945 the wing was flying up to twenty-five daily services to points in France, the Benelux, Scandinavia, Germany, Italy and the Channel Islands,

Seen here in war-time camouflage, Railway Air Services' de Havilland Rapide G-AGLP was the first civilian aircraft to land in the Channel Islands after liberation. (Richard T. Riding)

with further weekly services to Prague and Athens; preference was given to military passengers, freight and mail, but civilian passengers with the right level of priority could also travel.

Channel Islands Airways, Railway Air Services and No. 110 Wing, all would soon just be part of history, as Lord Winster stood up in the House of Lords on that November evening and announced his plans for the future.

Avro 19 G–AGUE of Railway Air Services. (Richard T. Riding)

Newly acquired by Jersey and Guernsey Airways, de Havilland Rapide G–AGPI does not wear camouflage, but still bears nationality stripes under its registration marks. (Richard T. Riding)

TWO

DEPENDING ON GOVERNMENT FAVOURS
1946–48

THE GOVERNMENT'S PLANS

So state ownership was to be the overruling principle. But, otherwise, Lord Winster merely re-hashed the Swinton plan which had been put forward in March 1945, entrusting future airline services to three airline corporations, each endowed with a monopoly in its geographical sphere of influence; the difference was that all of them would be wholly owned by the government. The first, structured around BOAC, would continue operating Commonwealth and transatlantic services; the second, British European Airways (BEA), was designated for European services, and would take over the aircraft and operations of the railway-owned airlines flying the internal routes; the third, British South American Airways (BSAA), renamed from BLAIR, would develop services to the Caribbean and South America. The three corporations would not compete with each other – 'healthy rivalry' would suffice. As a general policy, the corporations would have to use British built aircraft. Prudently, the minister gave himself powers to underwrite the corporations' losses over the next ten years; he could eliminate any deficits through Exchequer grants.

Even though they were now barred from flying scheduled services, there were some scraps of comfort for independent airline operators. The ban on private flying was to be lifted on 1 January 1946. Although the corporations would be empowered to engage in charter flying, they would not have a complete monopoly. The government, having in mind pre-war charter services which had been operated by small aircraft with limited range and payload, decided charter flying should still be open to private operators, a small but fortuitous loophole. However, even if it was not proposed to exclude private operators from charter work, the government made it clear that an air taxi must be an air taxi and not 'a pirate bus', and that no attempt to run regular scheduled services would be tolerated. Lord Winster, as he continued his November statement, admitted that it could not stop any operator flying services until legislation was in place, but warned that, 'such an operator should bear in mind that legislation will be coming along, and that, when it does, no claim for compensation in respect of services so started will be entertained'. Compensation would be paid to those companies in existence on 1 November 1944 for physical assets taken over, but not for any goodwill. Unlike the Swinton plan, there would be no financial participation by existing surface transport interests in the arrangements contemplated. Not that the railway companies cared; they already had an idea as to their fate, bruisingly adumbrated in the Labour Party's manifesto:

> Co-ordination of transport services by rail, road, air and canal cannot be achieved without unification. Any unification without public ownership means a steady struggle with sectional interests or the enthronement of a private monopoly, which would be a menace to the rest of the industry.[1]

Indeed, shortly afterwards, on 19 November, the government announced its plans for the nationalisation of the railways, the road haulage industry, ports and docks and the canals. The bus companies were spared for a time.[2]

The reaction to Lord Winster's plans was muted. Predictably, there was criticism from the Conservative Party, now in opposition, although the Labour Party's plans closely followed those that had been put forward by Lord Swinton in March, and it was the pre-war coalition government that had established BOAC. The *Daily Mail* called it a 'rash adventure', the *Daily Express* thought that the government was showing a 'terrifying blindness to the needs and interests of Britain's postwar future'.[3] Lord Balfour, formerly under-secretary of State for Air, observed in the subsequent debate that the determining factor was the fulfilment of a political theory, that 'public ownership shall be the overruling principle in air transport' – not efficiency, not economy, not safety of operation, not the achievement of results. He also criticised the plan as 'bureaucracy gone mad'; Lord Reith, in the same debate, pursued his concern that the minister should give the corporations freedom of management. There was some sympathy for the pioneers of aviation who had risked much to establish air services in the country, but their constituency was small. Captain Fresson, the managing director of Scottish Airways, came away from a meeting with Lord Winster thinking that state ownership could be made to work, 'but I failed to take into account the scheming and jockeying for power which eventually reared its ugly head and the type of individual who would hold control against which there would be no appeal. In other words, civil aviation was to be operated under a dictatorship.'[4] As Fresson went on to remark ruefully, Lord Winster did not stay long as minister and his successor was less appreciative of the efforts that had been made to keep Scotland's air services operating throughout the war. Journalists and commentators were largely opposed to the total nationalisation of Britain's civil aviation, again expressing support for the pioneers and fearing the effects of a top-heavy and bureaucratic approach, something that the British had learned about during the war. But they were also resigned to it. 'We have no faith whatever in national ownership of a form of transport in which speed in every form counts for so much – speed of aircraft on the routes, speed of getting going, and speed of decision', was the opinion of *Flight* magazine, and it continued, 'We still do not believe in nationalisation, but the present government was put in by a misguided electorate with such powers that it is fairly useless to keep crying over spilt milk. The most that can be done now is for everyone concerned to do his (or her) utmost to make the best of a bad job.'[5] The one group which had most to lose, the railway companies that owned the airlines, had their own battles to fight, for they were next in line for nationalisation. Whatever the views of a small minority, the future of civil aviation was not one that stirred great passions in the British public, particularly one that had endured six years of war, was unlikely to fly anyway, and had just voted in a socialist government that had made no particular secret of its desire to bring transport operations under state control. Although individuals may be quite severely affected in situations such as these, this will rarely outweigh public indifference unless it is presented successfully as a David and Goliath struggle. There was, in any case, little that they could do about it. 'The air services are being nationalized', said a *Flight* editorial, '...no rules, regulations, good advice, or even goodwill can alter the fact that, from the moment when the [proposed Civil Aviation] Act becomes law, the government is all-powerful. And the charter companies must operate from hand to mouth, depending finally on government favours.'[6]

THE 1946 CIVIL AVIATION ACT

When the government came to publish the Bill, it provoked further derogatory comment:

> There is no half-heartedness or half anything about the Government's Civil Aviation Bill. This is nationalisation. Every effort has been made to ensure that not even a dog-cart or pony-trap of private enterprise can be driven through any of its clauses. After reading the Bill one has the impression that a determined roller-skate would have little chance of splitting a single infinitive.
>
> The Bill creates Lord Winster, minister of Civil Aviation, supreme dictator of Britain's commercial air. He can order air services to be stopped or started, and tell the three corporations just what they can or cannot do. But if Lord Winster has become an absolute despot, he prefers to give jovial assurances that while he will be zealous and jealous in guarding the monopolistic privileges of nationalisation, he has every intention of being benevolent. Armed with such complete powers, Lord Winster can well afford to be benevolent. Only the incautious or stupid will invite what Lord Winster has himself alluded to as 'menacing gestures'.[7]

The Bill fleshed out the proposals, and even made a stab at defining what a scheduled service was, so that there should not be any doubt, or at least, not much: 'The expression "scheduled journey" means one of a series of journeys which are undertaken between the same two places and which together amount to a systematic service operated in such a manner that the benefits thereof are available to members of the public from time to time seeking to take advantage of it.' However, the interpretation of this clause 23(2) of the Act when it came into effect, was at the core of the many disputes between Britain's independent airlines and the government. The government chose to frame the Act under the penal code, so successful prosecution in a criminal court by the government on this issue could lead to imprisonment and a fine of £5,000. The possibility of incurring such heavy fines certainly deterred some would-be entrepreneurs; the old PSIOWA was one airline which decided that discretion was the better part of valour and turned instead to aircraft manufacturing. The Bill was rushed through Parliament, steered through the House of Commons by Ivor Thomas, the Minister's Parliamentary Secretary – as Lord Winster sat in the House of Lords, the Ministry needed a parliamentary spokesman in the House of Commons – with the government giving no hostages to fortune and declining to define too closely what charter companies could, or could not, do: 'The only thing that emerged from Mr Ivor Thomas's bantering, and sometimes trite, replies seems to be the fact that, until such time as the government has seen its three corporations functioning and has been able to determine which way the charter cat will jump, it has no intention of making the charter operator's position clear "beyond all reasonable doubt".'[8] Another uncertainty, that the corporations would be able to use their deficit guarantees to compete against and undercut private airlines, was met by an assurance from Lord Winster that the corporations would not be allowed to use the resources of the state to the disadvantage of the private operators. One concession, far-reaching as it happened, was that charter companies could be booked by travel agencies to run air tours; it was to be some time before the inclusive tour industry took full advantage of this concept.

The Bill received the Royal Assent on 1 August 1946 and passed into law, becoming the Civil Aviation Act, 1946.

1 JANUARY 1946

The first day of 1946 was significant for all those engaged in British civil aviation. The ban on private flying was revoked, but at first petrol was strictly rationed to allow each aircraft to fly only sixty hours a month. Charter operators and flying clubs were able to resume or start operations. Cambrian Air Services was quick off the mark, claiming to operate the first charter flight, though its load was largely symbolic: a cargo comprising wire rope and a prototype aircraft seat which Captain Eric Symmons flew from Cardiff (Pengam Moors) to Bristol (Filton) in a hired Auster Autocrat. Hunting Air Travel also had one of its Percival Proctors in the air on 1 January. Heathrow Airport, although unfinished, was handed over to the Ministry of Civil Aviation (MCA), and Air Vice-Marshal Bennett, managing director of BSAA, took off from its new runway on 1 January in an Avro Lancastrian, the first of a number of route-proving flights to South America. The British European Airways Division of BOAC, the forerunner of BEA, was formally constituted and arrangements were made to take over the United Kingdom–Continental services previously operated by the RAF's No.110 Wing, 46 Group.

THE CORPORATIONS IN 1946

Events moved on quickly. The BEA Division took over the services operated by No.110 Wing on 4 February, and transferred them from Croydon to Northolt. BSAA became a wholly owned subsidiary of BOAC on 1 August 1946, the same day that BEA was established, but regular services to Buenos Aires had already started on 15 March 1946, and the new airline went on to develop a network covering both east and west coasts of South America as well the Caribbean. BSAA was quick to exploit charter opportunities, too, to North and South America as well as freight charters to Europe.

Things began to return to normal. Aircraft no longer appeared in war-time camouflage and aircrew no longer wore RAF uniforms. Actually getting a seat on flights was another matter. The allocation of seats was controlled by the Air Transport Priorities Board, and there was a desperate shortage of seats for passengers insufficiently high on the priority list, particularly on long-distance flights. The shortage of seats and the heavy demands of the Priorities Board created a short post-war boom for charter and air-taxi companies, as both individuals and companies with overseas interests availed themselves of the freedom to travel abroad again; chartering an aircraft was often the only way to secure a passage, especially on longer routes. Railway Air Services and the other railway-owned airlines in the meantime continued to operate; RAS inaugurated direct service between Croydon and Glasgow on 15 April, the first non-stop scheduled service between the two cities, and by May was using Dakotas on its major trunk routes. After BEA was vested, RAS continued to fly domestic services under charter to the new corporation, which allowed BEA to concentrate on its European services. BEA's fleet of twenty-one Dakotas was augmented by the arrival in September of new Vickers Vikings, and the corporation began to expand its European network. BOAC reopened its services to the Far East and Australia with flying boats and Lancastrians, and launched regular passenger services between London and New York, using Lockheed Constellations, the first of many so-called 'stop-gap' purchases from American manufacturers. There were further boardroom changes at BOAC following the resignation of General Critchley, with two of the directors now earmarked for BEA: Sir Harold Hartley as chairman and Gerard d'Erlanger as chief executive. Both had aviation backgrounds; Hartley had been chairman of RAS, and d'Erlanger came to BEA through BOAC and his earlier banking interest in the erstwhile British Airways. An interesting appointment to the board of BEA as deputy chairman was Whitney Straight, an American-born entrepreneur who had invested in various British municipal airfields before the war; he had taken over Western Airways in 1938, and so was also an independent airline operator. There were also changes in the government following the first post-election Cabinet reshuffle in October 1946. Lord Winster was succeeded as Minister by Lord Nathan; George Lindgren replaced Ivor Thomas as Parliamentary Secretary.

The Bristol Aeroplane Co.'s Type 170 Wayfarer demonstrator G-AGVB was leased to Channel Islands Airways for the summer of 1946. The Wayfarer lacked the nose-opening doors of the better-known Bristol Type 170 Freighter. (A.J. Jackson Collection)

THE INDEPENDENTS

Other airlines had not wasted time either. Channel Islands Airways introduced a chartered Bristol Wayfarer on its London–Jersey services on 1 July 1946; the Wayfarer was a passenger-carrying version of the Bristol 170 Freighter and, with thirty-four seats, boosted capacity on the route significantly. Great Western & Southern reopened the Cardiff–Weston-super-Mare services, the route originally pioneered by Western Airways before the war. Scottish Aviation chartered its aircraft to BEA to provide extra capacity on domestic routes. There was little incentive for independents to launch new scheduled services as impending nationalisation would merely see these routes taken away from them. Only Channel Islands Airways and Allied Airways (Gandar Dower) vigorously opposed nationalisation. Channel Islands Airways felt they had a special case in view of the relationship of the Channel Islands to the British Crown, and argued that their position was not dissimilar to Malta or Ireland, neither of which were covered by the proposed nationalisation plans. But in truth, although the islanders regarded the airline as 'their' airline, it was now wholly owned by the Great Western & Southern Railways, themselves about to be nationalised. As for Allied Airways (Gandar Dower), Eric Gandar Dower was an individualist who would not brook such interference from the state, or anyone else for that matter; he even managed to have himself elected as a Member of Parliament, and his voice was heard many times during the various debates on the Civil Aviation Bill.

That was the situation on 1 February 1947 when BEA formally took control over all the domestic services previously flown by the railway group companies. Neither Channel Islands Airways nor Allied Airways (Gandar Dower) had as yet succumbed, but they would not hold out forever as the government resorted to some determined coercion. Despite resolutions calling for a separate Channel Islands airline, the Home Office was not to be deterred, pointing out to the island authorities that the British Government had given considerable financial assistance to the islands since the war, and that therefore they should not be obstinate.[9] The threats worked, and BEA duly took over the services on 1 April 1947. In turn, Eric Gandar Dower had to relinquish his services from Aberdeen on 12 April, and thereafter devoted much time and energy to pursuing his claims for compensation over the loss of the airline's rights and the expropriation of Dyce, the airport he had built at Aberdeen, which were only finally settled in 1973. BEA had published ambitious plans for developing domestic services, but at first could only try to consolidate what it had inherited in the way of post-war services, establishing an impressive bureaucracy in the process. BEA then suffered aircraft equipment shortages during the winter of 1946–47 when its new fleet of Vikings had to be grounded due to icing problems. This was rectified in due course, but the next blow came in the autumn of 1947 when the government banned all foreign travel for leisure purposes outside the sterling area. The airline then got cold feet over the development of the turbine-engine Vickers Viscount and decided to order piston-engine Airspeed Ambassadors; now two British aircraft manufacturers

Vickers Viking G-AJBV of British European Airways was named *Viscount*. The corporation chose to name its Viscounts the Discovery Class. (A.J. Jackson Collection)

KLM, the Royal Dutch Airline, introduced its Convair 240 PH–TEF into service during 1948. Pressurised and seating forty passengers, the modern American built airliner offered formidable competition to British European Airways's fleet of smaller, unpressurised Vickers Vikings. (MAP)

were developing to BEA's requirements two completely different short-haul aircraft of similar size. Meanwhile, European airlines, led by KLM, were already introducing into service new American built Convair 240s; it would be some years before BEA could compete with this modern pressurised aircraft. Nor were the financial results encouraging. In its first eight months of operation, BEA lost over £2 million.

OUR STATE CORPORATIONS SEEM TO MAKE SUCH HEAVY WEATHER OVER EVERYTHING THEY DO, AND THEY LOSE AN AWFUL LOT OF MONEY IN THE PROCESS[10]

'Another dismal and disheartening chapter to an already depressing story', wrote *Aeronautics*,[11] referring to the latest reports and accounts of the three corporations for the year ending 31 March 1948, which revealed combined losses of over £11 million, 'these show that, like the stone that starts as a landslide and becomes an avalanche, the Corporations are still thundering downhill into the valley of financial loss'. All three corporations made a loss; the biggest was BOAC's at £7 million, but at least that was down from the previous year. BEA lost more than in the previous year, but then its staff numbers had increased from 2,428 in 1946 to over 7,500 two years later. BEA's losses included an astonishing £2 million on domestic services, which it now seemed to regard as a social service. It is small wonder that aviation commentator John Longhurst was unable to hide his anger:

Merging a dozen or so small companies into one State Corporation had lost the taxpayer over £2,000,000. The same services, had they been run by private companies, could have been run without any cost to the taxpayer at all. The net route mileage had dropped since 1937, and there is little doubt that had the internal routes been left in the hands of private companies in the 10 years from 1937–47 traffic would have more than doubled. Jersey Airways Ltd alone had budgeted to carry 135,000 passengers a year had they continued to run independently.

As we have seen, there seems to be a case for subsidising Britain's external air services until they can pay their way, for they are of importance to our trade and for strategic reasons. But where we are paying out £2,000,000 for the running of services which private operators are prepared to run without any subsidy at all, and in a country where there is an excellent alternative transport network of railways and roads, then there appears to be no case for nationalised internal air services and the sensible thing to do to save taxpayers money would be to hand all the internal services back to private enterprise and let them make what they can of it.[12]

Amongst the services most affected were those in Scotland. In a debate on 1 March 1949 Eric Gandar Dower said that the service in Scotland had diminished since nationalisation, and part of the problem was that BEA had reduced the payload of the Rapide to five passengers, whereas in his airline's service the Rapide had carried seven, eight and nine passengers and had been able to operate profitably at lower fares. Captain Fresson, another successful and profitable airline operator in Scotland before the war, makes the same criticism – that BEA did not look after the Rapide aircraft sufficiently carefully with the result that their payload became restricted. The Rapides needed to be replaced; there were off the shelf aircraft available – indeed, two of the Brabazon types were specifically designed as Rapide replacements, the Miles Marathon and the DH Dove, but BEA found numerous reasons why they were not suitable, and instead issued proposals for yet another different aircraft that in the end was never built.

BRITISH SOUTH AMERICAN AIRWAYS (BSAA)

The one corporation that could afford to smirk a little, albeit not for long, was BSAA, which managed to return a profit in its first year. When questioned about this in the House of Lords, Lord Nathan had to deprecate its achievement somewhat. BSAA only operated two types – five Lancastrians and eleven Yorks – he said, on two main trunk routes to South America, and they were only paying £2,000 a year for the hire of the Lancastrians. BSAA continued to acquire aircraft at competitive rates, however, when it took delivery of a number of Avro Tudors, a type which had been rejected by BOAC; by so doing, BSAA saved the government and the manufacturers some embarrassment. The first Tudor service operated out of Heathrow on 31 October 1947.

BSAA had a poor safety record, however; in the sixteen months between August 1946 and November 1947 the airline had seven accidents, three involving fatalities. But the airline became notorious for the unexplained losses of two of the Tudors over the Atlantic. The first, *Star Tiger*, disappeared on 30 January 1948 en route from the Azores to Bermuda. The MCA grounded the Tudors, and for their pains were criticised by the chief executive, A.V.M. Bennett, in an interview he gave in the *Daily Express*. So he was dismissed, having refused to resign. During the subsequent debate in the House of Commons on 18 February, Lindgren, the minister's Parliamentary Secretary, had some scathing things to say about the airline, whose safety record had already been the subject of study by his department: 'I do not think that the high accident rate is unrelated to the fact that the operations of the Corporation [BSAA] are very near to the bone. The inference has been made, with some justification, I think, that training and maintenance standards were not so high as they should have been', and he went on to suggest that other incidents, involving the arrival of BSAA aircraft in Bermuda with almost dry tanks, had a bearing on the lack of confidence of the Board in their chief executive. Bennett fought back: 'I have been sacked for speaking my mind. The minister has made it clear that those in anything like a responsible position in nationalised industry are very much muzzled with regard to the details of management and to their political views. In other words I was not the "Yes-man" who alone can fit into a socialist structure. I will fight to the utmost against socialist strangulation.'[13] He went on to form a charter company, Airflight, which operated two Tudor tankers during the Berlin Airlift.

Avro Lancastrian G–AKMW *Star Bright* of British South American Airways. (MAP)

Avro Tudor 4 G–AHNN *Star Leopard* of British South American Airways. (BOAC photograph, British Airways copyright, via MAP)

BSAA, meanwhile, carried on, falling back on its Yorks and Lancastrians. In due course, in the absence of any proof as to the cause of the loss of *Star Tiger*, the Ministry relented and allowed the Tudor to resume operations, first as a freighter and then from August 1948 carrying passengers, flying the long way round via Gander in Newfoundland. As it turned out it was lucky for the government and BSAA that the type was cleared as a freighter. Very soon, every available large four-engine aircraft was needed to help in the Berlin Airlift, and BSAA was swift to respond to the challenge, taking over newly built but undelivered Tudor 5s as well as Tudor 1s from BOAC,[14] which it operated intensively on the airlift, carrying fuel. Looking ahead, BSAA ordered the de Havilland Comet and expressed strong interest in the huge Princess flying boats; but BSAA's plans, as we shall see, came to nought following the unexplained disappearance of a second Tudor early in 1949.

THE BERMUDA AGREEMENT

One of BSAA's destinations, Bermuda, was the setting for a meeting between Britain's government negotiators and their American counterparts during January and February 1946, to pick up the threads that had been left hanging over air service rights since the 1944 Chicago Conference. The Americans were still in a strong position. They had it within their power to deny the British use of the modern transatlantic airliners that BOAC needed; at the same time the British were also trying to negotiate a huge post-war dollar loan in Washington. The British still wanted controls: over fares, routes, frequency of services, division of capacity, fifth-freedom rights.[15] After three weeks of negotiations, the two sides concluded what became known as the Bermuda Agreement, on 11 February 1946. On the whole, the Americans prevailed. The British conceded frequencies, division of capacity and fifth freedom rights, albeit with some restrictions. The Americans agreed to control fares, mainly through the machinery of the International Air Transport Association (IATA), and they also accepted limitations on routes and route access. But the British got their Constellations and Stratocruisers, and many of the subsequent bilateral agreements, especially those with European countries, were more to their taste. US airlines may not have had to share the traffic 50/50, or put up with restrictions on the number of weekly flights to the United Kingdom, but many European airlines had to accept them – not that they minded. As British airlines were to discover over time, European governments turned these same restrictions to their advantage, successfully using the 50/50 formula to block expansion into their markets by British carriers.

LORD DOUGLAS AND PETER MASEFIELD

In June 1948 a new Minister of Civil Aviation was appointed, Lord Pakenham (later the Earl of Longford); hitherto he had been Chancellor of the Duchy of Lancaster in charge of German affairs. With a clear view of his mission – 'No Minister of Civil Aviation, so long as subsidies are paid, could possibly content himself with pursuing a policy of non-intervention'[16] – he tackled the problems of the corporations with some vigour and not a little success, replacing the upper hierarchies of both BEA and BOAC in quick order. He fired Gerard d'Erlanger from BEA, and appointed Lord Douglas of Kirtleside as chairman. Lord Douglas's appointment was interesting. A veteran of the Royal Air Force,[17] he had been A O C-in-C Fighter Command from 1940 to 1942, and latterly British Military Governor in Germany, where he had had dealings with Lord Pakenham. He was known to have left-leaning views, and his elevation to the peerage in 1948 had been thought to presage a closer association with political affairs, possibly leading to his appointment as Defence Minister. John Longhurst wrote, 'The application of Lord Douglas's talent to civil air transport was not altogether expected, seeing that he had spent a lifetime in the military service'.[18] But once installed at the corporation, he pugnaciously fought BEA's corner, and his appointment heralded the start of better times for BEA, as did the appointment of its new chief executive, Peter Masefield.

SIR MILES THOMAS

Better times, too, for BOAC, now with a more competitive fleet and, from July 1949, a new chairman, Sir Miles Thomas, its fifth chairman in nine years. Thomas was a hard-headed businessman and his comments on what he found at BOAC are illuminating:

Stratton House, which was the headquarters of BOAC when I joined, had originally been built as a block of costly Mayfair flats, and there was an atmosphere of luxury that I found strangely out of accord with the dreadful financial result of the Corporation… It had been early borne in upon me that the whole operation was too stragglingly untidy for words and needed drastic pruning. There was, moreover, a cloying sense of lushness; that money did not matter.[19]

Lord Pakenham had asked Thomas to undertake a review of the corporation, and together with its recently appointed chief executive Whitney Straight (speedily transferred from BEA), he began to tackle some of its equipment problems, boosting the mainline fleet by buying twenty-two Canadian-built variants of the Douglas DC-4, the Canadair C4, known in BOAC service as the Argonaut. Thomas, a veteran of the Nuffield Organisation and war-time production demands, knew how to get his way:

Canadair DC-4M Argonaut G-ALHD *Ajax* of British Overseas Airways Corporation (A.J. Jackson Collection)

Lockheed Constellation G-AHEM *Balmoral* of the British Overseas Airways Corporation. (MAP)

On our way to the Ministry meeting I said to Whitney: 'Look, it's no good us asking for a nice round number. If we ask for twenty-five they'll want to cut it down to twenty. Equally, if we ask for twenty they'll probably want to cut down to fifteen. Let's quote a figure which is a silly, odd sort of number and then they will be impressed by the fact that we have done some precise reckoning instead of some round guessing!' All that we both wanted was to be allowed to purchase twenty or more Argonauts. After some preamble at the meeting we solemnly stated that we had come to the conclusion that 23 Argonauts was the exact number we required. We had done forward analysis and cross-checking, and by correlating the expected growth of passenger traffic and the extrapolated increase in route mileage and a few other bits of jargon, including the number of pence per ton mile and suchlike, we asked for twenty-three. As expected there was an argument. The civil servants had to justify their watchdog duties, but finally we happily got away with twenty-two.[20]

The Argonauts joined BOAC's front-line fleet of American built Stratocruisers and Constellations; nevertheless, the future still looked promising for the British aircraft manufacturers. The Handley Page Hermes had been ordered for services to Africa, and there were no less than three types envisaged for longer-range routes: the Bristol 175, which evolved into the turbo-prop Britannia; the Comet, the world's first jet airliner; and the massive Bristol Brabazon.

ECONOMIC CRISIS[21]

'To the victors belong the spoils of the enemy.' Hardly the case as far as Britain was concerned, which faced the brave new world with its empire in tatters and a mountain of debts, huge dollar-denominated debts. Of necessity, Britain had had to import increasing amounts of food, equipment and raw materials from the dollar area while exports to this same area dwindled. Although Lord Keynes had negotiated a large dollar loan from the US and Canada, its terms were less generous than Britain had wished, and among its provisions was the stipulation that the pound should become fully convertible by July 1947. Things started to go badly wrong early in 1947. Exports began to stagnate at the same time as dollar imports were rising rapidly. There was a sharp increase in domestic consumption, which diverted resources away from exports, which were further reduced anyway by the severe winter of 1946–47. Britain also had to spend much more on its extensive military commitments overseas. But most significantly there was a serious capital drain due to the looseness of the arrangements which had been made to tie up the sterling balances. European countries could earn convertible sterling by joining the transferable account area before July. By restricting imports from Britain and increasing their own exports, these countries were then able to enlarge their sterling surpluses, thereby transferring their dollar problems to Britain; after the pound became fully convertible in July 1947, holders of sterling quickly took the opportunity to convert them into dollars, drawing down still further on the post-war loans to such an extent that the decision was taken to suspend convertibility only a few weeks later, on 20 August 1947. Among the controls that the Prime Minister, Clement Attlee, was obliged to introduce was a severe cut in tourist allowances outside sterling areas. At first allowances were reduced to £35 per year, and then in October they were abolished altogether. Business people were allowed to take out more for business trips, up to a maximum of £8 per day. There was no restriction for countries in the sterling area, but there were not many such destinations in Europe: only Ireland, Gibraltar, Malta and Cyprus. These travel restrictions had an immediate impact on BEA, coming during the winter season when demand was in any case weaker and at a time when the airline was trying to promote leisure travel.

Matters improved in 1948, however. Britain received $2,694 million in Marshall Aid between April 1948 and the end of 1950, and without such aid the prospects for the British economy would have been very bleak indeed. With the help of this American aid the economy surged ahead, with production, exports, consumption and the national income rising. There was a budget surplus, even a surplus on the international currency account. Helpfully, the government finally removed the system of priority control over seats on the corporations' aircraft; and the Chancellor announced that tourist travel would be permitted, from 1 May 1948, to Austria, Denmark, France, Italy, the Netherlands, Norway, Portugal, Switzerland and Sweden with a currency allowance of £35 per person. But Marshall Aid was mainly used to cover the cost of dollar imports, such as sugar, petroleum, cotton and aluminium; with hindsight, maybe it could have been put to better use: 'The government must be blamed for its almost complete failure to appreciate the seriousness of the disinvestment in British railways that was taking place, at the same time as the war-devastated railways of France, Germany, Holland, Belgium and Italy were being reinstated with modern equipment including electrification. Marshall Aid from the USA, which in Europe was largely devoted to restoring and improving the national transport infrastructure, in Britain was diverted elsewhere.'[22]

PURCHASE OF AMERICAN AIRCRAFT

Britain's economic problems, and the scarcity of dollars, inevitably had an impact on aircraft purchases. Once opportunities opened up for charter airlines to enter the market, they wanted to buy American aircraft, too. Initially, restricting the availability of dollars was one way to ensure that charter airlines did not become too competitive or get ideas above their station; requests for dollars to buy Dakotas from the US Liquidation Commission, and other US-built aircraft, were turned down. But after the passing of the Civil Aviation Act, the Treasury could afford to be more lenient.

Up to date we have refused all applications from private individuals or organisations for exchange to purchase American aircraft. This is in accordance with [the Chancellor's] ruling when the purchase of Constellations for BOAC was sanctioned. At that time the decision was also welcome to the Ministry of Civil Aviation since they feared that certain private charter companies, if allowed to acquire American aircraft, might use them to challenge the government's policy of reserving scheduled services for the public corporations which had not then got statutory backing. But now that the Civil Aviation Bill is through both we and the MCA think that some relaxation is desirable...

... wrote the Treasury on 4 October 1946.[23]

It duly made $1½ million in exchange available up to the end of 1947 for the purchase of surplus US aircraft and spares. One of the first beneficiaries of the new policy was Freddie Bosworth, founder of Gulf Aviation. His appeal for dollars to buy a Fairchild Argus from the US Liquidation Commission illustrates the harsh realities facing small entrepreneurs with not a lot of money when they are trying to turn a good idea into something more tangible:

> I am the founder, promoter and manager of a commercial venture known as the Iraq Flying Centre, based in Baghdad, and plans for the venture include the purchase of initial aircraft namely two trainers and one four-seater for taxi and charter work. I have been attempting to purchase a British four-seater for work in Iraq but have been without success. It should be pointed out at this stage that, necessarily, my finances are limited and I am unable to pay the astronomical figures now being asked for new and/or used machines available on the aircraft 'black market' and unable to postpone the execution of my venture until these conditions change or are changed. I have exhausted every avenue which will lead to my being able to purchase a British aircraft and am compelled to make this request for your sponsorship of an American machine.[24]

The main beneficiary of the Treasury's change of heart was Scottish Aviation, which drew down $374,000 to purchase and refurbish Dakotas for resale in the commercial market. Air Transport Charter (CI) and Kearsley Airways also purchased Dakotas, but the allocation as a whole was underspent and the MCA were able to surrender over $600,000 when the Treasury reimposed exchange restrictions in 1948. BOAC and the government were then obliged to come up with some novel solutions when the airline wanted to buy more American aircraft. Additional Constellations were bought from the Irish airline, Aerlinte Eireann, which accepted payment in sterling but at a premium to the purchase price; BOAC paid £315,000 for each aircraft in sterling, even though the Irish had only paid the equivalent of £250,000 in dollars. Similarly Stratocruisers were bought off the production line from the Swedish airline SILA and again paid for largely in sterling. The most complex deal involved buying the twenty-two Canadian-built Argonauts in 1948. Although Canada is in the dollar zone, the purchase was structured so as to minimise the actual disbursement of dollars. Some of the equipment was paid for in sterling, including the engines, and the government was able to cover the dollar element by postponing repayment of its dollar debt to the Canadians and using those dollars to cover the aircraft purchase.

THREE

CHARTER FLYING
1946–48

CHARTER AIRLINES

Before the war, Britain's airlines had earned their living mainly by flying scheduled services, and by and large that was still their intention after it was over. By stopping the private airlines from operating these services, the government hoped that, even if it could not stifle the new-born airlines, it would at least keep the infant industry confined within the playpen: in this it failed. The airlines that grew up after the war had to struggle to survive, but against the odds they found new markets, developed new skills and contrived to offer consumers a choice. Maybe John Longhurst had both the private airlines and state corporations in mind when he wrote: 'The best results in any form of activity are usually born of adversity and not from over-indulgence.'[1]

There was an immediate and short-lived opportunity for charter airlines to exploit the enormous demand for travel as soon as the war ended. The government had revoked all the licensing regulations during the war, so there was no regulatory impediment to anyone who wanted to start services. Aircraft had to be bought and made airworthy to the satisfaction of the Air Registration Board and flight crew had to be licensed by the Ministry – both of these procedures pre-dated the war. The Civil Aviation Act did not come into effect until later in 1946, so there was a brief inter-regnum when an operator could carry passengers with few restrictions apart from those imposed by a war-time bureaucracy, covering, for example, the export of currency and the need for visas. With war-surplus aircraft becoming available, many former RAF aircrew were keen to start their own charter airlines; by the end of 1946 there were eighty-five firms engaged in air charter work.[2] At an early stage the charter airlines formed their own lobbying organisation and support group, the British Air Charter Association (BACA), which first met on 28 August 1946 at the premises of the Royal Aeronautical Society in London, 4 Hamilton Place. The main problem they all faced, apart from government obstructionism, was a shortage of petrol and a shortage of aircraft.

The pent-up demand for overseas travel could not be met by scheduled services alone; there was only very restricted availability of seats on passenger flights, which were in, any case, erratic. The situation as regards shipping was not much better. Most ships were still required to carry returning forces' personnel from the various war zones, and were in a very run-down state; passenger vessels would need extensive refitting before they could be returned to regular service. British companies with overseas interests needed to send staff out, to resume contacts that had been either ruptured or curtailed during the war; there were many special charter flights out to China, the Far East, the Middle East and Africa, some involving epic journeys of many months' duration in quite small aircraft. There was a simpler demand for people just to emigrate from war-torn Britain, especially to South Africa; a number of the air-taxi operators took advantage of the lack of shipping space to fly small parties and families on the one-way journey south. Some pre-war business opportunities were quickly resumed, with charter companies again able to fly press photographers and newsreel cameramen at short notice; and newspapers returned as a staple on special early-morning charter flights.

There was great interest in carrying air freight, a wholly new market; it was thought that civil aviation could emulate the British shipping industry and develop an expertise in freight tramping operations, with aircraft flying from airport to airport, picking up and discharging loads wherever the business took them. Perhaps the most welcome development, from the public's point of view, was the large-scale import of fruit and vegetables from Italy, Spain and France. With European railways still disrupted through war damage, and lacking refrigerated wagons, continental fruit growers began to look for different markets and for different ways to serve them. Before the war Italy's fruit surplus had gone to Germany; now it came to English markets. The Handley Page Halifax could carry around 7 tons of fruit, the Lancastrian 5 tons, and so every return flight to the United Kingdom was guaranteed a load out of French and Italian airports. The Italians went so far as to build a special airport at Verona in the middle of the fruit-growing district. Between September 1946 and August 1947, over 3,620 tons was imported by air.[3] For the British consumer the war must have seemed finally over when rare fruit like peaches, pears and grapes appeared for sale on London's streets. Not everyone, however, was pleased with this development; a senior Treasury official harrumphed:

My Times this morning reports that today 8 transport aircraft are flying 9 tons of apricots from Madrid to London. I bought a Camembert yesterday which had a silhouette of a 4 engine plane on it and the statement that it was flown in from Brittany. You will recollect the story of the carp flown on ice from Belgrade a few weeks ago that arrived so promptly that it started jumping round the counter of a North London fishmonger and had to be taken to the zoo.

Are these really valuable uses for petroleum, aluminium, engineering capacity, and government expenditure on airfields? I want to get the IPC to have a crack at this fantastic industry soon. But can we foment any righteous indignation elsewhere?[4]

The traffic was not all one way. Aside from more traditional exports, charter airlines began flying livestock out of the country, with the first recorded large-scale movement being flown on an Air Contractors' Dakota from Croydon to Cologne in June 1947. Racehorse owners were quick to appreciate the benefit of flying their animals rather than sending them by rail and lorry. In other sectors new business opportunities were seized. Britain still had a large merchant marine despite war losses, and was a major industrial producer with much of its infrastructure still intact. There was strong demand for shipping, and ship owners knew that ships laid up in port, waiting for replacement parts, cost them money. They quickly learned that the extra cost of an air charter was outweighed by the charges and demurrage that a ship would continue to accumulate whilst awaiting the delivery of a replacement part by sea. When the Lancashire Aircraft Corporation flew a ship's propeller tail shaft out to Singapore in October 1947, it saved the owners of the SS *Lake Chilco* over £10,000. The cost of the Halifax to carry the 5½-ton shaft out to Singapore was around £6,000, and took four days. To ship the new shaft out by sea would have taken around sixty days; meanwhile, the ship would have remained out of commission at Singapore, accumulating charges of £300 a day, a total of at least £18,000.

In its February 1947 issue, *Air Transport and Airport Engineering* magazine wrote about one of the new breed of charter airlines:

Apart from a slight seasonal drop in passengers carried, charter companies have started the new year with very satisfactory bookings to all parts of the world. For those companies who carry cargo in bulk there has been no seasonal easing of consignments, in fact an increase of freight loads is more the order of the day, and charter companies see a great future in this direction. Witness the expansion of London Aero and Motor Services Ltd, who, starting in a small way with a few light aircraft for passenger carrying, and then branched into the air cargo business last August with excellent results. LAMS purchased six Halifax Mk8's to start with and such was their success that a further 10 have been ordered.

LAMS has now taken the unique step of leasing Stansted Aerodrome in Essex as an operating base solely for the use of its cargo aircraft. From August until the end of December, 1946, LAMS was chartered to carry 1,000,000 ton-miles of freight. Its Halifaxes made trips covering most of Europe, North Africa, and Middle East. A thoroughly modern and novel step was taken by the company when it secured the services of ML Bramson, who is the only private owner of a civil Spitfire in this country. He will visit all parts of Europe in his Spitfire and study local needs on the Continent which can be filled by British air exports. He will also book cargoes from Europe for return flights.

LAMS claims to be the first company to fly freight aircraft direct from Nice to London with cargoes of flowers. The company is under contract to carry 10 tons each week during February and March. The transport of flowers by air started early in January, when they were flown from Paris to London. For the United Nations Relief and Rehabilitation Administration, LAMS has been carrying medical supplies to Vienna, Prague and Belgrade. Thirty tons has been carried to date. At Christmas, 'Port of Oslo', one of the LAMS Halifaxes, carried five tons of vaccines, packed in ice, to Belgrade, to combat a local epidemic of diphtheria. The flight was made non-stop from Heathrow in 5hrs 10mins, from take-off to touch-down.

One year later, *World Aviation Annual 1948*[5] recorded eighty-one British charter airlines operating a total of 484 aircraft. Four types, Rapide, Consul, Proctor and Auster, accounted for approximately half the total:

Seventy-four de Havilland Rapides
Fifty-nine Airspeed Consuls
Fifty-four Percival Proctors
Forty-nine Austers
Thirty-six Douglas DC–3 Dakotas
Thirty-two Avro Ansons
Thirty-one Handley Page Halifax and Haltons
Twenty-two de Havilland Doves
Twenty-one Miles Geminis

Other notable types in the charter fleets were ten Miles Aerovans, thirteen Avro Lancastrians, eight Vickers Vikings and six Douglas DC-4s. There was a preponderance of single engine and light twin types, reflecting the short-haul requirements of many of the smaller air-taxi charter companies; in defiance of the popular belief that many such companies were single-plane operations, however, only twenty had fewer than three aircraft in their fleets.

By the end of 1947, the immediate post-war flying boom was ending, hurt by the government's decision to restrict the import of fresh foodstuffs following the economic crisis that summer, and the ban on foreign travel. But the government did help the charter airlines by using their aircraft to fly milk from Northern Ireland to Liverpool, milk churns and all. There was a surplus of milk production in Northern Ireland and there was a shortage in England; it was taking four days for the milk to arrive by ferry, by which time most of it had turned sour. A York could carry around 1,450–1,500 gallons per trip, a Lancastrian around 950–1,000 gallons, and the government was subsidising the cost of a pint to the tune of 2d to 3d, but it kept the consumers – and the voters – happy.

Although statistics at this period are a little rough and ready, it is interesting to compare output in 1947 between the two main sectors, the corporations and the charter airlines. *The Aeroplane* estimated that 250,000 passengers flew on charter services, 585,000 with the corporations, and the charter airlines carried 3,000 tons of cargo, as against 4,678 tons carried by the corporations.[6] It was to be expected that the corporations would carry more; after all they had a monopoly on scheduled services, but the charter airlines were carrying 40 per cent of both the total passenger and cargo business.

AVIATION OUTPOSTS

Charter firms were not confined to London and the big metropolises – a number developed specialised businesses around Britain's shores. Offshore islands were quick to benefit from the resumption of charter activities; doubtless there was also a measure of island pride in seeing a local airline established at its airport.

By 1948 the Isle of Man boasted two charter airlines at Ronaldsway, Manx Air Charters and Mannin Airways, both flying Rapides, both evoking memories of the pre-war Isle of Man Air Services. The Channel Islands, which had been especially hostile to the nationalisation of 'their' airline, ascertained that the Ministry in London had no powers to regulate inter-island services, so soon saw a new airline, Island Air Charters, operating Rapides between Jersey, Guernsey and Alderney; it was linked to another charter airline, Air Transport (Charter) (Channel Islands), of which more later. Maldwyn Thomas, a Welshman, started charter operations out of Jersey in 1949, again using Rapides. He could not register the name Jersey Airlines as it was too similar to the late lamented Jersey Airways, so he called his airline Airlines (Jersey) and painted the title 'Jersey Airlines' on the aircraft anyway. Guernsey had two short-lived charter companies, Air Transport Association and Guernsey Air Charter, neither of which survived beyond 1947.

Closer to home, rival airports on the Isle of Wight fielded rival airlines. Bees Flight, flying Miles Geminis, operated out of Sandown (Lea) when it reopened in 1948; renamed Isle of Wight Airport, Sandown became the main commercial airport on the island, seeing many domestic services during the 1950s and into the 1960s.[7] Ryde, the most important destination for PSIOWA's ferry services from Portsmouth before the war, had been closed for some time, but Somerton (Cowes) had remained open during the war, and was used by Somerton Airways until both closed down in 1952.

Seen at Liverpool, Ulster Aviation operated the diminutive Miles Aerovan G-AJKU on charter services. (MAP)

In Northern Ireland, Lord Londonderry founded his own charter airline, Londonderry Air Charter, in December 1946. Based at Newtownards, where Miles Aircraft built the Messenger club aircraft, the airline relied on Miles for much of its work, carrying aircraft assemblies and spares between Newtownards and Miles's other base at Woodley, near Reading; aircraft used included a fleet of Miles Aerovans and Messengers. But by late 1947 production of the Messengers had ceased and the airline had to look elsewhere for business. Two Rapides were acquired for passenger work, mainly weekend charter flights to the Isle of Man, and the name was changed to Ulster Aviation. Further change came in 1949 when Ulster Aviation and Mannin Airways joined forces to form North-West Airlines, based at Ronaldsway, which took over the assets of the two airlines. But that was a short-lived venture and in 1950 North-West was bought out by Lancashire Aircraft Corporation.

Wales had its own flourishing airline, Cambrian; but in Scotland the pioneering spirit had been extinguished. The inter-island network in Orkney was not resumed, but BEA flew the remaining internal services; Scottish Airlines, the operating division of Scottish Aviation, was a respected charter airline flying all over the world and specialising in contract services, but it had had to surrender its domestic services to BEA.

SOME AIRLINES TO REMEMBER

'Large streams from little fountains flow, tall oaks from little acorns grow.' Maybe, but the metaphor does not seem to apply to Britain's charter airlines; it was to be many years before some of them even reached the height of saplings. These charter services are listed below:

Air Charter

Air Charter started in 1947 at Croydon and operated Rapides and Geminis until 1950, when charter services were suspended. Operations resumed in 1951 when a young entrepreneur, Freddie Laker, took over the airline under the auspices of his engineering company, Aviation Traders.

Air Kruise (Kent)

Formed by Wing Commander Kennard at Lympne in Kent, Air Kruise was the first operator of the Miles Messenger, to which he soon added a Percival Q6 and a Proctor. The airline developed a network of cross-channel charter services, developing an early relationship with a leading tour operator, Fourways. In 1950 Air Kruise opened a three-times-daily service from Lympne to Le Touquet, using Rapides, and Kennard quickly spotted the potential for offering a cheaper service between London and Paris. By catching a train at either end and using the Rapide connection across the Channel, travellers saved an hour over the conventional rail–ferry–rail service, and it was marginally cheaper. Holidaymakers for Le Touquet also used the service, as did day-trippers, and it was the forerunner of the 'coach–air' services that developed in the later 1950s and 1960s.

Air Transport (Charter) (Channel Islands)

A small airline with a big name, which merits attention because its business activities, and its subsequent fate, serve as a template for the evolution of post-war charter operations. Its Rapides and Dakotas carried holidaymakers from the United Kingdom to the Channel Islands during the summer months; at other times of the year they made long overseas trips, mainly to Africa, with freight, livestock and passengers. The airline participated in the Indian airlift in 1947, and in 1948 operated fruit flights as well as milk charters from Northern Ireland; later it flew for three months on the Berlin Airlift until all the Dakotas were withdrawn as a result of a policy decision. The airline was allowed to operate scheduled services within the Channel Islands, which it started in January 1949, using the Rapides.

Wing Commander Kennard's airline, Air Kruise, was the first to use the Miles Messenger when it bought this aircraft, G-AHZS. (A.J. Jackson Collection)

Dakota G–AKIL of Air Transport (Charter) (Channel Islands). (MAP)

Derby Aviation

Formed as 'Air Schools' in 1938, a reserve flying school established at Burnaston, near Derby, it was subsequently joined by a second flying school at Wolverhampton. Some 14,000 pilots and navigators were trained during the war, and afterwards flying training continued; and as so often happened, the light aircraft used by the school and the Derby Aero Club were made available for charter work. The first such commercial flight was made on 21 August 1947, when a Miles Messenger was chartered to take three passengers to the TT Races on the Isle of Man. The name Derby Aviation was registered in 1949 and operations continued with a Rapide and an Aerovan. Like many other small charter operators, the airline flew summer services to Jersey.

East Anglian Flying Services

Started by Squadron Leader R.J. Jones, and registered as a company in August 1946, it was the first operator to be based at Southend's new municipal airport, taking up residence on 5 January 1947 with an Airspeed Courier, an Auster and a Puss Moth. At first the company relied on pleasure flying, but in order to put the airline on a firmer footing, the Squadron Leader began to look for more charter work and to this end bought a Miles Aerovan, once even sending it down to Cyprus. With the arrival of Rapides, the airline began a regular series of charter flights across the Channel to Ostend.

Eagle Aviation

Eagle operated its first flight on 9 May 1948, carrying a load of cherries out of Verona in a Halifax. Started by Harold Bamberg, a young entrepreneur and pilot who went on to dominate the industry in the 1960s, the airline took over the Bovingdon-based freight airline Air Freight, and continued to operate fruit flights during the first summer of its existence; it was well-placed to help out in the Berlin Airlift when the charter airlines began to participate in the autumn of 1948. Bamberg's other company was Air Liaison, an airline passenger and freight agency which also acted as general travel agents. Even at this early stage Bamberg was concerned to market and sell his airline's services professionally.

Hunting Air Travel

Formed in December 1945, its directors, members of the Hunting family, also sat on the board of Percival Aircraft, and based a fleet of three Proctors at Luton. Hunting Air Travel was in the air on 1 January 1946 as the ban on private flying was lifted, flying a charter for the Daily Mail. New Vikings and Doves were ordered to supplement the fleet, which grew to include Rapides and Ansons, and the company switched its base to Gatwick, then Croydon, before settling for the time being on Bovingdon. The mix of business was typical for a charter airline of the period, with fruit flights, occasional long-haul charters and regular flights to holiday destinations.

De Havilland Dove G-AJDP *Thames* of Hunting Air Travel. (MAP)

Island Air Services

Started in June 1946, it was an early charter operator to and from the Scillies, carrying flowers to the mainland during the season. But by the end of 1948 its focus changed, when, under its redoubtable chairman and chief pilot, Miss Monique Agazarian, it gained the joy riding concession in London, first from Northolt, then at Heathrow, flying Rapides on pleasure flights from the public enclosure. Two types of flights were offered. A long flight around the Heathrow circuit cost ten shillings: and for a pound the flight took in London as well, which could be extended to the London Docks for an additional fifteen shillings.

Lancashire Aircraft Corporation

Owned by Eric Rylands, an important figure in the post-war airline industry, it quickly established itself in 1946 at Squire's Gate, the new airport for Blackpool, flying DH Rapides. Bearing the red Lancastrian rose, the fleet expanded rapidly so that by mid-1947 there were over twenty aircraft: Rapides, Consuls, Proctors, Austers and the first of many Halifaxes. The latter were converted by the airline's sister maintenance organisation, and as there was insufficient work for them in the north of England, they were based at Bovingdon, mainly flying fruit from the Continent together with the occasional ship's charter and other long-haul freight flying.

Morton Air Services

This was the first charter airline to introduce the Airspeed Consul into service, but also made extensive use of the Rapide. Based at Croydon, and founded by Olley's former chief pilot, Morton's first flights early in 1946 included two return flights to

Rome, a seventeen-day tour of Europe arranged for two British and two United States businessmen engaged in reviewing prospective markets, and a 5,735-mile flight from Bombay to London for an Indian Maharajah. In September one of his Airspeed Consuls flew four passengers down to South Africa, taking six days to cover the 7,000 miles. The Rapides were well adapted to air-ambulance work, with a large door that allowed easy stretcher access, and Morton's operated many air-ambulance flights from the Continent, including skiing accident casualties from Switzerland during the winter season. In 1948 Morton's, together with Air Enterprises, were contracted by the United Nations Truce Commission in Palestine to provide seven Consuls for courier and patrol services, with an engineering base at Beirut. This contract lasted until 23 April 1949.

Scottish Aviation Ltd

The owner, developer and operator of Prestwick Airport in Scotland, it had ambitious plans to develop a network of services post-war, which were cut short by the government's plans for nationalisation. Scottish Aviation lost out on both counts, as the airport was taken over by the Ministry of Civil Aviation, and the formation of BEA precluded any scheduled service development. Nevertheless, under its energetic founder Wing Commander McIntyre, an airline division was nevertheless started, Scottish Airlines, which obtained Dakotas and Liberators for charter work. These operated contract services for BEA out of Glasgow's two airports, Renfrew and Prestwick, and also flew extensively for European airlines, including Iceland Airways, KLM, Luxembourg and Hellenic Airways; they were also used to develop holiday charter services to the Isle of Man. Scottish Aviation built up a formidable business maintaining and refurbishing former military transports, mainly Dakotas.

Airspeed Consul G-AHJX of Morton Air Services. (A.J. Jackson Collection)

Transair

Transair may be said to have taken over from where Wrightways and Air Dispatch left off, resuming after the war the role of specialist newspaper carrier, to which end it bought a fleet of converted Ansons. The first newspaper services were to Paris, starting in October 1948, and were followed by further contracts to Brussels, Dublin and the Channel Islands. No doubt impressed by the efficiency and regularity of Transair's services, the Royal Mail also decided to start using the airline, awarding it mail contracts from 1950 to France, Belgium and the Channel Islands.

Operated by Scottish Aviation, in whose colours it appears, Liberator SX-DAB was flying on behalf of Hellenic Airlines of Greece in 1949. (MAP)

With its windows blanked off, Transair's Avro Anson G-ALFD was used regularly on newspaper delivery and Royal Mail flights. (A.J. Jackson Collection)

SKYWAYS

One charter airline that set out to challenge the corporations and develop a significant presence in the charter sphere, was Skyways, an airline that had some big ideas and an impressive board which included General Critchley, formerly director-General of BOAC, and Sir Alan Cobham. *Flight* said admiringly:

> Apart from the fact that it is good to see a start being made by private enterprise in the only field open to it, there is a deal of poetic justice in the formation of the new charter company, Skyways Ltd, by Sir Alan Cobham and Gen. Critchley. Sir Alan was, before he introduced his schemes of refuelling in flight, a blazer of trails on the Empire route, and General Critchley has had applied to him the term 'filibustering'. Sir Alan never tired of hammering home the point that commercial flying will not amount to anything until it ceases to be news, and General Critchley, whatever may have been his faults while he was with BOAC, is a man of ideas with terrific drive. Both are thus well fitted for guiding the operations of tramp services.[8]

The company had originally been established in 1929 but was reformed as an airline in 1946 and, although Cobham quickly became disillusioned and quit the company soon after, he left a more lasting memorial in the airline's name:

> When faced with the attraction of becoming involved with airline operations, Cobham had, as his earlier endeavours have shown, rarely been able to resist 'waggling his wings'. So, when Captain Ashley, one of his former pilots from the NAD [National Aviation Displays] tours approached him with a glowing proposition concerning aerial charter work his interest was immediately awakened. Ashley explained that the potential for such work in Egypt, Africa and the Middle East was enormous, and that there were literally thousands of people employed by the oil companies needing repatriation after several years spent abroad during the war. Furthermore, Ashley had secured an undertaking from BOAC that, should he be able to form a proper company, they would be prepared to act as agents and offer the support of its ground organisation. Faced with such an attractive prospect, Cobham produced a surprise of his own. In the early Thirties he had favoured the name 'Skyways' for his operations, but had found himself pre-empted by a small firm based in Norfolk. In 1936 however, his diligent solicitor, William Morris, had noted that the company was no longer operating and that Cobham could purchase the deeds and title for a very small sum if he wished. This is how, ten years later, he was able to present an aptly-named and already registered company to his co-venturers.[9]

Skyways immediately obtained valuable contracts with Anglo–Iranian Oil Co. to fly personnel, stores and equipment out to Basra in the Persian Gulf on a twice-weekly basis. Anglo–Iranian, the forerunner of BP, had over 5,000 expatriate staff together with their families based at its Abadan oil refinery in Iran; regular services were needed to take staff out there on appointment, on leave and for business travel. Skyways also launched so-called 'aerial cruises' on behalf of Sir Henry Lunn, precursors of the package tour. Travellers were flown out to Zurich in Switzerland, transferred to a hotel for a two-week stay and then flown back to England, all for an inclusive price of £75.

At the time of Skyways's first flight to Basra in May 1946, the government had still not enacted the new civil aviation legislation and was obviously nervous about the possible uncontrolled development of new airlines. As the following account from *The Aeroplane* magazine makes abundantly clear, it resorted to other means to exert pressure:

> We gave full details of this new company's activities and its contract with Anglo–Iranian in [a previous issue]. We also said that we hoped the government would not crab charter companies' activities, because of the great contribution they can make all over the World to the volume and scope of British air transport.
>
> But, sure enough, the crabbing has started already. Skyways Ltd has made an arrangement with BOAC that the latter should be its traffic-handling agents throughout the World. Therefore they sought to despatch the York from Northolt on May 14, Croydon being unsuitable for York operations with a full passenger load. But, oh dear no, that would have made it too easy for Skyways, and the Ministry of Civil Aviation said Skyways could not use Northolt, because it would mean letting all the other operators in as well, for which Northolt is not yet ready. 'All right', said Skyways Ltd and its handling agent, BOAC, 'let us use Hurn'. Another excuse was thought out to veto the use of Hurn, and the long and short of it was that, through the kind assistance of Hawkers, Skyways Ltd has to put the passengers on board at Langley, BOAC traffic staff having to cart over there from Northolt to handle the departures and arrivals, then before departure from England the aircraft has to land again at Manston, a Customs aerodrome, to sign out for departure overseas.
>
> Two things are certain, first that the MCA can produce all the necessary excuses and provide chapter and verse to convince themselves that they are right, and second that in a few months time the matter will be cleared up and Skyways Ltd will get settled at Heathrow or Northolt. Meanwhile most people seemed to agree that the obstacles are really unnecessary, and that this sort of thing contradicts the official policy of expanding British air transport with utmost despatch.[10]

The good relationship with BOAC continued, however. Very soon Skyways's Yorks were flying scheduled services on behalf of BOAC, five such flights to Singapore being flown during August. By the end of 1946 the Yorks were flying an average of around 2,000 hours per year. Nor did the company ignore smaller loads, using its Rapide, based at Manchester Ringway, to fly newspapers to Dublin. By the time of its first anniversary, in May 1947, Skyways seemed to be well established. The airline employed over 1,300 people at Dunsfold, near Guildford, many of them living in quarters on the base. The Anglo–Iranian contract continued, and the airline had taken delivery of the first of four Douglas DC-4 Skymasters, bought from KLM,

Seen at London Air Port, Skyways's Douglas DC-4 G-AJPM *Sky Freedom* flew on behalf of British Overseas Airways Corporation as well as the oil companies. (A.J. Jackson Collection)

the Dutch airline. At a time when even BOAC had to struggle to get permission to buy American built aircraft, it says much for the formidable clout that Skyways was able to wield that the airline was able to persuade the Treasury to disgorge sufficient foreign currency, in this case guilders, to buy the aircraft. The Treasury was persuaded by the argument that Skyways would earn many times the initial purchase cost in foreign currency, through the oil contracts. BOAC was indignant and wrote to the minister to tell him so, speaking of its grave concern that 'it will appear to the staff as to outsiders that the Corporation has been outwitted by Skyways'.[11] By October 1947 Skyways had all the DC-4s in service and a typical week's operation for the company gives some idea of the scope of its business. Between 1 November and 8 November 1947, the DC-4s, equipped to carry thirty-six passengers, performed two passenger flights London–Abadan–Kuwait–London and two freighter versions were employed on the same route. A thirty-seat Avro York flew London–Dar-es-Salaam and completed local flying in Africa for the United Africa Co. A York flew London–Lydda–London for Anglo–Iranian Oil, and another York flew to Abadan, as did two Lancastrians. Another Lancastrian, equipped for fifteen passengers, flew Cunard passengers from Hurn – Paris. There were further Lancastrian freight flights to Saigon, Naples and Dar-es-Salaam. In

Avro York G-AHFI of Skyways. (MAP)

addition, a Dakota, chartered by Unilever, was engaged in a tour of China that lasted several weeks.

When BOAC withdrew its flying boat service between Southampton–Bahrain, it started flying the route with Skyways's DC-4s from May 1948, later adding Abadan, Damascus and Baghdad to the network.

AIRFIELDS

Skyways's problems at Heathrow and Northolt highlighted an important issue; at the end of the war there was no airport near London suitable for long-distance flights. Passengers had to go to Hurn, near Bournemouth, until London Airport, later known as Heathrow, was ready. Croydon was brought into use again, although its terminal was by now outdated, it had only a grass runway and was in every way unsuitable for long-haul flights. Northolt was lent to the Ministry of Civil Aviation by the RAF, and became the principal airport for European services, used by BEA and the European airlines. Charter airlines continued to use Croydon, but many established engineering bases at airports in the greater London area, some of which were also

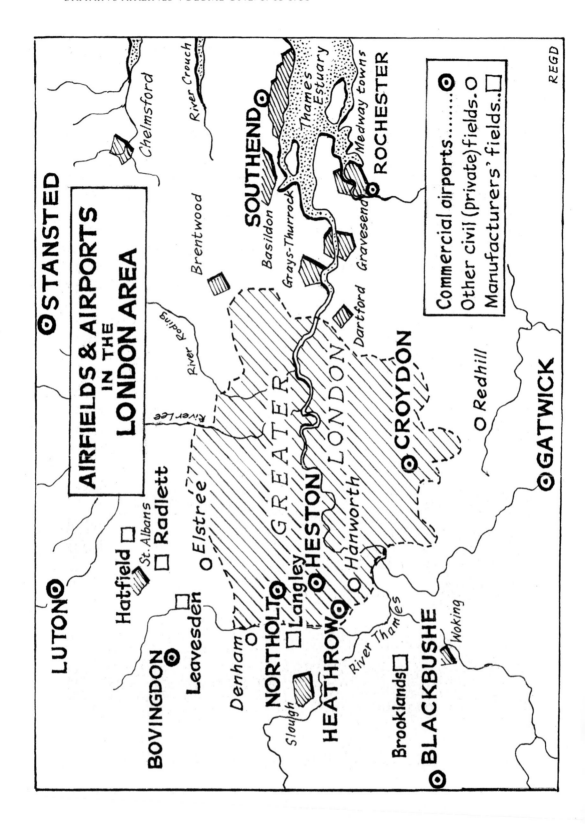

AIRFIELDS & AIRPORTS IN THE LONDON AREA

REGD

Commercial airports........ ◉
Other civil (private) fields. ○
Manufacturers' fields.. □

used for passenger and freight services: Bovingdon in Hertfordshire, Gatwick in Surrey, Blackbushe in Hampshire, and latterly Stansted in Essex, were all used for charter flights.

AIRWORK

Airwork had spent the war training pilots, manufacturing components, and working on military maintenance contracts, overhauling aircraft at its engineering base at Gatwick; it soon switched to civil contracts, converting military Dakotas to civil standards for BOAC and the Dutch airline KLM. Under its managing director Myles Wyatt, and its commercial director Sir Archibald Hope, the company sought out new business ventures quickly and aggressively. With its extensive world-wide contacts, the company was asked to help develop a sales organisation overseas for British transport aircraft like the Bristol Freighter and the Vickers Viking. Airwork sold six Vikings to its protégé, Indian National Airways, before acquiring Vikings of its own, which were based at Blackbushe. They were used by the Polytechnic Touring Association (PTA) for what were called tourist flights to the Continent, starting during the summer of 1947. These were among the first inclusive tours, and over 2,000 passengers were carried to Switzerland during that summer. The PTA was no stranger to promoting tourist flights abroad; as early as 1932–33 it had chartered a Handley Page HP42 from Imperial Airways for all-inclusive holidays to Switzerland. By the end of 1947 Airwork was also involved in the Hadj, the pilgrimage to Mecca, flying over 100 pilgrims between

For a time, Airwork operated Vickers Viking G-AJFT on behalf of the new Pakistan Government, and it is seen here in the hangar at Karachi in 1947. (MAP)

Mombasa and Jeddah. They based a Viking in Kuwait to fly on behalf of the Kuwait Oil Co., and another in Karachi to fly for the newly formed Pakistan Government. Elsewhere in the Middle East, Airwork continued its association with the major oil companies forged before and during the war; it maintained and operated five Rapides and two Doves for Anglo–Iranian Oil, and a further three Rapides and two Doves for Iraq Petroleum. The company also obtained a valuable three-year contract in South America, operating two Bristol Freighters and various smaller aircraft on behalf of Shell in Ecuador, flying heavy equipment such as caterpillar tractors, scrapers, drill collars and bits, trucks and jeeps into remote drilling strips, as well as cement and food supplies. Despite the rundown of war-time contracts, Airwork maintained its specialised government contract services, including the training of pilots at Perth, now a Reserve Flying Training School.

AIRWORK AND THE SUDAN

Just as Airwork had assisted in the formation of the Egyptian airline Misr Airwork before the war, so it too helped the Sudan Government establish Sudan Airways after the war, using DH Doves. These contacts in the Sudan had far-reaching results, leading to a major commitment to operate the Sudan Government's leave flights for many years, the core of this airline's early business ventures. As soon as the war was over the Sudan Government had to address the problem of granting home leave to its many British officials. Sudan was jointly administered by Egypt and Great Britain. The Governor was British and so were many of his staff and government officials; they were entitled to ninety days of home leave every year, as Sudan was considered a hardship posting. During the war it had been just about possible to send everyone back home once, but the situation did not improve after the war, when, as we have seen, there were severe restrictions on both air and sea passages. With a backlog of 450 home passages to resolve, the Sudan Government was desperate to find a solution, and begged the Ministry of Civil Aviation to release an aircraft to BOAC so that it could operate special charters, without success. As the months went by, the situation did not change. By April 1946 the Ministry noted, 'the Sudan Government had been in touch with the BOAC's local manager, who had explained the difficulties of meeting the request for charter services owing to shortage of aircraft and crews. Mr Cribbett[12] has so far given a non-committal response, but has promised that we will do our best to persuade BOAC to help them when the aircraft and crew position improves.'[13] Part of the difficulty was that there was a similar problem with government officials in India who also required home leave and who were just as hard pressed to get passages, but colonial sensitivities being what they were, it would have been tactless to point out that the Indian civil servants rated more highly than those in the Sudan. The Sudan Government then decided to take matters into its own hands, chartering a Bristol Wayfarer from Airwork for a series of flights out of Cairo, and also using a converted B-17 bomber operated by the Swedish airline SILA. On 25 August 1946 the Bristol Wayfarer flew the first of many leave flights for the Sudan Government to London. The series of flights were to continue for the next ten years, soon graduating to bigger aircraft, Vikings and later Hermes, and operating out of Khartoum. The Sudan Government was well pleased with its solution to the problem of organising leave flights, having complete control over the capacity and the services of its own reliable airline. Contracts went out to competitive tender but Airwork was always the carrier of choice. That did not please BOAC, once its aircraft shortages began to ease, particularly when Airwork began selling off spare seats on the flights. By 1948 it was making trouble at the Ministry. 'The main point of issue [with the tender] is Paragraph 2. (2) (a) and (b) which I think we agreed was a tacit invitation on the part of the Sudan Government to flout Section 23 of the Act', wrote BOAC to the Ministry, continuing, 'I understood you to say that you would examine this point with a view to having someone send the Sudan Government at least a "reproach".'[14] But the British Government was not very cooperative. Having taken advice from the Treasury Solicitor and the Director of Public Prosecutions, it realised the Sudan Government was within its rights to tender, and that it was then up to the contracting airline not to commit a breach of the regulations. Moreover, carrying return passengers on a fill-up basis did not constitute a 'systematic service available to the public', and could not therefore be regarded as a scheduled service. BOAC tried to force a ministerial direction which would have required the traffic to go on BOAC, but that course of action was deemed inappropriate. As an internal minute records, it might have led to some awkward repercussions:

> BOAC proposed to quote a price equivalent to the ordinary fare less a 20% rebate. They had assumed that the Ministry would want the Corporation to capture this traffic, which is, after all, legitimately theirs, and that we [the MCA] would agree to issue the necessary 'request' to carry the Sudan Government official leave personnel in question at a rebated fare. It could be argued that this was no more than a device to cut out Airwork who had some moral claim to the job, unless BOAC or any other operator could offer a genuinely competitive quotation. In this particular case, it appeared that the Ministry would, in effect, be 'requesting' BOAC to so adjust their price so as to beat Airwork. This might be regarded as sharp practice and the critics, perhaps even Airwork themselves, might regard our action as aiding and abetting BOAC to the detriment of a charter operator who, by virtue of his initiative, was entitled to some consideration.[15]

So the government merely told BOAC to try harder at winning the contract, and made consoling noises when it did not. But later, in November 1948, the Ministry was again agonising over the issue, as well as the complex relationship between the government, the corporations that the government owned, and the independent airlines whose well-being was also recognisably a part of the government's responsibility.

> If, as a result of action taken by us, [Airwork] lose the Sudan contract now, they will certainly find themselves in a very difficult position and may be unable to proceed with the other promising schemes they have to hand. The late Minister [Lord Nathan] said repeatedly in public that he regarded himself as Minister of Civil Aviation and not merely Minister for the Corporations. If we feel that we here have any responsibility for the wellbeing of the British charter industry,

there are reasons for allowing the Sudan work to go to Airwork for one year more, it being clearly understood that if a similar situation arises a year from now, we shall have no hesitation in taking the work away from Airwork and giving it to BOAC if it is at all possible.

If the contract goes to BOAC and Airwork are disposed to make trouble, they may allege with some force that BOAC are only able to undercut them on what is essentially a charter job because BOAC are a public Corporation financed from public funds. They would go on to allege that this was contrary to assurances given at the time when the Civil Aviation Bill was going through the House to the effect that the Corporations would not be allowed to use their subsidy to compete with charter companies in the charter field.

If we authorise BOAC to quote on the basis proposed and they get the contract (it is not yet clear that on the basis proposed their offer would necessarily undercut that of Airwork) we shall certainly be criticized and the matter may be raised in the House. If it is, I think that a defence could be put up which, though not fully satisfying our critics, would be regarded as reasonable by papers of the standing of the Economist and the Times.

If we feel in MCA that we have a serious responsibility to the more reputable charter firms, there are I think urgent reasons for allowing Airwork to have the contract for another year. If we authorise BOAC to quote against them on the basis proposed and BOAC get the contract, our action I think will be generally interpreted as meaning that the interests of the Corporations will always come first with MCA and the interests of the others nowhere. I think this would have a depressing effect on the charter field whose future is already precarious.[16]

A lot of 'ifs'. Despite the implied threat, BOAC never won the Sudan contract, but both the government and BOAC learned their lesson from this experience. When the Nigerian Government proposed a similar service using Skyways's DC-4s, the request was firmly turned down and instead BOAC put on a service with its Haltons, limited to ten passengers over the long trans-Sahara sector, which operated at a loss to the corporation of £9,500 a week.[17] And after the International Refugee Organization awarded a significant contract to Airwork in 1948 to carry refugees from Germany to Canada, the government, through a mixture of incompetence and foot-dragging, was able to scupper that deal, too.[18]

SILVER CITY AIRWAYS

The exotically named Silver City Airways joined the growing number of long-haul charter operators when it launched service in December 1946, flying Lancastrians and Dakotas, on behalf of its parent company, to South Africa, Burma and Australia. The airline was closely associated with British Aviation Services (BAS), backed by the constituent companies of the British Aviation Insurance Co., which performed appraisals, accident surveys, aircraft-ferrying and the like. Through BAS, Silver City acquired its managing director, Air Commodore Powell, formerly of RAF Ferry Command, the organisation which had ferried aircraft over from the US and Canada during the war; ferrying aircraft must have been in his blood, because at first a large part of BAS's activities consisted of

Silver City used Avro Lancastrian G-AHBV for the long flights to Australia and South Africa on behalf of its proprietors, the Zinc Corporation and the Imperial Smelting Corporation. (A.J. Jackson Collection)

taking war surplus aircraft back to Canada and elsewhere. BAS managed the new airline for its two owners, the Zinc Corporation of Broken Hill, New South Wales, and the Imperial Smelting Corporation in Australia, which had mining interests in Burma and South Africa as well as in Australia, and needed to transport freight and staff – especially their South African mining staff – between the various locations. But problems arose after the independence of India in 1947; the Indian authorities began to make difficulties for South African engineers on their way to Burma, causing long delays and negating the value of these private flights. Later it became possible to route South Africans west-about to Australia on commercial airline services avoiding India; the Zinc Corporation no longer needed such specialised charter services and so the airline sold its Lancastrians. The Zinc Corporation, later to become Rio Tinto–Zinc, continued to use Silver City's other aircraft both in the United Kingdom and Australia, but early in 1950 sold the airline to British Aviation Services. Something of the flavour of these long-haul charter flights can be obtained from Commander Hurren's account of a trip in a Silver City Lancastrian, which was published in *The Aeroplane*, 18 July 1947:

Day by day in the coveted columns of the front page of the *Times* appear the names of air charter companies offering transport to romantic centres of the world where the sun shines in more senses than one. Only a few companies figure in these announcements, presumably for space reasons, and it may not be realized generally that some 100 charter companies are in being, offering air charter services.

Recently I made a trip to the Great East in an aircraft of one of the more important of these charter companies, Silver City Airways, which is a subsidiary of British Aviation

Services. And as this company is in the front rank of those carrying the British flag overseas, yet outside the officially sponsored organization, it may be of considerable interest to recount some features of the journey.

First, the aircraft – a converted Lancastrian. Now, the make-shift-and-mend policy forced upon us by War conditions is not anywhere near as bad as many have been led to believe. I can state categorically, for example, that the food and drinks served on the Silver City Lancastrian are just as good as those with BOAC and better than some other lines, so far as my experience goes. And since most of the passengers are soon lulled into a state of mental torpor, knowing nothing technically about the air services, the food and drink question rates high.

The same applies to seating. Indeed, the adjustable seats of the Lancastrian are far better than the fixed seats in BOAC Dakotas, some of which have been devised by a direct descendant of the Grand Inquisitor.

A very simple formula gives the answer to the equivalence of the services of BOAC and the leading British air charter companies: overseas, they tap the same facilities. What happens is that the senior charter companies rely on, and pay a fee for, BOAC services; and hence, they carry not only their own efficiency and prestige but have the immensely influential backing of the State air lines.

I think the thing that next impressed me much was the lack of meaning embodied in time-schedules. Flying East (or West), there is always much juggling with the clock. To say a lunch departure from London Airport meant breakfast in Basra and dinner in Karachi on the next day, therefore, conveyed to the ordinary passenger far more, I thought, than the bald statement of times.

Anyone who denies the need for fast aircraft should be forcibly sent on a long trip. The World, despite glib phrases, remains a big place; and the tedium of sitting nine or more hours for one hop is something Nature did not provide for. Nor was it only a question of a nine-hour flight. For example, in round terms, it takes six hours direct to Malta, and then, after an hour's halt for refuelling, a further nine hours to Basra; where, after another hour's halt for breakfast, a further five hours to Karachi. In other words, and correctly, 22 hours transit travel non-stop. Now in 22 hours' travel non-stop, there is towards the closing stages only one thought uppermost in the traveller's mind: when the hell do we get there?

By that time, all interest in the landscape and seascape below has long passed away. You cannot see much from 10,000 ft in any event, but vast stretches of wilderness, of sea, of forest and mountain soon take on an unbearable degree of monotony. Hence the speed of the Lancastrian or York is something which the experienced traveller weighs off carefully against possibly more comfortable but slower aircraft. Incidentally, why do we still have windows to aircraft? Why not a saloon with an observation car or compartment? Most people doze uneasily and ignore the windows except for the few minutes when near the ground.

And now, shed of some technical aspects, what about the passengers? Who travels by charter, when BOAC supplies? The answer is that BOAC schedules hold out faint hope of a passage, for non-priority passengers, some months ahead. The charter companies frequently have a spare seat, and any such are eagerly snapped up.[19]

Commander Hurren and the passengers spent the night at Karachi, staying in the relative comfort of the BOAC mess, before proceeding to Singapore the next day; night stopping of both passengers and crew was a normal procedure.

CROSS-CHANNEL CAR FERRY

But Silver City's future lay not in far distant lands; it found its true purpose flying the shortest of routes over the narrowest stretch of the English Channel. Silver City is forever associated with the vehicle ferry services which they operated with Bristol Freighters, carrying cars and their passengers across the Channel with speed, reliability and efficiency. I do not know who had the idea first. In *The Aeroplane* of 13 June 1947, 'Commentator' remarked:

> I saw somewhere the other day that it costs £8 10s to ship a car across to France by sea, and that all the shipping space for this purpose is now booked up for July and August. Which charter company will be the first to establish a regular car ferry service across the Channel, using a Bristol Freighter?

And, just over a year later, he was able to say, 'There has been no rush to accept my suggestion, for nearly 12 months have elapsed, but I am glad to hear that Silver City Airways has a project in hand to do this'.[20] Maybe his words did set minds thinking, because even Air Commodore Powell in his autobiography fails to attribute the inspiration to anyone in particular. Silver City had a Freighter, a demonstrator on loan to the company, but recognised that Dakotas were more suitable for passenger work. Nevertheless, the company wanted to find a use for the aircraft, and conducted tests with ramps, demonstrating that cars could be driven straight on board. The Air Commodore explained what happened next:

Bristol Freighter G-AIFM of Silver City is poised, with nose doors open and loading ramp in place, to accept its next load of cars. (A.J. Jackson Collection)

The war had been over for two and a half years and war conditions were gradually being left behind. Continental holidays showed signs of being an attractive relief in spite of the £50 foreign travel allowance restriction. In retrospect I suppose we should have foreseen the Continental travel explosion after the drab years of war. Of course it was a very mini explosion compared with what was to happen 25 years later but it quickly became a feature of the travel trade with the sea ferries by no means ready for it. The shipping companies had been left at the end of the war in the same state as the airlines – very short of equipment and substantial additions to the cross-channel fleets were years away. In any event there were many bothersome features; the paperwork involved in taking a car to the continent involved delays and even apprehension at the terminal ports. Customs Carnets or Temporary Export Permits were essential and both English and continental Customs officers went through – with diligence – the rigmarole of not only finding chassis and engine numbers but also checking them with travel documents to be sure that a six had not been upside down and that sort of nonsense.

I thought therefore that if we could fly private cars across the Channel two at a time the mere fact that there were only two would save hours of time because of the short flight and because there would be no queue at the Customs points. Fortunately we had an air route staring us in the face – a short channel hop from Lympne near Folkestone on the English side to Le Touquet in France. With only 47 miles between them it was only a 20-minute flight and both airports had good road connections from London and Paris.[21]

Interpreting the regulations flexibly, (the service was called an 'all-inclusive Car freighting Service', and if push had come to shove, the company would have said the car owners had chartered the aircraft), Silver City was ready to launch by mid-summer and on 7 July 1948 inaugurated the service, flying the Air Commodore's Armstrong Siddeley Lancaster saloon to Le Touquet. They brought a Bentley back, and he was pleased to see that the Freighter could comfortably carry two large cars as well as eleven passengers.

LACK OF OPPORTUNITIES IN 1948

But for other charter airlines, business was bad. Fruit flights resumed in 1948, although not soon enough to help LAMS which, after some unhappy round-the-world tramping experiences, had been forced into receivership, just weeks before the start of the Berlin Airlift when the airline's experience could have been put to good use. Charter rates were not as good in 1948 as in the previous year. Rates from northern Italy in 1947 for Halifaxes had started at £800 and were about £700 by the end of the season; in 1948 the rates remained fairly steady at between £400 and £500. Passenger bookings were down, too; most flights headed for the Channel Islands as the foreign travel allowance was so small. There was, however, a resumption of the milk flights from Northern Ireland to Blackpool and Liverpool, using a number of carriers to transport 50,000 gallons of milk a day. The larger charter airlines had their fixed contracts which ensured some continuity. By mid–1948 Airwork was flying for the Sudan government, Iraq Petroleum, Kuwait Oil Co., the Overseas Food Corporation and had extensive business for Shell in Ecuador. Skyways had its major contract with Anglo–Iranian, and had started flying for BOAC. But there was a downside to charter operations.

CHARTER AIRLINES BEHAVING BADLY

'Mushroom development of charter services to cash in on the overflow from the airlines and the lack of shipping space is giving aviation a bad name', was the candid comment from *Aeronautics*, which went on to castigate the 'I couldn't care less' attitude of many pilots, who did not seem to rate passenger comfort and convenience very highly. 'The survival of the fittest operates in air transport quite as effectively as the jungle, and it is unlikely that many of these casual concerns will still be going in a year's time. Meanwhile they are queering the pitch of the old-established charter companies who know the business from A to Z and give their clients service.'[22] A reflection, surely, of the British class system, but there was a growing two-level structure to the charter airline industry. There were those airlines which were deemed reputable: Airwork, Hunting, Scottish Aviation and Skyways. Then there were the smaller operations, largely air-taxi companies, managed enthusiastically if not always very soundly by an owner/pilot; these were much lower down the social order. 'Oh, so you're in the racket', remarked a politician to a Skyways employee, causing the latter to conclude in an article in *Flight* that this comment was born, 'of an inverted form of snobbery and… a complacent smugness which rejoices in its own security, while condemning the foolishness of those unwary enough to seek their fortunes outside the realms of Government control'.[23]

The rapid development of charter flying worried the government. The 1946 Act tried to spell out what charter operators could not do, but the minister was evasive when it came to defining their legitimate activities. Consequently, much time was wasted as operators engaged the various departments of the Ministry in daily question-and-answer sessions, seeking advice on possible flight bookings. Having framed the 1946 Act under the penal code, the government could only test the Act in the courts, so the Ministry started examining charter flights with a view to early prosecution. Its objective had been to guarantee state-controlled airlines a monopoly of all scheduled services, but in the hectic post-war rush it suspected that many of these passengers were being diverted to charter airlines. Weekend services to the Channel Islands in particular were suspect; there seemed to be just too many 'charter services' and surely not all of them could be legitimate? A questionnaire sent out to some charter airlines in 1948 asked, 'How did the passengers know that seats were available? Was the first approach made by the passengers to your company, or by your company to the passengers? How was that approach made? Whom did the passengers pay for their seats?' 'Commentator,' in *The Aeroplane*, dismissed the questionnaire as 'a typical product of a Civil Servant who has nothing to do and all day to do it in'.[24] Other concerns were: whether the flights were systematic, that is, performed on a regular basis; whether spare seats could be sold off to fill up an otherwise properly chartered flight; and just who were 'members of the public'? The Ministry was able to supervise the activities of charter airlines fairly closely through its control of many of the airports that the airlines had perforce to use, and the corporations were not above making mischief either. 'I regarded this as a case rather of pique on the part of BEA who were annoyed at their prices being undercut in respect of flower trade', writes the Treasury Solicitor with regard to a complaint about some flights from the Channel Islands by British Air Transport.[25] But following the first prosecution in May 1948, involving Ciro's Aviation, the magistrate had some sarcastic comments to make about the minister as he fined the airline a nominal £10:

> These are terrific powers given to a Minister. No private individual shall compete with a nationalized undertaking. If they do so, they shall be required to give full particulars of the offence. They shall convict themselves at the arbitrary order of the Minister who can fix his own time for the information to be supplied.[26]

Ciro's Aviation was regarded as somewhat louche by the Ministry: 'Complaints which have reached the Ministry in the past suggest that the operating standards of this company are not high. As its name suggests it had connections, at any rate originally, with the night club of the same name.'[27] So next time round the Ministry prosecuted the more respectable Hunting Air Travel for regularly flying passengers to Jersey during the summer of 1948. The Ministry must have been disappointed when the court stated that the airline had 'rendered yeoman service to the public in general', and fined them only £1 on each of the two summonses, rather than the impressive amounts, up to £5,000, that the law allowed.[28] The lack of success in the courts became embarrassing and the Ministry was increasingly reluctant to prosecute. In desperation the Treasury Solicitor suggested that Section 23 of the Act should be redrafted in the form of an absolute prohibition, subject to exemptions, but this proposal was turned down by the Ministry, which was unable, or reluctant, to determine exactly what activities the charter companies should be allowed to undertake. Sir Thomas Barnes, the Treasury Solicitor, wrote to Lord Shawcross, the Attorney General, offering another solution: 'It is extremely difficult to frame the appropriate statutory provision without going too far and stopping bona fide charter business. I have always thought that a licensing system is the proper remedy, but the Ministry dislike it for administrative reasons. It may be that, if no prosecution is undertaken in this case, it would be advisable for BOAC to institute proceedings.' To which Lord Shawcross replied: 'The only satisfactory course appears to be to take civil proceedings as suggested in order to get a ruling from the Courts. My own feeling is that the... plan is an infringement of the section but obviously we must test the matter and I think it better to do that in civil proceedings than in criminal ones.'[29] But the corporations were reluctant to do the Ministry's dirty work, believing that it was for the government to test the legislation. The government had to deal with largely unsympathetic magistrates, so was unable to develop any satisfactory case law as a result. As Lord Shawcross hints, the penal code was not appropriate for many of these cases; the government had the proverbial sledgehammer to crack a rather small nut.

SOUTH AFRICA

Also part of the 'racket', and again one which the Ministry found hard to control, were foreign-registered charter airlines. If British charter airlines erred, the Ministry could try to prosecute them under the 1946 Act, but they held no such powers in respect of foreign carriers, much as they would have liked them. Tiresomely, not all overseas governments were as hostile to charter airlines as was the British Government. Indeed, the South African Government rather thought that charter and scheduled airlines could co-exist, and saw nothing wrong in allowing South African charter airlines to operate low-fare services between England and South Africa, recognising the legitimate need for such services, and preferring to control rather than curb them. The British Ministry watched unhappily as airlines like Alpha Airways, Mercury Aviation, Pan-African Air Charter and Suidair International Air Charter began making regular appearances at British airports, carrying on average seventy passengers a week between London and Johannesburg. Complaints were made to the South Africans but they fell on deaf ears, so the Ministry took matters into its own hands, requiring prior approval for all flights, and when that did not work, banning the supply of fuel to the aircraft and threatening the travel agents who took the bookings. The airlines tried to circumvent the restrictions by flying to and from European airports, usually Paris, and offering a 'free' connecting flight to London operated by a British airline. Eventually the government did prosecute Ackroyd's Air Travel for carrying passengers on charter flights to Paris to connect with Mercury's flights to South Africa, but again met with an unsympathetic response: the Chief Magistrate, Sir Laurence Dunne, merely fined Ackroyd's £5 on each count, saying he was very sorry that he had to impose a fine and that he thought the flights were a benefit to the public.[30]

WHAT HAPPENED TO THE PRE-WAR AIRLINES?

Although all charter airlines had been obliged to close down during the war years, a number resurfaced when operations were allowed to resume; but like so many of the charter airlines which sprang up after the war, few survived beyond the end of the decade.

Looking first at those airlines which had also operated scheduled services before the war, as recounted in the previous chapter, Allied Airways (Gandar Dower) had gone down fighting, but had gone down nevertheless. North Eastern Airways sold the goodwill of its network to the railway companies for £100,000 and never reopened any of its services. The Hon. Mrs Bruce had kept Air Dispatch busy during the war as a Commercial Repair Organisation, and afterwards wanted to resume her Inner Circle service, linking all the major London area airports, but was unable to do so after the plans for nationalisation were announced, so, like many others, she started building bus bodies instead. Renamed Bruce Coachworks, and based in Cardiff, the company lasted another six years before it closed.[31] PSIOWA spent the war overhauling and repairing aircraft, and had ambitious post-war plans to build up the Isle of Wight air services with Doves, but these were forestalled by the government's actions, and it, too, switched to building bus bodies, although it remained in the charter business with a simpler name, Portsmouth Aviation. Western Airways, still owned by Whitney Straight, by this stage a key figure in the BOAC hierarchy, started flying charters with Ansons; when the restrictions on scheduled services were relaxed in 1948, it was back flying the Cardiff–Weston-Super-Mare route, this time in conjunction with Cambrian Air Services. In order not to identify too closely with Straight after he became deputy chairman of BOAC, the Straight Corporation was renamed Airways Union in 1949. The Weston–Cardiff route was handed over entirely to Cambrian in 1949, but the airline continued to operate charters until 1953. Lundy and Atlantic Coast Air Lines never resumed operations, but Devonair operated a charter link with Lundy Island during the 1950s.

As for the pure charter airlines, Birkett Air Service Ltd was back in business in 1947, operating charters out of Croydon with two Rapides and a Leopard Moth. But by the early 1950s it, too, had closed down. Cambrian, which as we have already seen was in the air on 1 January 1946, continued to derive its revenue from charter

Cambrian Air Services' Percival Proctor G-AHEV, with one of the company's de Havilland Rapides in the hangar behind. (MAP)

flying, some maintenance work, aerial photography and flying instruction. There was also pleasure flying from Pwllheli, most of the passengers being holidaymakers at the nearby Butlin's Holiday Camp. Surrey Flying Services resumed operations after the war, as an aircraft overhaul and maintenance organisation, and was taken over by Freddie Laker's Aviation Traders. Wrightways, famous for its newspaper flights before the war, never restarted, but carrying newspapers was to become big business again for other charter airlines.

OLLEY AIR SERVICE

Olley Air Service provides the thread, the unbroken link with the pre-war commercial activities of the charter airlines. During the war it was not closed down, but it was bought out by the railways. Its chief pilot, Captain Morton, left to form his own airline and started operations out of Croydon. Olley's also resumed charter services from Croydon; Captain Bebb, now chief pilot, was still flying G-ACYR, the Rapide he had used to carry General Franco back in 1936. Olley's was in an anomalous position; it was now wholly owned by a nationalised undertaking, British Railways, themselves under the control of the British Transport Commission, but it was not part of the dowry handed over to BEA as by this stage it was not flying any scheduled services. It continued to operate independently, introduced Doves in 1947 and specialised in charter flights to race meetings.

AIRLIFTS

The creation on 15 August 1947 of two self-governing dominions, India and Pakistan, out of what had been British India, required an evacuation by air of government officials and their families in September; this was to be the first major exercise in co-operation between the government, the state corporations and the charter airlines. With BOAC acting as co-ordinating agent, Scottish Airlines, Silver City and Westminster Airways positioned a total of nine Dakotas out to Karachi to assist BOAC in evacuating 7,000 people from Delhi to Karachi over a three-week period. By the end of the year British charter airlines were back in India, engaged in a much bigger airlift which saw them carrying over 41,000 refugees between October and November, many from remote airstrips. The refugees in this case were mostly transport officials, desperately required in order to arrange the much larger evacuation of the respective Hindu and Muslim minorities by surface transport. Again BOAC was the co-ordinating airline, contributing six Dakotas to the operation, but this time the charter airlines between them provided a further fourteen Dakotas and one Wayfarer. Scottish Airlines provided six Dakotas, Westminster Airways, Air Contractors and Air Transport (Charter) (CI) two each, and Sivewright and Kearsley Airways one each: the Wayfarer, a passenger-carrying version of the Bristol Freighter, came from

Silver City. The operation was based at Palam (Delhi). Every morning the aircraft would leave with refugees bound for Pakistan, clear immigration at Lahore, and then proceed to a designated airstrip in Pakistan. The aircraft captains would offload their passengers, and negotiate to bring out more passengers for the return, who would be flown to either Amritsar or Ambala, again via Lahore. The aircraft then positioned back to Palam at night. The pressure was on to maximise passenger loading, given the circumstances of the refugees' plight. Westminster Airlines carried sixty-nine passengers in one of their Dakotas; Air Contractors managed a creditable sixty-five.

All this was but a prelude to the following year's events, when the Soviet Union blockaded the western sectors of Berlin, which were controlled by the Americans, British and French but isolated within the Communist zone of Germany. Then the charter airlines were called on to mount a major airlift that was to last many months.

FOUR

THE BERLIN AIRLIFT
1948–49

REFLECTIONS

The Berlin Airlift of 1948–49 is important at many different levels. The endless stream of aircraft bringing in essential supplies from the British and American zones of Germany flew over cities, not least Berlin itself, which had been flattened by Allied bombing less than five years previously – but there was no irony. The Western allies were determined not to repeat the mistakes made after the First World War; the Airlift was a manifestation of their positive approach to post-war reconstruction and of a genuine desire to rebuild Germany in a modern and essentially democratic idiom. The first major post-war confrontation between the Western powers and their erstwhile ally, the Soviet Union, the Airlift also demonstrated convincingly the technical and logistical superiority of the United States and its partners.

At another level, the Airlift had a significance which parallels the subsequent development of the Western world. The United States, despite its enormous resources and wealth, could not mount the operation on its own and did not disdain the considerable help given in the performance of its execution by its allies: the British, members of the Commonwealth, the French, and of course the Germans themselves. Britain's government, in turn, could not meet its commitments by relying solely on its own resources. Although the RAF shouldered the bulk of Britain's transport obligation, it depended to a certain extent on Commonwealth aircrew and, for many of the specialist tasks, in particular the carriage of liquid fuel, the British contribution relied on the independent British charter airlines.

The Airlift was important for the British charter airline industry, too. Despite having helped out in India, the charter airlines were still regarded with suspicion by the civilian ministries, which remained reluctant to use them further. But the airlines did work out a good relationship with the military which was to stand them in good stead later; and once the initial operational difficulties were overcome, they went on to provide an invaluable contribution to the British share of the Airlift. The airlines benefited not just from the steady income that the government contracts provided, including many hours of winter flying, but also from the greater organisational demands that participation in the Airlift brought with it. The airlines learned how to fly an intensive and repetitious programme which required high standards of flying, maintenance support and logistics. Harold Bamberg, Freddie Laker and Eric Rylands came out of the Airlift with their reputations and bank balances enhanced and stayed the course longer than the other participants, for, contrary to popular belief, the Berlin Airlift was not the making of the charter airline industry. In all, twenty-three charter airlines participated in various phases of the Airlift, contributing over ninety aircraft and flying, between them, 19,278 sorties,[1] but most of the airlines which flew the Airlift were unable to re-adjust when it was over, leading to their early demise. Paradoxically, it was the airlines that did not participate – at least not in a significant way – Airwork, Hunting and Silver City, which came to dominate the sector in the following decade.

OCCUPATION OF GERMANY AND BERLIN

The division of Germany after the war into different zones, each administered and governed by one of the major powers, was agreed at the Yalta Conference of February 1945, attended by Stalin, Roosevelt and Churchill. A further condition was that Berlin, the capital of Germany, should in turn be divided into separate sectors and likewise administered by the occupying powers; surprisingly, even though Berlin was located in the middle of the Soviet zone, no explicit right of access to Berlin from the other zones was agreed. To co-ordinate the administration of occupied Germany, the Commanders-in-Chief of the occupying forces formed the Allied Control Commission; in Berlin there was an inter-Allied Governing Authority, known as the Kommandatura. Initially the occupying powers comprised the USA, USSR and Great Britain, but agreement to include France was also reached at Yalta, and a French zone in Germany and a French sector in Berlin were carved out of the agreed zones and sectors of the Americans and British.

The Russians had fought their way to Berlin and raised the Soviet flag over the Reichstag on 2 May 1945. By the time of the German surrender on 8 May, the Allied forces had stopped roughly along the line of the Elbe and, under the terms of the Yalta agreement, had to withdraw to the west, quitting Thuringia and Saxony. This withdrawal was not made conditional on the Soviets granting unrestricted right of access to Berlin, although the Soviets were already making difficulties in arranging for the first US forces to reach Berlin. General Lucius Clay, the US Military Governor, later recorded, 'I think now that I was mistaken in not at this time making free access to Berlin a condition to our withdrawal into our occupation zone, but I did not want an agreement in writing which established anything less than the right of unrestricted access'.[2] After a number of setbacks and delays, the first American troops arrived in Berlin on 1 July, followed shortly afterwards by the British. The Russians insisted that the Western powers had to feed their own sectors of Berlin, so the allies began the formidable task of provisioning the population, and restoring the services and manufacturing industry; foodstuffs and goods had to come from the Western zones, across the Soviet zone, by train, by truck and by barge. In most areas of civil administration the Soviets were unco-operative, with one notable exception.

THE AIR CORRIDORS

Although the Soviets would give no guarantees over land and river access, over which the allies were reluctant to press them, the Soviets did agree, in November 1945, to allow access by aircraft to Berlin along three air corridors from the Western zones. Each corridor was 20 miles wide, and rose from ground level to 10,000ft. The two shortest corridors were connected to the British zone – the northern corridor for Hamburg covering 95 miles of the Soviet zone, and the Hanover corridor, which was 117 miles long. The longest corridor, 216 miles, connected the American zone and was the most southerly. All corridors terminated in the Berlin Control Zone, a circular area of 20 miles radius centred on the Allied Control Commission Building. There was one airfield in the British sector, at Gatow, which initially just had a single pierced-steel planking (PSP) runway, although a concrete runway had already been started and was completed in July 1947. The Americans had Tempelhof, the magnificent showcase airport and terminal built before the war, but also used Gatow. During the blockade an airfield was built at Tegel, a former airship station in the French sector, which opened at the end of 1948. The Soviets had a number of military airfields.

THE BLOCKADE

From the very beginning, relations between the Soviets and their former allies were tetchy. The consolidation of the Western zones into what eventually became the Federal Republic of Germany, the Marshall Plan (whereby the USA gave massive aid to the battered economies of Western Europe), and the different aspirations of the two major world blocs, all led to further estrangement. The Iron Curtain came down across Europe and what we know now as the Cold War started. By 1948 the Soviets were severely hampering and disrupting rail, road and barge traffic to Berlin, imposing checks and restrictions, often causing the suspension of military and civilian trains. Nevertheless, the allies went ahead with their own plans for the rebuilding of the West German economy and in June announced major economic reforms, including the introduction of the Deutsche Mark to replace the Reichsmark. In retaliation, the Soviets withdrew from the Kommandatura, cut the grid carrying electricity supplies to the western sectors and then announced on the evening of 23 June that from 6 a.m. of the next day all passenger and freight traffic to and from Berlin would be halted, 'because of technical difficulties'. The blockade had begun.

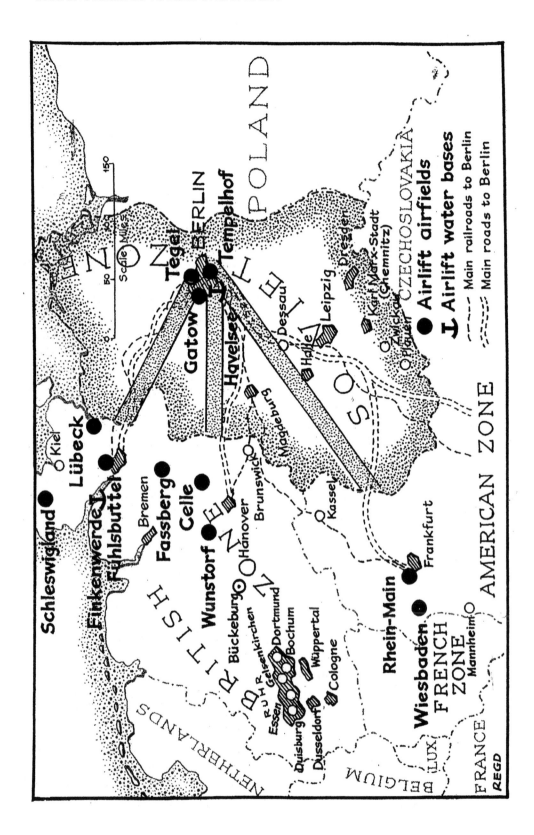

THE AIRLIFT: EARLY DAYS

Original plans called for the supply of just the military garrisons by air; the British used RAF Dakotas from No.46 Group to bring in around 58 tons a day in an operation code-named 'Knicker'. But very soon it was realised that rather more than that would be needed if Berliners were not to starve or freeze. Sending armoured columns down the Autobahn was out of the question; it would surely have provoked an aggressive reaction from the Soviets and the consequences of that could not have been predicted. The daunting task of supplying all of Berlin's needs had to be faced; Berlin's daily requirements had been around 10,000 tons a day. The senior RAF officer in Berlin, Air Commodore Waite, thought it possible that supplies could be brought in by air, and persuaded the British Military Governor, General Sir Brian Robertson, to discuss the plan with Ernest Bevin, Britain's Foreign Secretary. Bevin, in turn, persuaded the Americans.[3] The American operation was code-named 'Vittles', and the British named theirs 'Plainfare'.[4] Neither the British nor the Americans were really prepared for the enormous task that lay ahead: 2,100,000 Berliners needed, at a minimum, well over 4,000 tons of supplies daily. A Dakota could carry 2½ tons. Both countries had been drastically reducing their military establishment since the end of the war, so the net had to be cast far and wide to assemble enough military transports. Eventually the United States had to bring in C-54s, as military DC-4 Skymasters were known, from Alaska, the Pacific, Japan and China; the RAF cancelled its scheduled York services to the Middle and Far East, which were taken over by BOAC. The ubiquitous Dakota was the initial choice for both air forces; very quickly its payload was increased to over 3 tons. The British aimed for 160 sorties a day from their base at Wunstorf, near Hannover; the Americans had further to fly from their bases at Rhein-Main and Wiesbaden, but were soon lifting over 1,500 tons a day. Then the RAF began to introduce Yorks and the US Air Force (USAF) its C-54s, both types capable of carrying up to 8 tons. By mid-July the Allies were flying in 2,250 tons per day.

Inevitably, the first weeks of the Airlift were disorganised, but matters changed at the end of July when the Americans appointed General Tunner, a veteran of the war-time airlift from India to China known as 'The Hump', in command of the entire Combined Airlift Task Force. His deputy was Air Commodore Merer, Officer Commanding No.46 Group, RAF Transport Command. Soon General Tunner had the US contribution standardised on C-54s, with over 200 usually available for flying and many more undergoing maintenance and repairs; the C-54s were sent to Burtonwood, near Manchester, after every 200 hours, and back across the Atlantic every 1,000 hours. The Americans used two bases in the British zone as well, Fassberg and Celle, to take advantage of the shorter distances through the northern corridor. Rigorous air traffic control and operating procedures were imposed, and the central and southern corridors were made one way, going north inbound along the southern corridor, and west outbound along the central corridor. The northern corridor remained two way. The USAF carried mainly coal, flour and dehydrated potato.

Royal Air Force Handley Page Hastings C.1 TG535 at Schleswigland in 1948. (MAP)

Backbone of the Royal Air Force's contribution to the Berlin Airlift, the Avro York C.1 proved an efficient load-hauler. MW285 shows its squadron recognition marks YY-M at Schleswigland in 1948. (MAP)

The British never achieved such a homogenous operation; the RAF used a mix of forty Dakotas, thirty-five Yorks and, later, fourteen Handley Page Hastings, as well as Sunderlands. The Sunderlands, with their anodised skins, were well suited to carrying salt, and together with the Sunderlands of Aquila Airways, used the Havelsee next to Gatow, until it froze over (salt supplies resumed with Halifaxes that had had their fuselages specially treated). But the RAF was soon short of manpower; training of aircrews had to be resumed if numbers were to be made good again. Transport Command's training establishment, depleted for the Airlift, had to be re-established, leading to the withdrawal of ten Yorks and twenty Dakotas together with thirty-six aircrews, and a consequent significant reduction in capacity. An appeal went out to the Commonwealth for help, with the result that the Royal Australian Air Force, the South African Air Force and the Royal New Zealand Air Force agreed to provide twelve, ten and three crews respectively.

The charter airlines were ignored. Eventually, the Air Ministry and the Foreign Office had to be reminded that there was a pool of aircrews and between 130 and 150 aircraft available in the United Kingdom which could be used on the Airlift.

THE START OF THE CIVIL AIRLIFT

There was some question as to whether civilian aircraft could use the corridors, but the Foreign Office overcame its doubts. The first civil aircraft to be chartered in were Flight Refuelling's Lancastrians, in response to an immediate need to carry liquid fuel into Berlin – they joined the Airlift on 28 July. After his barnstorming days, Sir Alan Cobham had pioneered the development of in-flight refuelling and was actively engaged in experiments with BSAA and BOAC to refuel aircraft in flight, so his company had a number of Lancastrians already adapted to carry petrol. The next stage was to charter additional transports, which the Foreign Office asked BEA to co-ordinate through its charter superintendent, Colonel Wharton. BEA acted as agents of the Foreign Office in the administration of the civil airlift and provided ground facilities at the aerodromes in Germany.[5] By the beginning of August Wharton had contracted ten Dakotas, two Sunderlands, a Liberator and a Halifax from a variety of sources; BEA, through its manager in Germany, Edwin Whitfield, arranged for liaison officers to be posted to the various stations where the civil operators would be based, to help in administrative matters as well as providing the link with the RAF. The motley assembly of charter aircraft just added to the varied fleet assortment, flying at different speeds and carrying different payloads. The companies involved at the beginning were: Scottish Airlines (three Dakotas and one Liberator); Bond Air Services (one Halifax); Westminster Airways (one Dakota); Kearsley Airways (one Dakota); Ciro's Aviation (one Dakota); Trent Valley Aviation (one Dakota); Air Contractors (three Dakotas); Air Transport (Charter) (CI) (one Dakota); Aquila Airways, a new flying boat operator (two Sunderlands).

Flight Refuelling already had aircraft converted for the carriage of fuel when the Berlin Airlift started. Avro Lancastrian G-AKDR is smartly turned out in Cobham Blue in 1948. (MAP)

Inevitably there were problems; for example, the civil Dakotas were only certified to carry 6,000lb, rather than the 7,480lb the RAF Dakotas could carry, and it took ten days before the Air Registration Board approved the increase. Many of the companies were very small, with limited resources; much of the administration fell to the aircraft captains, and rather more to the BEA liaison officers. The charter companies were regarded as a nuisance, and treated as such; although the charter airlines knew they would be paid eventually, and could expect to make some profit, they did not know how much they would be paid, or when, nor did they know for how long they would be required. Most airlines flew on the basis of nothing more than a letter setting out terms, and some companies did not have firm contracts even as the Airlift was ending. Maintenance and spares provision was difficult, and the individual airlines were at times over-stretched. As the Airlift continued, it became extremely hard to find parts for Dakotas, leading to the decision to withdraw all civil Dakotas by the end of the year. The civil airlines were shunted around from pillar to post, with the Dakotas being based first at Fassberg, then moved to Lübeck at the end of August, then on to Fühlsbüttel, the civil airport at Hamburg, at the beginning of October. The Liberator and Halifax were based at Wunstorf, but the Liberator was withdrawn at an early stage due to serviceability problems. The Halifax went on to greater glory, and forty were used eventually by the charter airlines on the Airlift. In an astute move, Laker bought eleven Halifaxes from BOAC (known by the corporation as Haltons) in July 1948; three he sold on to Westminster Airways and the remaining eight were leased to Captain Treen of Bond Air Services, with Aviation Traders remaining responsible for their maintenance. More Dakotas joined the operation, one each from British Nederland Airservices, Hornton Airways and Sivewright, two from Ciro's and three from BOAC. At the beginning of September, following the successful trials with Bond's first machine, more Halifaxes appeared at Wunstorf; two more from Bond and one from Skyflight; two Bristol Wayfarers were contributed by Silver City Airways and, for a short time, two Vikings from Trans-World Charter. September also saw the arrival of the first Tudors; A.V.M. Bennett, now in charge of his new airline, Airflight, arrived with a Tudor 2, and his former employers, BSAA, contributed two Tudor 1s handed over to them by BOAC. They all operated out of Wunstorf, carrying freight.

Weekly sorties and tonnages were increasing, and there were some notable feats of endurance; Captain Treen of Bond Air Services made six return trips in a Halton in twenty-six hours. But in a way such enthusiasm caused its own problems. The charter airlines would generate great bursts of activity, then stand down whilst aircraft were maintained and crew had much needed rest, so preventing an even flow of goods. The ratio of crews to aircraft was low – on average 1.3 crew per aircraft – though crew shortages were a problem for the RAF also. Sadly, Airflight's senior captain, Captain Utting, was knocked down and killed by a lorry on the tarmac at Gatow in December. A.V.M. Bennett was the only other pilot qualified to operate the Tudor at night, and for the next two months flew two or three sorties every night – a tribute to his mental and physical endurance, and his astonishing sense of duty.

But matters got better over time. BEA improved its liaison with the RAF and regulated the flow of aircraft more satisfactorily, which did much to improve the co-ordination of the Airlift as a whole. Standardised cargoes were agreed: 7,500lb (3 tons) for the Dakota; 14,112lb (6 tons) for the Halton/Halifax; 1,500 gallons or 5¼ tons for the Lancastrian; over 20,000lb (just under 9 tons) for the Tudors; and 7,400lb (3 tons) for the Wayfarer. Turnaround times at Berlin were reduced: twelve minutes for a Dakota, thirty-three minutes for a Tudor, fourteen to twenty minutes for a Halton/Halifax and twenty-one minutes for a Flight Refuelling Lancastrian. Larger aircraft began to arrive in October, with more Haltons coming from Bond, and Halifaxes from two new operators on the Airlift, Lancashire Aircraft Corporation and Eagle Aviation; one of Eagle's aircraft, G-ALEF, had been acquired from a defunct Norwegian airline, Vingtor, and came resplendent in its previous owner's all-over red livery, being duly named *Red Eagle*. On 11 November 1948, the civil Airlift had completed 100 days of operations, performing 3,944 sorties.

THE CIVIL AIRLIFT: SECOND PHASE

By now it was clear that the Airlift was going to have to continue for the foreseeable future and so further changes were made in its organisation. To ease congestion at Gatow, it was decided that only the larger civil aircraft would be used. Following the example of the USAF, which had withdrawn its C-47s at the end of October, all the civil Dakotas were withdrawn from the Airlift during November, incidentally releasing these aircraft back into the British charter market for other work where they were sorely needed. The civil contribution now relied on four-engine aircraft, ably backed up by Airwork's Bristol Freighters which joined the Silver City Wayfarers but had the nose opening doors; they proved useful for carrying bulky and out-of-gauge freight. Wunstorf became an all-Avro airfield, hosting the Lancastrians of Flight Refuelling and the Tudors of Airflight and BSAA, and now joined by Yorks from Skyways. The Halifaxes of Lancashire, joined in time by further Halifax tankers from British and American Air Services and Westminster Airways, were moved up to newly re-opened Schleswigland, a horrible airfield near the Baltic coast, and at three and a half hours flying from Berlin – compared to two and a half hours from Wunstorf and only two hours from Hamburg – the most distant of the civil airfields, which reduced the number of sorties that could be performed in a day. The operators shared their misery and Schleswigland's bad weather with the newly delivered Hastings of RAF Transport Command. Bond and Eagle remained at Hamburg, where they were joined in March by Flight Refuelling.

With the arrival of the Hastings and the departure of the civil Dakotas, the emphasis for the civil operators now turned towards carrying liquid fuel supplies. By the end of 1948, Berlin's fuel supplies, petrol, kerosene and diesel, were practically exhausted; 220 tons needed to be flown in daily, and the race was on to convert sufficient tankers. A.V.M. Bennett's Airflight had its two Tudors converted, and BSAA, still in existence, was allowed to use five converted Tudor 5s (which had been grounded since the unexplained losses of its two Tudor 4s); they contributed significantly to the 'wet' lift. Flight Refuelling already had its fleet of Lancastrians; now they were augmented by five Lancastrians from Skyways and up to thirteen Halifax tankers from Lancashire Aircraft Corporation. Tony Merton Jones describes the Lancashire operation:

> Each Halifax was capable of uplifting 1,300 gallons of diesel oil per sortie, and by January 1949 Lancashire was flying twelve Halifax tankers into Berlin, representing half the total number of all Halifaxes then flying into Berlin. The Lancashire Aircraft Corporation was able to carry out all the necessary maintenance and conversion work on the Halifaxes in its own workshops. The installation of all radio and navigation equipment, together with the overhaul of the Halifaxes, was performed by the corporation's own engineers at Bovingdon, while the construction of the internal fuel tanks was carried out at Leeds by Yeadon Engineering – a Lancashire subsidiary company. To fly the dozen Halifaxes, Lancashire employed sixteen fully trained air crews, and to maintain these aircraft, one hundred engineers were based in Germany. These engineers could carry out all necessary maintenance, except major overhauls, on a twenty-four hour basis. When a Halifax required a major overhaul or renewal of its certificate of airworthiness, then the aircraft returned to Bovingdon for this work to be carried out. The airline maintained a shuttle service of flights between Blackpool, Bovingdon and Schleswigland with its Airspeed Consuls carrying spare parts and personnel in order to support this vast operation. In order to cope with the demand for spare Hercules engines and other parts, the airline had acquired a total of twenty two Halifax B.6 aircraft and broken them up for spares recovery, thereby ensuring a handsome inventory to support its aircraft on the airlift.[6]

What emerges from the above account is the changing nature of the charter airlines' operations. Instead of using a large number of very small operators, with only one or two Dakotas each, the Foreign Office was now contracting larger organisations which were well able to support their operations from their extensive maintenance facilities. Laker's Aviation Traders looked after Bond Air Services and others; Skyways, Lancashire, BSAA and Flight Refuelling all had large maintenance organisations in England, to which the aircraft returned on a regular basis (aircraft still had very restricted time between overhauls, as little as fifty hours in many cases, and never more than 500 hours). It is, nevertheless, a credit to the smaller operators without such large maintenance organisations that they, too, kept their aircraft in the air. Some of the Halifaxes had seen intensive use before the Airlift; and the Lancastrians and Yorks were never designed for the constant landings and take-off cycles of an essentially short-haul operation. Because aircraft had to return to base if they were unable to land at Gatow, they had to carry 200 per cent fuel, so that every other landing was at maximum landing weight. Keeping them serviceable in the harsh conditions of the Airlift and German winter demanded extraordinary efforts.

AIR BRIDGE

In 1951 the English author Hammond Innes published the novel *Air Bridge*,[7] based on his experiences of the Airlift. In the extract below, he describes the arrival at Wunstorf of a new crew who are due to start flying Tudors, and their first flight to Berlin. The crew members are called Carter, Westrop, Field, and the pilot, Fraser:

We went in search of our rooms. It was a queer place, the Wunstorf mess. You couldn't really call it a mess – aircrews' quarters would be a more apt description. It reminded me of an enormous jail. Long concrete corridors echoed to ribald laughter and the splash of water from communal washing rooms. The rooms were like cells, small dormitories with two or three beds. One room we went into by mistake was in darkness with the blackout blinds drawn. The occupants were asleep and they cursed us as we switched on the light. Through the open doors of other rooms we saw men playing cards, reading, talking, going to bed, getting up. All the life of Wunstorf was here in these electrically lit, echoing corridors. In the washrooms men in uniform were washing next to men in pyjamas quietly shaving as though it were early morning. These billets brought home to me more than anything the fact that the airlift was a military operation, a round-the-clock service running on into infinity.

We found our rooms. There were two beds in each. Carter and I took one room; Westrop and Field the other. Field wandered in and gave us a drink from a flask. 'It's going to be pretty tough operating six planes with only two relief crews', he said. 'It means damn nearly twelve hours flying a day.'

'Suits me,' I replied.

Carter straightened up from the case he was unpacking. 'Glad to be back in the flying business, eh?' he smiled. I nodded.

'It won't last long,' Field said.

'What won't?' I asked.

'Your enthusiasm. This isn't like it was in war-time.' He dived across the corridor to his room and returned with a folder. 'Take a look at this.' He held a sheet out to me. It was divided into squares – each square a month and each month black with little ticks. 'Every one of these ticks represents a trip to Berlin and back, around two hours' flying. It goes on and on, the same routine. Wet or fine, thick mist or blowing half a gale, they send you up regular as clockwork. No let-up at all. Gets you down in the end'. He shrugged his shoulders and tucked the folder under his arm. 'Oh well, got to earn a living, I suppose. But it's a bloody grind, believe you me.'

We were briefed by the officer in charge of Operations at nine o'clock the following morning. By ten we were out on the perimeter track waiting in a long queue of planes, waiting our turn with engines switched off to save petrol. Harcourt [owner of the aircraft] had been very insistent about that. 'It's all right for the RAF', he had said. 'The taxpayer foots their petrol bill. We're under charter at so much per flight. Cut your engines out when waiting for take-off.'

The last plane ahead of us swung into position, engines revving. As it roared off up the runway the voice of Control crackled in my earphones. 'Okay, Two-five-two [aircraft callsign]. You're clear to line up now. Take off right away.' I taxied to the runway end and swung the machine into position.

We took off dead on time at 10.18. For almost three quarters of an hour we flew northeast, making for the entry to the northern approach-corridor for Berlin. 'Corridor beacon coming up now', Field told me over the intercom. 'Turn on to 100 degrees. Time 11.01. We're minus thirty seconds.' That meant we were thirty seconds behind schedule. The whole thing was worked on split-second timing. Landing margin was only ninety seconds either side of touchdown timings. If you didn't make it inside the margin you just had to overshoot and return to base. The schedule was fixed by timings over radar beacons at the start and finish of the air corridor that spanned the Russian Zone. Fixed heights ensured that there were no accidents in the air. We were flying Angels three-five – height 3,500 feet. Twenty miles from Frohnau Beacon Westrop reported to Gatow Airway.

As we approached Berlin I began to have a sense of excitement. I hadn't been over Berlin since 1945. I'd been on night raids then. I wondered what it would like in daylight. Westrop's voice sounded in my earphones, reporting to Gatow Airway that we were over Frohnau Beacon. We switched to contact with Traffic Control, Gatow. And then I was looking out of my side window at a bomb-pocked countryside that merged into miles of roofless, shattered buildings. There were great flat gaps in the city, but mostly the streets were still visible, bordered by the empty shells of buildings. From the air it seemed as though hardly a house had a roof. We were passing over the area that the Russians had fought through. Nothing seemed to have been done about it. It might have happened yesterday instead of four years ago.

Over the centre of the city Field gave me my new course and Westrop reported to Gatow Tower, who answered: 'Okay, Two-five-two. Report at two miles. You're Number Three in the pattern.'

There was less damage here. I caught a glimpse of the Olympic Stadium and then the pine trees of the Grunewald district were coming up to meet me as I descended steeply. Havel Lake [Havelsee] opened out, the flat sheet of water across which the last survivors from the Fuehrer Bunker had tried to escape, and Westrop reported again. 'Clear to land, Two-five-two', came the voice of Gatow Control. 'Keep rolling after touchdown. There's a York close behind you.'

I lowered the undercarriage and landing flaps. We skimmed the trees and then we were over a cleared strip of woods dotted with the posts of the night-landing beacons with the whole of Gatow Airport opening up and the pierced steel runway rising to meet us. I levelled out at the edge of the field. The wheels bumped once, then we were on the ground, the machine jolting over the runway sections. I kept rolling to the runway end, braked, and swung left to the off-loading platform.

Gatow was a disappointment after Wunstorf. It seemed much smaller and much less active. There were only five aircraft on the apron. Yet this field handled more traffic than either Tempelhof in the American Sector or Tegel in the French. As I taxied across the apron I saw the York behind me land and two Army lorries manned by a German labour-team, still in their field grey, nosed out to meet it. I went on, past the line of Nissen huts that bordered the apron, towards the hangars. Two Tudor tankers were already at Piccadilly Circus, the circular standing for fuel off-loading. I swung into position by a vacant pipe. By the time we had switched off and got out of our seats the fuselage door was open and a British soldier was connecting a pipeline to our fuel tanks.

THE THIRD PHASE

In January, civil aircraft from Hamburg and Schleswigland began using Berlin Tegel, another grim airport, with few facilities, no Ground Control Approach, an inoperative control tower and no phone lines to the Berlin Air Safety Centre; it also developed an undulating runway after several months of hard use, which was particularly trying for tail-wheel aircraft which tend to bounce on landing. However, it was operationally more satisfactory as aircraft could now use the northern corridor for both arrivals and departures, and it avoided impinging on the airspace around Gatow and Tempelhof. In February, the Bristol Freighters and Wayfarers of Airwork and Silver City were withdrawn, and Scottish Airlines made a reappearance with two Liberators converted for fuel, based at Schleswigland. The Foreign Office by this stage had been contracting civil airlines for six months, but the government's distaste at having to deal with these exponents of free enterprise was still evident. Foreign Secretary Bevin wrote the following to the Prime Minister on 4 February 1949:[8]

> My attention has been drawn to the problems which arise in relation to the civil portion of the airlift. The civil airlift is admittedly a comparatively small part of the whole, but it is important not only because it is a significant part of our contribution but also because it provides the whole of the wet lift for liquid fuel into Berlin. The airlift is in fact a military operation and it is difficult, if not impossible, to fit into such an operation a number of small segments of private enterprise. The civil operators, of whom there are upwards of a dozen, are of differing types, but for all of them the operation is a commercial venture. Difficulties arise not only from the impossibility of securing orderly operations but also from the problem of making contract terms which provide an adequate incentive without leaving a loophole open for excessive profits at the expense of the Crown.

Even if the civil contribution was merely 'a commercial venture', it continued to play an increasingly important part in the Airlift. On 20 February 1949 the civil airlift had completed 200 days of operations, and had carried 44,883 tons in 7,802 sorties. There were four main loads carried by the civil aircraft: petrol, 10,508 tons; kerosene and diesel fuel, 7,038 tons; food, 21,359 tons; coal, 5,126 tons and miscellaneous cargo, 852 tons. The daily number of sorties flown rose to seventy a day, serviceability had improved, the worst of the winter was behind them and over 350 tons of liquid fuel was being flown in every day. The civil fleet by then comprised thirty-nine aircraft, divided into tankers and freighters: of the 'Wet' tankers, Airflight had two Tudors; BSAA, five Tudors; Flight Refuelling, seven Lancastrians; Skyways, two Lancastrians; Lancashire, eight Halifaxes; British–American, two Halifaxes and Westminster Airways, one Halifax; the 'Dry' freighters were operated by Skyways, three Yorks; Westminster Airways, one Halifax; World Air Freight, one Halifax; Eagle Aviation, two Halifaxes; and Bond Air Services, five Halifaxes. Over the same period, the RAF carried 200,866 tons in 36,442 sorties;[9] the civil contribution comprised just under 20 per cent of the British effort. In March, Flight Refuelling transferred its base to Hamburg;

Freddie Laker bought Handley Page Halton G-AHDO from the British Overseas Airways Corporation just in time for use on the Airlift. It was operated for him by Bond Air Services and carried over 2,000 tonnes to the aid of the Berliners. (MAP)

Avro Tudor 5 G-AKBZ of British South American Airways flew 517 sorties during the Airlift as a fuel carrier. (MAP)

plans were made to boost the tanker fleet further by adapting more of the Tudors and Lancastrians. Eagle was flying its Halifax on three sorties a day, the big Airflight Tudor 2 was averaging 3.8 flights per day. Weekly and monthly tonnages began to soar. By now the Airlift was bringing in over 5,000 tons daily, helped by better than average winter weather. It will be recalled that when the Airlift was first mooted, the daily minimum requirement was estimated to be 4,000 tons. In one twenty-four-hour period, ending at midday on 16 April, the Combined Airlift Task Force had brought in 12,940 short tons of food, coal and machinery on 1,398 flights.

THE FINAL PHASE

On May 11/12 at 12.01 a.m., the Soviets lifted the blockade. The Soviets had watched in wonderment as the Airlift proceeded along its seemingly unstoppable flightpath. Ominously, at the beginning of May, the USAF had introduced the first of its Boeing C–97 Stratofreighters, capable of carrying 26 tons, almost three times as much as the C–54. On the global stage, on 4 April 1949, twelve nations had signed the North Atlantic Treaty, including the United States, the United Kingdom, Canada and France, leading to the establishment of NATO; it was becoming increasingly difficult for the Soviet Union to pick off individual countries. Besides, there were major developments in China where the Nationalist Government was being driven out of mainland China by Mao Tse-Tung's Communist forces; it became more important for the Soviets to bind China tighter to its cause than to watch helplessly as the Western allies flaunted their logistical and technical superiority in the skies over Berlin.

Discussions were held at the United Nations and agreement was reached on 4 May. On 8 May, exactly four years after Germany's unconditional surrender, the Parliamentary Council in Bonn adopted a constitution for the new Federal Republic of Germany. On 9 May, the new Military Governor of the Soviet zone, General Chuikov, issued the order lifting all traffic restrictions on 12 May. And, at 12.01 a.m., as the lights came on again in the western sectors of Berlin, the first Allied trains and convoys crossed into the Soviet zone. At this point the civil airlift had flown in 86,252 tons in just over ten months.

But the story does not end there. The operation of the Airlift, involving many thousands of people on two continents, was too big and dynamic to be wound down overnight. Moreover, the Soviets almost immediately began placing new restrictions on the movement of West German commercial vehicles, and required all trains to be hauled by Soviet Zone locomotives. To make matters worse, the 15,000 West Berlin railway employees of the Soviet-controlled Deutsche Reichsbahn went on strike on 20 May, utterly paralysing the railway system in the Soviet Zone until the beginning of July. The Western Allies decided to keep the Airlift running at the same intensity until all the road, rail and barge connections were secure and fully restored, and to allow a reservoir of supplies to be built up. In June, the British were flying in, on average, 1,700 tons daily. Even without the Airflight Tudors, the daily average was 586 tons of fuel, reflecting sterling contributions from the Schleswigland tankers and Flight Refuelling. But on 13 July the contracts for the Schleswigland carriers were cancelled, and four days later it was the turn of the Skyways Lancastrians. The decision to run down the Airlift was taken at the end of July, and the last civil flight was performed by Eagle Aviation in the early hours of 16 August, when Halifax G-AIAP landed at Tegel with 6½ tons of flour. By early September the RAF and USAF had also drastically reduced their commitment, following the disbanding of the Combined Airlift Task Force on 1 September, and the return of HQ No.46 Group to the United Kingdom.

THE ACHIEVEMENT AND THE ACHIEVERS

Between 26 June 1948 and 30 September 1949, the Western allies flew 2,325,809 short tons[10] into Berlin. The United States was responsible for 1,783,573 tons (76.7 per cent), the RAF 395,256 tons (17 per cent), and the British civil airlift for 146,980 tons (6.3 per cent). Of this total, 1,586,530 tons, and by far the greatest proportion, was coal; food accounted for 538,016 tons, and 92,282 tons was liquid fuel. A considerable quantity of cargo was also carried out of Berlin, just under 71,000 tons, being mostly goods produced in the beleaguered city, and more than 227,000 passengers were carried out of the city, usually by the RAF. BEA continued operating its scheduled services throughout the Airlift, using Vikings, and achieved almost total self-reliance, even flying in enough for its own fuel needs. As for the civil airlines, Flight Refuelling, Skyways, BSAA, Bond Air Services and Lancashire Aircraft Corporation together accounted for 72 per cent of the civil airlift contribution, but Eagle and Bennett's Airflight, with much smaller fleets, made heroic contributions. The Tudor tankers, only seven all told, accounted for 30 per cent of the liquid fuel carried, the rest being carried by up to seventeen Lancastrians, twenty Halifaxes, two Liberators and a Lincoln, teaching the government a lesson in productivity. When the time came for the government to consider what steps it should take to hold some airlift capacity in reserve, the unsold Tudors still with Avro were the first choice.

The United States shouldered the bulk of the Airlift, carrying over three-quarters of all goods inbound; its aircraft were larger and deployed more effectively, and the USAF achieved a much higher ratio of crews per aircraft. In a parallel operation, American civil carriers, including American Overseas Airlines and Seaboard and Western Airlines, carried in many tons of relief packages assembled by CARE, the Co-operative for American Remittances to Europe.

The contribution of the RAF was impressive, given the resources available. As well as keeping its aircraft in the air, the RAF was also hard at work on the ground, building new runways and improving existing facilities; six of the eight dispatching bases were in the British zone, and Gatow was the most heavily used of the Berlin airports. But the RAF was hampered by a shortage of crews and inferior equipment, and for the foreseeable future was never going to be able to achieve more than its modest target of flying in 1,000 tons a day. Although the Hastings were coming on line, Dakotas still carried a large part of the RAF's share to the very end. The RAF had hoped to obtain C-54s to replace the Dakotas, but the United States was unable to release any; and although there was vague talk of acquiring, with Canadian aid, Canadair DC-4Ms, nothing came of that either. A telling assessment of the RAF's contribution appears in an Air Ministry assessment, written in April 1949:

> Almost from the beginning of operation 'Plainfare' virtually the whole resources of Transport Command have been committed to the operation. The scheduled services of Transport Command have been entirely discontinued, airborne training for the Army has been reduced below the minimum War Office requirements, and a number of transport crews have been borrowed from overseas commands to reinforce the 'Plainfare' squadrons. A valuable contribution, totalling about 23 crews, has been made by the RAAF, SAAF, and RNZAF. The Hastings replacement for the York is steadily coming into service and is already operating in considerable numbers on the Airlift. The limiting factor, however, as far as the RAF is concerned, is the supply of trained transport crews. Drastic measures have been introduced to improve the supply of crews for the Operational Conversion Units for four-engine aircraft, but this process of "barrel-scraping" can now go little further. Nor will it be possible for the Commonwealth Air Forces, with the possible exception of a small contribution by the Royal Canadian Air Force, to increase the number of crews supplied.
>
> Altogether it is not possible for the RAF to undertake to lift more than 1,000 short tons (2,000lb) per day into Berlin in future. It is therefore clear to us that the chief, and perhaps the only, source of a material increase in the British contribution is civil aircraft.[11]

Had the Airlift continued into the following winter, the United States was proposing a much bigger operation, aiming for a daily airlift total of just under 8,000 tons, to allow for 5cwt of coal for every household. The British contribution would have risen significantly and, as we have seen, the increase would have had to come from the civil airlines. The Foreign Office agreed to the conversion of ten more Tudors for the carriage of dry goods. All the various ministries involved hoped that the Tudors would be operated by a reputable airline, namely the state-owned BSAA – ironic in view of that airline's deplorable operating and safety record elsewhere – but once the blockade was lifted, the ministries began to have second thoughts, by which time work on the conversions had already started. Exchanges between the Foreign Office and the Ministry of Civil Aviation over which department should pay for the work became increasingly acrimonious.[12] Then the Treasury, which had always been difficult over the contracts, began to get a little shrill about the cost of maintaining the civil airlift, which it regarded as an unnecessary expense; in its 'view' using civil aircraft was much more expensive than the marginal cost of flying additional sorties with RAF aircraft. So the civil contracts were terminated, while the overstretched RAF struggled on, wearing out its equipment and aircrew. Because the RAF had actually worked at close quarters with the civil airlines, the service could appreciate the value of their work. On completion of the tanker contracts, the AO C-in-C British Air Forces of

Occupation in Germany, Air Marshal Williams, had this tribute to make:

> On termination of contracts as tanker operators in Operation 'Plainfare', I wish to extend to you on behalf of the Royal Air Force our sincere thanks and warmest appreciation of the part you have played in helping to supply Berlin. I think the greatest lesson we have all learned has been the ability to co-operate under all conditions of flying, maintenance and living and working together, and you have played your part in full. Good luck in the future.[13]

But the government was plainly embarrassed by its inability to fulfil its commitment to supply Berlin within its own resources, and so was characteristically ungenerous in recognising the contribution of the civil airlines, leading the British Air Charter Association to complain about the apparent 'deliberate attempt to belittle the efforts of the British air charter companies on the Berlin Airlift'.[14] Twenty-one British civilian air crew lost their lives during the Airlift, as did eighteen serving members of the RAF. Most of the Airlift participants were out of business by the beginning of the next decade. BSAA, Bond Air Services, Skyways and the many smaller operators had their futures cut short. Lancashire Aircraft Corporation bought the name and good will of Skyways and it lasted into the early 1960s; Eagle went down in 1968. Laker went on to greater glory, too, before meeting his nemesis in 1982. But Flight Refuelling survives to this day, as part of the appropriately named Cobham plc; and so does Kearsley Airways, no longer flying aircraft, it is true, but employed in building and maintaining aviation electronic equipment at Stansted. Restrictions on flying into Berlin continued until the reunification of Germany in 1990; up until then only American-, British-, Soviet- and French-registered aircraft could operate to and from the airports in West Berlin, so providing British charter airlines with a welcome and lucrative source of business, carrying Berlin holidaymakers on inclusive tour charter flights. Perhaps the final word should be left to Air Commodore Merer, who had been the senior British air officer throughout the duration of the Berlin Airlift. In a lecture to the Royal Aeronautical Society on 13 April 1950, he reflected on the contribution of the British charter airlines, neither glossing over the difficulties nor disparaging the achievement:

> Apart from the diversity of aircraft types, the companies themselves differed considerably in material resources, personnel strength, operating standards and technical efficiency. In the early days some of the aircraft lacked de-icing equipment and the requisite radar navigation aids. The supply of spare parts for some of the aircraft types was a source of anxiety right up to the end of the air lift. With all these factors it was difficult indeed in those days to assess the operational potential of the fleet, but by the spring of 1949 most of the uncertainties had been resolved. Thereafter an intensive, if occasionally somewhat irregular, effort could be counted on. The experience of the air lift showed that the civil charter companies can provide a highly effective contribution in strategic air transport operations alongside the RAF if certain principles are observed; and emphasised their importance as a potential strategic reserve.

FIVE

AIRCRAFT: BUYING BRITISH

MANUFACTURING

Airlines, passengers and freight were all ingredients in the civil aviation formula; so too were the aircraft manufacturers and the airliners they built. When the war ended, there were twenty-seven firms in the United Kingdom designing and manufacturing aircraft; there were also eight companies building aircraft engines. They were privately owned, independent, widely dispersed, and they all needed to make the change from meeting war-time requirements to coping with post-war retrenchment. First, though, let us go back and look at what happened to aircraft design and manufacture as a result of the war.

LOST OPPORTUNITIES

By 1939 the development of three new aircraft and one flying boat was well underway:

(a) The Short S.32 Airliner, a four-engine, all-metal airliner weighing 70,000lb, intended primarily for North Atlantic services, but also for Empire service generally. Two versions were ordered from Short Brothers by Imperial Airways.

(b) The Fairey F.C.1, a four-engine, all-metal airliner weighing about 35,000lb. Fairey Aviation was designing a thirty-seat aircraft with tricycle undercarriage and pressurisation for European services, and twelve had already been ordered by British Airways.

(c) The de Havilland DH95 Flamingo, a twin-engine, all-metal aircraft weighing 17–18,000lb and carrying twenty passengers.

(d) The Short G Class flying boat, an enlarged version of the successful C Class.

Progress on the design of British transport aircraft came to a standstill at the beginning of the war, as the country concentrated on building fighters, bombers and trainers.

The development contracts for the first two of the aircraft types were cancelled, but the de Havilland Flamingo had started commercial operations during 1939 with Guernsey and Jersey Airways, and a military adaptation of the type, the 'Hertfordshire', was used successfully during the war. The G Class flying boat gained its certificate of airworthiness in 1942, but two were subsequently lost. The third, *Golden Hind*, continued in service until 1948, flying to Cairo.

Most of the transport aircraft used during the war, the vast majority of them Dakotas, came from the United States; American manufacturers were able to develop new transport designs and take advantage of the accelerated technological advances that war-time brings. British manufacturers concentrated on producing warplanes in large numbers, although towards the end of the war Avro built the York four-engine transport aircraft, derived from the Lancaster bomber, and Handley Page built a variant of the Halifax bomber as a transport aircraft.

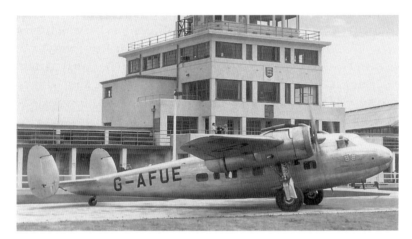

De Havilland Flamingo G-AFUE was used by Guernsey and Jersey Airways during the summer of 1939, seen here outside Jersey Airport's new terminal. (Richard T. Riding)

Short G Class G-AFCI *Golden Hind*. Bigger than the C Class Empire flying boats, with more powerful engines and greater range, *Golden Hind* saw service after the war before being scrapped in 1954. (MAP)

THE BRABAZON COMMITTEE[1]

As we learned in Chapter 1, the Brabazon Committee, reporting on 9 February 1943, recommended the development of five new types, and the production of suitable so-called 'interim' conversions of the Lancaster and Halifax bombers and of the Short Shetland flying boat. These recommendations led to the appointment of the Second Brabazon Committee with the following terms of reference:

> To consider the several aircraft types recommended for post-war civil air transport and to prepare, with due regard to traffic needs and economy of operation, a list of requirements for each type in sufficient detail to provide a working basis for design and development, and to make recommendations accordingly.

In a series of reports issued between August 1943 and March 1945, the committee expanded on its first recommendations and proposed the development and production of seven new types of aircraft:

Type 1	A multi-engine aircraft for a London–New York direct service.
Type 2A	A twin-engine aircraft carrying thirty-six to forty passengers, for European and other medium-stage services.
Type 2B	A twenty-four-seat aircraft, powered with four gas-turbine engines, for European and other short- to medium-range services.
Type 3	A four-engine aircraft with accommodation for twenty passengers in sleeping berths, or forty passengers by day, for use on Empire services.
Type 4	A jet-propelled aircraft, for express services.
Type 5A	A fourteen to twenty-seat aircraft, for feeder services.
Type 5B	An eight-seat twin-engine aircraft for feeder, taxi and charter services.

In addition, the committee recommended the development and production of the Avro Tudor, derived from the Lincoln bomber, to replace the Avro York. Late in 1944 the Vickers Viking, a development of the Wellington bomber, was initiated by the Ministry of Aircraft Production and later endorsed by the committee.

Shortly after the government pronounced on the fate of the airline industry, Ivor Thomas, the Parliamentary Secretary to the Minister of Civil Aviation, introduced in the House of Commons on 24 January 1946 the government's plans for the aircraft industry, outlining three stages of development for the manufacture of civil aircraft. The first stage would be to rely on straightforward conversion of bombers, like the Halifax and the Lancastrian. During the second stage, airlines would use civil developments of military types: the Tudor and Viking already mentioned above, and the Handley Page Hermes, which traced its ancestry back to the Halifax.

The third stage would be a complete break from previous designs, with aircraft specifically designed for civil use. The Ministry of Civil Aviation accepted the recommendations for the seven new Brabazon types, but recognising that the

Type 1 proposal was for a very large aircraft which would take years to develop, the committee subsequently modified the Type 3 proposal to allow for a somewhat smaller transatlantic aircraft to be designed, to be known as the Type 3A; the original shorter-range 'Empire' aircraft then became the Type 3B for which the contender was a variant of the Tudor with a longer fuselage, the Tudor 2. The importance of the North American market was pointed up by the fact that there were now three transatlantic designs, the Type 1, Type 3A and Type 4, all of them to different timescales and specifications.

Twelve types – the seven Brabazon designs, the two Tudors, the Hermes, the Shetland flying boat conversion and the Viking – were launched in 1945: a big wish list and a tall order. And that was by no means all. In 1945 the Ministry of Civil Aviation and the Ministry of Supply added a further five types for initiation in 1946:

(a) A twin-engine aircraft for charter work.
(b) A helicopter, to promote the development of helicopters in the UK.
(c) An eight-seat amphibian aircraft.
(d) A medium- to long-range transport aircraft of 150,000lb for Atlantic and Empire services.
(e) A large flying boat for long range services.

At the same time private enterprise launched the Miles Messenger, the Miles Aerovan, the Miles Gemini, the Avro 19 and a civil version of the Percival Proctor.

BUILDING THE AIRCRAFT

All seven of the new aircraft types that the Brabazon Committee recommended were built, but the process was, on occasion, torturous:

Type 1
This became the Bristol Brabazon, and a prototype of this giant 100-seat aeroplane flew in 1949 and the early 1950s. Development was discontinued when it became apparent that a smaller aeroplane could do the same job more economically, and the Brabazon never entered service.

Type 2
The Type 2 requirement was split into two, with the original Type 2A design being met by the piston-engine pressurised Airspeed Ambassador, now somewhat larger than the Dakota it was intended to replace. Eventually, the modified Type 2B requirement was met by the four-engine turbo-prop Vickers Viscount. The development of the Viscount, and its Rolls-Royce Dart engine, was protracted, but the design benefited enormously from the input of BEA and another early customer, Trans-Canada Airlines, and evolved into an aircraft that could be sold in North American and world markets.

Bristol Brabazon G-AGPW in flight. (MAP)

Type 3

This is the sorriest tale, for progress on the design was delayed whilst resources and effort were diverted to the interim design, the Tudor 1. As Avro was also the designated manufacturer of the Type 3A (Avro 693), and resources are in the end finite, it is not surprising that there was delay and procrastination. The Brabazon Committee was seriously sidetracked on this recommendation. Writing of the Tudor 1 in 1943, Lord Brabazon argued:

> We realise this Lancaster conversion[2] would not be an effective substitute for Type 3A on the Atlantic, but it would do the job as a stop-gap machine fairly well, even though not very economically... Nevertheless, we recommend that intensive study be devoted to this Lancaster conversion immediately... Although trusting that the new Types 3A and 3B will be studied and proceeded with... we feel that the exigencies of the situation force us to suggest that design work on the conversion takes pride of place.[3]

There were alternatives. As we have seen, before the war both Imperial Airways and British Airways had ordered new designs of transport aircraft. Imperial Airways had turned to Shorts, manufacturer of the Empire flying boats, for the S.32, a large four-engine, pressurised all-metal aircraft, with a massive centre section frame and tail-wheel undercarriage. More promising was the design by Fairey, the F.C.1, which was smaller than the Shorts aircraft, but had a tricycle undercarriage and a fuselage 4in wider than the Douglas DC-4; it had a triple tail, rather like a Constellation. Peter Brooks laments the lost opportunity:

The F.C.1 would have required some 'stretching' to make it fully competitive in developed form with the DC–4 and Constellation series, but the design held great promise. It had the added distinction of being the first transport aeroplane in the world to be ordered into production which incorporated all the major features which were later to characterise the 'DC–4 Generation.' If the F.C.1 and S.32 had had their chance, American long-range transport aircraft might not have had such a clear field in the years after the War.[4]

Whatever the reasons, the Brabazon Committee chose not to resurrect either of these proposals, even as an interim design; of course war does hasten the progress of technology, so that pre-war designs, though only six years old, may have seemed prematurely obsolescent. But the decision to back the Tudor seems perverse, given that at least one British aircraft manufacturer had produced a more sophisticated design six years earlier. The Type 3B requirement would be met by the Tudor 2, although for good measure, a rather similar design, the Hermes, was ordered in parallel to the Avro design.

The Type 3A aircraft was never proceeded with. The project was cancelled in 1947 and, as related below, BOAC refused to accept either variant of the Tudor, although various marks of Tudor were built nevertheless. The whole experience traumatised Avro, which withdrew from the civil market for a number of years, and built large bombers instead. Eventually, Bristol was able to meet BOAC's requirements, formulated as the Medium Range Empire and Long Range Empire types, with the Britannia turbo-prop airliner, which entered service in 1957, some fourteen years after the Brabazon Committee's initial recommendation.

Type 4

This became the de Havilland Comet, and evolved from being a small transatlantic mailplane into a somewhat larger jet transport capable of flying the empire routes. The Comet promised so much when it first entered into service, flying fast and smoothly above the weather. In his book, *A History of the World's Airlines*, Ron Davies captures the excitement of the early days of Comet operations:

> The first official delivery to [BOAC] took place on the last day of 1951, and only just over four months later – less than three years after the first flight – the D.H.106, now named the Comet, with thirty-six seats, entered commercial service on 2 May 1952 on the route to Johannesburg.
>
> This was an important day not only for BOAC and de Havilland but for the British aircraft industry as a whole. A dream had become a courageous venture; once thought to be a wild gamble, it was now seen to be an astonishing success. Within a few months the startling saving in time which the 500 mph Comet was able to make compared with its piston-engine rivals, and the trouble-free regularity with which the schedules were achieved, impressed the airline world. The doubters were shamed; the critics were silent; de Havilland had the world at its feet.[5]

De Havilland's first Comet 1 G-ALVG about to land after another test flight. (MAP)

Orders for the Comet began to flow, plans were made to increase production, and even the mighty Pan American ordered the longer-range series 3 in October 1952, but then there were a number of crashes. Aircraft were lost overshooting the runway; another crashed near Calcutta in a storm. Then, inexplicably, on 10 January 1954 a BOAC Comet broke up shortly after taking off from Rome, coming down in the sea off Elba. The remaining aircraft were taken out of service and examined minutely but, as nothing untoward was found, Comet operations resumed on 23 March. But a few days later, on 8 April 1954, another Comet, leased to South African Airways, disappeared over the sea in similar circumstances off Stromboli in Sicily. The aircraft's certificate of airworthiness was withdrawn, and the long and ultimately successful search for clues to explain the catastrophe was begun. It says much for the soundness of the concept that de Havilland were able to proceed with the development of the longer-range Comet 4 despite the setbacks, and that it entered service in due course, just pipping the Boeing 707 to the post as first transatlantic airliner in 1958.

Type 5

The Type 5 designs, the small feederliners, had mixed fortunes. The contract for the larger aircraft, the Type 5A, was awarded to Miles for its fourteen/eighteen-seat Marathon; this was unfortunate as the Miles Aircraft Co. subsequently collapsed during the winter of 1947–48. The assets and design were taken over by Handley

Page, but both BEA and BOAC rejected the type and only a handful went to civilian operators, the bulk passing to the RAF. The Type 5B, however, had remarkable success as the private-venture de Havilland Dove, selling over 500 examples and establishing a considerable bridgehead in the United States. Ironically, its success was not as a feederliner but as an executive transport for businesses, and as a trainer and light transport with air forces worldwide.

Miles Marathon G-ALUB optimistically painted in British European Airways colours. The Corporation never accepted the type, even though it had allocated a class name – Clansman. (MAP)

Fine air-to-air shot of de Havilland Dove G-ALVS, used by the British Embassy in Washington, DC, during the early 1950s. (MAP)

FLYING BOATS

Fittingly, Britain also pursued its maritime heritage by persisting with the design and construction of large flying boats, and a number of transport flying boats were built after the war. As Peter Brooks says:

> Before the War, the Short Empire boats had shown the possibilities of this type of aircraft for use on routes deficient in ground facilities. Flying boats had also proved extremely useful during the War because of their independence of fixed bases. This past experience was responsible for the widely held belief that flying boats would continue to fulfil an important transport role. It took some years of operating experience to establish to the satisfaction of British operators – the Americans had reached this conclusion by 1940 – that the flying boat is not, in fact, economically competitive with the landplane.[6]

In the immediate post-war years the flying boats helped to ease the capacity shortage on routes to the Far East and Africa, and indeed Aquila Airways created a unique niche with its services to Madeira during the 1950s, but all the designs evolved from the war-time Sunderland, and whilst the concept may have been leading ultimately to a dead-end, it did not materially waste resources or design talent along the way. The same cannot be said of the Saunders–Roe design, the SR 45 Princess, a vast flying boat on the scale of the Bristol Brabazon, powered by ten Proteus engines, which languished on the beachfront and in the mind's eye for many years, a true white elephant which nevertheless caught the imagination. At the other end of the scale, Shorts built the five-seat Sealand, too small to be of much commercial use and unable to tackle rough sea conditions.

Saunders–Roe (Saro) Princess flying boat G-ALUN (A.J. Jackson Collection)

BRITISH AIRCRAFT: BRITISH AIRLINES

After the war the need for modern replacement aircraft was critical. The internal airlines mustered thirty-five de Havilland Rapides all told.[7] Dakotas had been supplied under Lend-Lease and the government bought a number of them outright so that they could be operated without restrictions; twenty-one were transferred to BEA which also acquired the Rapides that had been operated formerly by the railway group of companies. BEA then introduced the twenty-four-seat Vickers Viking during the summer of 1946; BEA operated seventy-three of them until they were replaced by the Brabazon types early in the 1950s – the Ambassador and the Viscount. One horrible mistake was the short-term use of captured Junkers Ju 52s, called the 'Jupiter' Class in BEA parlance, although this stopped after one crew was almost asphyxiated by carbon monoxide gas escaping from the engines.

BOAC was in a more desperate situation: BOAC needed aircraft now. By mid-1946, the corporation had 132 landplanes and thirty-five flying boats. Of these, over seventy were twin-engine Dakotas and Lockheed Lodestars; there were forty-nine four-engine aircraft, Lancastrians, Yorks and Liberators; the flying boats included nineteen Sunderlands and the remains of the 'Empire' C Class.[8] Modern long-range aircraft were badly needed, and the interim designs were just not adequate. There were two 'Brabazon stage one' designs – the Halton, which was a straightforward conversion of the Halifax bomber seating up to ten passengers, and the Lancastrian, a similar conversion of the Lancaster bomber, seating nine passengers on a longitudinal bench (and which could be converted to sleep six; one idly wonders what happened to the other three passengers at night). Lancastrians were put into service on the Australian route although their economics were hopeless; each flight to Australia cost the taxpayer around £9,000[9] even if it did take only sixty-three hours.

Stage two designs were slightly more sophisticated developments of war-time aircraft, like the York, developed from the Lancaster but with a capacious square fuselage. Yorks could fly down to South Africa, and flying boats would resume many of the other Commonwealth services, but the only aircraft with sufficient range for transatlantic services was the American built Liberator, mainstay of the Return Ferry Service, and their future long-term use was ruled out. Almost the first act of the new government was to agree to buy five Lockheed Constellations so that BOAC could start a daily service to New York. They were the first of a long line of American aircraft purchased as interim measures while awaiting delivery of new British designs. BOAC was duly castigated for spending dollars in a way not appropriate for what some people clearly regarded as a public utility. 'The argument that the available British aircraft would be uneconomical to operate, therefore BOAC would have to show a financial loss', wrote Air Chief Marshal Sir Philip Joubert to the *Times* on 9 February 1946, 'ought not to be of great importance to a nationalised service, especially when weighed against the obvious advantage of using British aircraft'. Nothing better illustrates the uneasy relationship between the state airlines and the British aircraft industry, which was to lead to quite unrealistic expectations on all sides.

Ever since Imperial Airways undertook to buy only British built aircraft, back in 1924, the fate and fortunes of both British airlines and aircraft manufacturers were almost inextricably linked. Although Imperial Airways ordered relatively large numbers of heavy, multi-engine, British built airliners, nobody else did.[10] Such export successes as were achieved before the war were down to enterprising manufacturers like de Havilland with their range of single- and twin-engine light transports. After the war, aircraft specified by the corporations also met with little success, apart from the Brabazon Committee's Viscount. By contrast, those airliners launched by the independent airlines turned out to be more commercially successful for their manufacturers: the BAC One–Eleven, Avro 748 and Britten-Norman Islander. In a further twist, the new aircraft that did emerge from the hangars of British manufacturers were to prove of greater benefit to the independent airlines than to the state-owned corporations. The corporations had to suffer the disappointments and delays, and the associated costs, of bringing these new aircraft into service. British independent airlines benefited from the early disposal by the corporations of these large fleets of well-maintained aircraft, some of them after disappointingly short service. Many of the aircraft which saw front-line service with the corporations – the York, Viking, Tudor, Hermes, Ambassador, Britannia and Comet – and even a number that did not, went on to have long second careers with Britain's other airlines. Indeed, the Comet, after all its trials and disappointments, went on to have a glorious fourteen-year career with Dan-Air.

Both during and after the war it was understandable that the government would wish to promote the aircraft industry, and redirect Britain's aircraft industry towards civil aircraft production as soon as possible. Aircraft manufacturing was important to the economy – it required modern skills and techniques and was a critical element in any developed country's industrial armoury. A country that stayed at the forefront of aircraft design and manufacture could remain ahead in the global economy. Building aircraft in Britain saved millions in precious foreign currency, usually dollars, when they were bought by British airlines. Furthermore, successful aircraft designs could be sold abroad, for dollars even, therefore actually improving Britain's balance of payments. There was a natural desire to preserve the jobs of skilled technicians and workers after the boom years of war-time production. One of the advantages of nationalisation, or so it must have seemed at the time, would be the ability of the government to direct the state-owned airlines to buy British aircraft. Perhaps there were resentful memories of British Airways before the war which had bought American built Lockheed aircraft. In any case, it is generally true that he who pays the piper calls the tune, and the government, having nationalised the major airlines, would have to approve and underwrite their purchases.

CUSTOMER FIRST?

That it did not quite work out as planned is inevitable, given the human condition. A Treasury minute from this period gives a surprisingly realistic assessment of the dangers of forcing the corporations to buy British built aircraft:

It is no doubt highly desirable that we should for strategic reasons alone maintain a large aircraft manufacturing industry, and it may be argued that this will not be possible unless it has an assured market for its products. It is also desirable, however, that this industry should be as efficient as possible and that British Air Lines should be able to use the best planes available. Both these desiderata are more likely to be achieved by allowing the air line operators to buy the aircraft that they prefer and by exposing the British aircraft manufacturing industry to the stimulus of foreign competition than by providing it with complete protection against such competition in its home market. In addition, if our manufacturing costs are competitive, and it has often been claimed that they are, we may hope to develop an export trade in aircraft so long as other countries do not prohibit the import of British planes.[11]

The airlines needed aircraft that were competitive, indeed, needed aircraft that would give them a competitive edge, if possible. The manufacturers needed to build aircraft that could be sold throughout the world; it helped if they were endorsed by the state corporations. But somehow this process was inverted. In too many cases the manufacturers built aircraft that were closely tailored to the narrow requirements of the corporations, and the corporations had requirements that were unlike those of most other major airlines. For a start, there were two of them, so BOAC purchased long-haul, BEA short-haul, aircraft. Flexible equipment which could be used on a mix of routes was not of any particular interest to the corporations – but it was to their competitors. Nor did either corporation excel at correctly specifying its needs; there was a sad tendency to get cold feet at crucial stages and so reduce the size, range and payload of proposed aircraft. BOAC never seemed to specify aircraft with sufficient range, preferring to operate long-haul services, for example the Empire routes, with frequent stops. The corporation was also intimidated by airport restrictions, so sacrificing range and payload for stunning airfield performance; but of course runways could be, and indeed were, extended to accommodate new aircraft types, making airfield performance much less of a priority. BEA favoured short-haul aircraft, of no great moment when propeller aircraft predominated, but unrealistic when the greater speed of jets pushed out the boundaries further, allowing passengers to travel greater distances for the same elapsed time. British aircraft manufacturers found themselves handicapped when they built aircraft specified for the corporations since those products did not find a ready market elsewhere. The manufacturing industry also faced other difficulties, and its relative decline cannot be wholly attributed to the role of the corporations. John Stroud, writing in January 1946, observed that British manufacturers needed to build aircraft that airlines wanted to buy, following a flight in a new Avro 19 between Glasgow and Stornoway:

The route mileage is 180, involving a flight over mountains, many of which are over 3,000ft high. Combined with turbulent air, this necessitates a minimum operational altitude of 6,000 ft., although heights of 8,000–9,000ft are desirable during strong winds. On this route for approximately one third of each year, there is a freezing level of 3,000ft or under, and it is therefore essential that aeroplanes operating this service should have full de-icing and anti-icing equipment. Lack of this equipment on the Avro XIX made a longer flight necessary on four of the twelve services operated. The need for de-icing equipment does not only apply to this route but to all internal and European routes for a considerable period each year.

British aircraft manufacturers have not grasped the importance of fitting this equipment, and for the most part say that de-icing equipment may be fitted if desired. This attitude is as reasonable as would be that of bus manufacturers if they said 'You can have treaded tires for buses in wet weather if you like but we don't make them as standard equipment'. This lack of understanding of the problems of air transportation by the British aircraft manufacturers is proving highly dangerous to the future well-being of British air transport and unless the designers and operators get together fast and discuss each other's problems then the leadership of the United States in air transport is guaranteed. One certain point is that the designer will have to stop being dogmatic simply because he has produced thousands of successful military aeroplanes, for there is no relationship between the military aeroplane and the civil transport type.[12]

CONTROL WITHOUT THE RESPONSIBILITY

Aside from the difficulties of switching from war-time to peacetime requirements, manufacturers had to contend with a new government organisational framework. British aircraft manufacturers had responded magnificently to the challenge of producing fighters, bombers and trainers during the war, and had learned to coexist with the government's purchasing agency, the Ministry of Aircraft Production. After the war it was assumed that the same relationship would be continued. The Ministry of Aircraft Production became the Ministry of Supply (MoS), and it remained an important constituent in the process, acting as a conduit for government funding of research and development, ordering and paying for aircraft from the manufacturers on behalf of the corporations so that production could be initiated. Once production had got underway, manufacturers would then sell the product commercially. There were, however, two further constituent parts in the post-war scheme of things, namely the corporations and the new Ministry of Civil Aviation. The corporations were expected to be the primary customers for many of the aircraft to be manufactured, yet BOAC failed to participate in the early design and planning stages of the new types, leading in part to the Tudor fiasco. Inevitably, there were turf wars between the two ministries. The dangers of having too many ministries involved are well illustrated by the following exchanges. In a related issue regarding the purchase of American built aircraft, which the Ministry of Supply would obviously try to discourage, it had complained to the Treasury, 'We consider that it should not be left entirely to the Ministry of Civil Aviation to decide whether a particular application should be granted... the condition with regard to the non-availability of British aircraft at comparable prices should be administered, in our opinion, by the Ministry of Supply'. To which the Ministry of Civil Aviation responded, 'Here we have the ugly head of dual control arising. We, in this Ministry, consider the main arguments for allowing purchases of American aircraft must rest on the requirements of civil aviation in the first place… We, in this Ministry, must keep aware of the market position for British types by direct touch with the sales side of the industry. Moreover, with the best will in the world, it will be impossible to avoid the slowing up of obtaining a decision in each case if dual control by two or more Departments is allowed.'[13] Judging from the following perceptive comments from BSAA, it is clear that dealing even with just one Ministry was dealing with one Ministry too many:

> It is necessary to state that the present system of ordering aircraft through the Ministry of Supply is entirely contrary to the interests of the Corporation. It imposes a third party between the user and the manufacturer, causing delays and misunderstandings. It takes control from the Corporation but leaves it with the responsibility. It adds to the cost of aircraft, as the manufacturer's price is loaded with departmental overheads. One of the prerequisites of successful airline operation is that the right aircraft shall be available at the right time at the right price. Under the present system, the Corporation has no control over prices, is in the hands of the Ministry of Supply as to priority of deliveries, and is subject to very considerable interference as to design.[14]

In early 1949 the government relented and decided that the corporations should be allowed to place orders direct with manufacturers, although the effect was slightly spoiled by its insistence that development work would still involve the 'closest collaboration' with two ministries, the Ministry of Civil Aviation and the Ministry of Supply, as well as the corporations and the aircraft manufacturers. The Ministry of Supply and the Ministry of Civil Aviation went on sniping at each other until 1960 when they were merged; doubtless even then the sniping continued.

THE TUDOR, BOAC AND BSAA

One of the unhappiest episodes in the immediate post-war era was the story of the Avro Tudor. The failure of this aircraft was bad enough, but more importantly, the insertion of this design into the post-war manufacturing schedule seriously delayed the development of the transatlantic airliners that Britain so needed to build if it was ever to compete with US manufacturers. There were two versions planned, the longer-range Tudor 1 for transatlantic services, which could carry twelve – yes, twelve – passengers, and the larger Tudor 2, for Commonwealth and South American services, which could be fitted with twenty-two bunks or up to forty-four seats. But, even before its first flight on 4 June 1945, it was obvious that this aircraft did not match up to requirements. BOAC had a requirement for a bread–and–butter machine, something that the very large Bristol Brabazon was not; and at the other end of the scale, the decision to go ahead with the Tudor meant that Avro did not have the resources to develop the original Type 3A specification, leaving it promoting a twelve-seat aeroplane. As the 1947 Tudor Inquiry (Courtney Report)[15] explained: 'The fuselage was to be designed so as to be capable of pressurisation and the passenger space was to be furnished for twelve sleeping passengers. This latter provision was inserted to meet the express wish of BOAC, who felt that this arrangement would enable the aircraft to attract passengers by providing greater comfort than the United States type [Douglas DC–4] with which it was thought at that time it would have to compete.' But by this time the Americans had moved on from the unpressurised DC-4; they were flying Lockheed Constellations, the pressurised Douglas DC-6 was about to enter service, and Boeing was building the Stratocruiser, based on the war-time B-29 Superfortress. They all flew further, faster and with more passengers. Indeed, BOAC had already been given permission to buy Constellations. Although pressurised, the Tudor still had a tail-wheel undercarriage, and was laid out for five cockpit crew, two pilots, a flight engineer, a radio operator and navigator, all for twelve passengers. *Flight* magazine, whilst bravely defending the design, was at a loss to justify the operating economics: 'Economically, the picture of the de luxe BOAC planned Tudor 1, arranged to carry only twelve passengers, trying to compete at standard rates on a North Atlantic service, is absurd. However there are probably more than enough government officials travelling to America to justify the service.'[16] The Tudor 1 then suffered a number of problems, including longitudinal and directional instability, which led to the fitting of a tailplane of greater span, and a much taller, and rather ugly, fin and rudder. The manufacturer laid much of the blame for the delayed entry into service on the shoulders of BOAC, which had indeed procrastinated and added to the general mess with late demands for more than 340 modifications. BOAC never got the aircraft it wanted and, clearly, by this stage did not want it anyway. Indeed, the corporation never put the type into service, rejecting it early in 1947 after a bizarre ceremony at Heathrow when HRH Princess Elizabeth named the flagship Tudor 1 *Elizabeth of England*. A truly shining example of the mismatch that can occur between public relations spin and reality, I cannot do better than quote John Longhurst's robust prose:

> As an instance of the apparent lack of coherence of policy permeating the whole of this question of BOAC's new aircraft fleet there was the extraordinary ceremony which took place, presumably at BOAC's insistence, at London Airport on January 21 1947, when HRH Princess Elizabeth was invited to christen the flagship of BOAC's future fleet of 22 Tudor 1 aircraft with the words 'I name this aircraft "Elizabeth of England". May good fortune attend her wherever she may fly'. Precisely 17 days after which event the Press were called together by the Ministry of Supply and told that BOAC had reported that as a result of its first long range tests in Nairobi, with the Tudor 1, the Corporation was not satisfied with the new aircraft. Various serious technical faults, which made the aircraft unacceptable, were alleged.
>
> To have invited the Heiress Apparent to a full-dress launching ceremony and a week or so later to have announced that the aeroplane was not technically suitable for service seems to have been the height of mismanagement. Had such a thing happened in Queen Elizabeth's reign, somebody's head would have been cut off.[17]

As the subsequent Courtney Report concluded, 'There was on the part of BOAC a lack of drive and determination to get the Tudor into service quickly'. That is no doubt true, but the airline had had little input during the early stages, and was in any case ill-equipped to cope with a problematical new airliner when it already had more than enough problems of its own. The Tudor 2 fared no better. BOAC, Qantas and South African Airways decided in 1944 to standardise on the type, and seventy-nine were ordered by BOAC. But after trials purported to show that the aircraft, which was some 25ft longer than the Tudor 1, could not operate beyond Calcutta on the eastern routes, and Nairobi on the African routes, Qantas and South African Airways decided not to use it. Orders were cut back to fifty, which were then further reduced to eighteen after BOAC pronounced itself not satisfied with performance after trials at Nairobi. BOAC did not even take those aircraft, although six were completed as Tudor 5s and were used on the Berlin Airlift. Sadly, the chief designer at Avro, Roy Chadwick, who had designed the Lancaster, was killed when the Tudor 2 prototype crashed shortly after take off on 23 August 1947; the accident was caused by incorrectly assembled aileron controls.

However, the Tudor did have two champions: A.V.M. Bennett of BSAA and Freddie Laker. BSAA introduced another version on its South American routes, the Tudor 4, which was 5ft 9in longer than the Tudor 1, carried thirty-two passengers and had more powerful engines. But after only a few months in service, G-AHNP *Star Tiger* disappeared on the night of 29/30 January 1948 and the type was temporarily grounded. Although the cause of the loss was not established, the Tudors were put back into service but, bafflingly, on 17 January 1949, another Tudor disappeared, G-AGRE *Star Ariel*, whilst en route from Bermuda to Kingston, Jamaica. The Tudor was again grounded, and in effect so was BSAA, which faced a serious equipment shortage as a result; the airline and its services were taken over by BOAC.

Its second champion, Freddie Laker, realised that the Tudor was a lower cost alternative to the DC-4 that could be useful as a freighter and on government trooping contracts. His engineering company, Aviation Traders, started buying and by February 1954 had no less than twenty, ten of which were intended to be operated, the others to be used as a source for spares. But the War Office would not accept Tudors for trooping, and instead Laker decided to use them as freighters, in the end converting six of them into Avro Super Traders which remained in service until the end of 1959.

FBA – FUNNY BRITISH AIRPLANES

It is easy for American audiences to be amused by the range of odd, and not so odd, aircraft that emerged after the war from the hangars of British aircraft manufacturers, perhaps forgetting that even some American designs, like the Constellation and DC-6, had troubled beginnings. Peter Brooks sums up the dilemma, and the problems that the British faced, in their race to catch up lost time:

The 'interim' types inevitably suffered, in comparison with contemporary American transports, from the lack of civil design experience of the firms which produced them. At the end of the War the American Douglas, Lockheed and Boeing companies had been building stressed-skin monoplane transports for from 10 to 15 years. This experience was also incorporated in the post-war Convair and Martin airliners. The British firms could only extrapolate their experience with military types into the civil field. This led to numerous difficulties and deficiencies, which gradually became apparent as the 'interim' types were used in airline service.

Unfortunately, the experience gained with the 'interim' aircraft was not, in many cases, learnt soon enough for full use to be made of it in the design of the Brabazon types. Thus, wings generally followed a single-spar design philosophy which led to fatigue troubles because of local high stress concentrations in vital structural members. Accessories gave a lot of trouble because military requirements had put insufficient emphasis, from the civil viewpoint, on long overhaul and scrap lives. Such matters as the reliability, ease and economy of maintenance, and overhaul life of engines required a new emphasis. Detail design required greater care and had to be based on new philosophies: particularly important now were durability, accessibility and ease of operation of such items as doors, hatches, refuelling points, cowlings, control locks and many other similar components. New types of radio, radar, and other navigational equipment had to be developed, and operating hazards particularly important in transport operation – such as icing – overcome. The whole field of interior layout and design, cabin air conditioning, soundproofing and passenger-seat design was virtually unknown. No wonder many in the airline business, who used British aircraft, felt that life could be made easier by turning to the relatively 'de-bugged' and trouble-free American types, which the vast majority of operators were using and–for this very reason– improving still further more rapidly than were the British designs.

The 'interim' and Brabazon types have had more than their share of difficulties for these reasons. Quite apart from the more spectacular disasters in service–such as the major structural failures in flight of the Bristol 170, Viking and Dove, the cabin failures and ground-stall of the Comet, the disappearances of the Tudors and the flap failure of the Viscount – there were the many other less-publicised troubles which afflict all undeveloped aeroplanes and cause irregular and unpunctual services, higher maintenance and operating costs, and expensive modification programmes. Only now, after long periods of service, have the survivors of the first British post-war generation attained fully competitive standards of reliability.[18]

Was the government's investment worthwhile? Some of the aircraft produced had noticeable success in the world market, like the Viscount and the Dove. Others, such as the Viking and the Bristol Freighter, had more modest success. The Comet and the Britannia were too late and sold only in very moderate numbers for front-line use, and the Ambassador and Hermes sold in even smaller penny numbers. In all, 1,170 Brabazon 'Types' were built; before and during the war, de Havilland alone had built over 1,100 of its airliners. At the time, the taxpayers may not have felt that they benefited much from the millions of pounds spent on the design and development of these aircraft, but they fulfilled a key role inasmuch as they kept British involvement in aircraft manufacturing current and effective, to the extent that the industry is still a worthwhile contributor to the national economy. Charter airlines benefited, too. It was the availability of inexpensive, relatively unused equipment, handed down from British and overseas scheduled airlines that underwrote their operations in the 1950s and 1960s, allowing them to create new opportunities for business, which ultimately led to sustained growth.

But if the aim was to provide Britain's state-owned corporations with the flagships of British industry that the Brabazon Committee clearly intended, the answer to whether investment was worthwhile has to be no. Luckily BEA had the Viscount, but the front-line equipment of BOAC remained stubbornly American built from 1946 until the introduction of the Vickers VC10 in 1965, with just a little flurry of Britannia/Comet activity at the end of the 1950s. BOAC's fleet of Constellations, Stratocruisers, DC-7Cs ('Seven Seas') and Boeing 707s, underpinned by the Canadian built 'Argonauts', reflect the true measure of the Brabazon Committee's success.

SIX

ASSOCIATE AGREEMENTS
1948–49

SECOND THOUGHTS

As the motley collection of transports and converted bombers flew across the plains of Germany to the relief of Berlin, there was a parallel development to this charter flying; one, moreover, that offered the private airlines the promise of a partial return of their birthright. When the airline networks of the railway-owned airlines, together with Channel Islands Airways and Eric Gandar Dower's airline, had been nationalised in 1947, the government determined that BEA, and only BEA, should fly domestic scheduled services; international services had to be shared with the other corporations and foreign airlines. There was much aggressive talk of air-charter services being permitted only if they resembled a taxi service rather than a pirate bus, and frequent mention of the penal code in respect of breaches of the relevant section of the Act.

BEA inherited a patchwork of internal routes, a few of them trunk routes, but many spread thinly around the British coastline: lifeline services to islands large and small, the Cardiff–Weston air ferry, holiday routes to the Channel Islands and Isle of Man. Nothing daunted, the corporation announced grandiose plans to introduce even more services, including new cross-country links.[1] But BEA quickly became over-stretched. Far from launching new domestic services as it had boasted it would, the corporation found itself having to retrench barely one year later. After accumulating a deficit of over £5 million in under two years, BEA announced in October 1947 that it was withdrawing from seven domestic routes: Belfast–Carlisle–Newcastle; Isle of Man–Carlisle; Bristol–Southampton; Cardiff–Bristol; Prestwick–London; Cardiff–Weston-super-Mare; and Prestwick–Belfast. To compound the problems further, the chairman, d'Erlanger, sacked three of the pioneers of Scottish aviation, first George Nicholson, followed in quick succession by Captain Fresson and William Cumming. 'Thus in a few months, and less than a year after the formation of this new corporation, Britain lost three men who knew more than most people about running internal services in Great Britain and who had made a great success of their companies before the War'[2]. That d'Erlanger was himself sacked a few weeks later was small consolation.

As the corporation took stock, someone there had the temerity to suggest to the government that perhaps the abandoned routes could be taken over by the independents, under proper supervision, of course.

'ANY CRUMBS WHICH MAY FALL FROM THE BOARDS OF THE THREE CORPORATIONS'

The government was nonplussed. One of its horses had fallen at the first hurdle, and it now looked as if a different jockey would have to remount and continue round the course part of the way. Such back-sliding from its doctrinaire approach was difficult to take, and was followed by several months of vacillating on the part of the government; if the independents were to be allowed to take over some of BEA's routes, then they had to be tied very closely to the corporation's apron strings. But a solution was found which allowed charter companies to take up the abandoned domestic routes, and any others not operated by the corporation, by exploiting the serendipitous wording of the 1946 Act. Under the Act an 'associate' was defined as an undertaking which provided air transport and was 'associated with the corporation under the terms of any arrangement for the time being approved by the Minister of Civil Aviation, as being an arrangement calculated to further the efficient discharge of the functions of the corporations'. On 2 April 1948, that is but a month before the start of the summer season, the government announced a six-month trial period for the coming summer. *Flight* was unimpressed by the apparent change of direction, but in its leader of 27 May 1948 coined the perfect expression of the charter airlines' fortunes:

> Private enterprise is to be given a six months' trial run. In these days of government monopolies, which mainly appear to mean the sole privilege of losing the taxpayers' money, the charter companies must, presumably, be grateful for any crumbs which may fall from the boards of the three corporations. An atmosphere of sweet reasonableness is introduced by the statement that BEA will not levy 'toll or tribute' on the private companies, which will take any profits and bear any losses.
>
> On the whole, there appears to be little cause for jubilation. The private firms will have to satisfy the Minister that the service for which application is made is desirable, and toe the line with BEA. After that they will be free to run the service as economically as they can. If some do make a profit in such conditions, they will have earned it.[3]

On any routes that BEA, or for that matter BOAC, did not want, charter airlines would be entitled to carry passengers and goods on scheduled services as 'associates' of the corporation; the charter airlines had to pay BEA a fee of £25 to become an associate, and then agree with BEA the timetables, frequency and fares, but remained responsible for their own traffic and aircraft handling, and of course any losses, or profits, that were incurred. But the corporations reserved the right to resume operation of the route themselves if circumstances changed, for example if the route began to show a profit! With development costs borne by another company, yet still retaining the right to take over operations under their monopoly powers whenever they wished, it was an almost perfect arrangement for the corporations. More significantly, in view of their subsequent history, it was the basis of the secondary and third level route networks with which independent airlines were cursed for the next forty years; for most of them there was no other option but to slog away at developing thin and difficult routes which the corporations had no interest in exploiting.

One of the first airlines to take advantage of the change was Western Airways, back operating the Cardiff–Weston-super-Mare shuttle service from 25 May 1948. The anomaly of that situation did not escape the notice of 'Commentator' in *The Aeroplane*:

> This new arrangement for independent airlines to run some of the internal services that BEA has wiped its hands of, is typical of the infinite capacity for compromise so many examples of which are part of this Island's story.
>
> A Bill is passed, backed by threats of a fine of £5,000 or two years' imprisonment to reserve regular air services to the Corporations. Within two years of the Bill's becoming law, the chocks under the independent wheels are kicked away. Can this new departure be taken at its face value or is it a pit set for the unwary? And could any other country boast a managing director of its leading Airways Corporation, Mr Whitney Straight, as owner of the private company, Western Airways, which is setting out to show the other leading Corporation how to suck eggs.[4]

Western Airways operated the service in co-operation with Cambrian Air Services, using Ansons and Rapides and offering seven flights a day over the fifteen-minute sector. They also managed to reduce the landing charges that were charged by the Ministry of Civil Aviation – something that BEA had been unable to achieve during its tenure. Whitney Straight got over whatever embarrassment he may have suffered by changing his group's and the airline's name to Airways Union.

A number of charter airlines followed suit, and applied for associate agreements on other routes. Those that actually operated services are listed below:

Air Enterprises Ltd	Croydon, Gatwick, Southampton–Cowes/ Somerton, Isle of Wight
Barclays International Airways	Cowes–Hurn
	Croydon–Cowes–Hurn
Brooklands Aviation	Shoreham–Southampton via Cowes
Cambrian; Western Airways	Weston–Cardiff
Lancashire Aircraft Corporation	Leeds–Isle of Man
	Blackpool–Southport
Northern Air Charter	Newcastle–Isle of Man
Patrick Aviation	Birmingham–Isle of Man
Scottish Airlines	Prestwick–Blackpool

In total, 12,896 passengers were carried in 1948. There was a certain fascination with the Isle of Wight, although Portsmouth Aviation, better known previously as PSIOWA, never resumed its services, leaving it to others to resume the short Solent crossing that it had pioneered before the war. Air Enterprises offered twice-daily flights from both London airports, and five flights a day for the ten-minute hop between Southampton and Cowes. Brooklands flew twice a day with its Rapides.

With rather less fanfare, the minister also allowed charter airlines to apply for Inclusive Tour Permits, again involving associate agreements between BEA and the respective airline, which allowed the latter to run inclusive tours at a price covering both fares and accommodation. Jersey was the main destination, but Airwork's flights for Polytechnic Travel were covered by a permit between Blackbushe and Basle, and Skyways had a permit from Northolt to Geneva. Almost by accident, inclusive tour charter flights could now be regarded as a legitimate activity for the independent airlines.

THE DOUGLAS REPORT

Lord Pakenham, the recently appointed minister, then asked his friend Lord Douglas to examine the working of the temporary agreements with the charter airlines which had been allowed during the summer of 1948, and to make further recommendations; in October of that year Lord Douglas submitted his report.[5] As it was never intended to be published, Lord Douglas's tone was bracing; indeed, he went far beyond his original remit – 'to examine the operation of those Sections of the Civil Aviation Act, 1946, which enable the Air Corporations to appoint associates or agents and to make recommendations' – and discussed at length the shortcomings of the corporations, especially those of BEA. Impressed by the vigour of his searching inquiry, Lord Pakenham decided to ask him to be BEA's new chairman – understanding its problems at least gave Lord Douglas a head-start in resolving some of them during his tenure.

Lord Douglas was critical of the Ministry for not explaining in greater detail what it thought the charter airlines were allowed to do, but argued against changing the Act, especially the contentious Clause 23, regarding it, and any subsequent case law, as sufficiently robust. He suggested giving a suitable licensing authority guidelines to handle the applications, as between them the Ministry and BEA were too slow in processing the requests for associate agreements; such an authority had existed before the war. Turning to the corporations, he criticised BOAC *en passant* for being over-staffed and having too elaborate an organisation, before putting his future charge, BEA, under the spotlight. His first remarks are telling:

> I doubt whether an organisation with so many General Managers, whose functions overlap, can be efficient: it would be considerably improved if all the traffic functions were combined under one head. Moreover, there appears to be a lack of drive in the management of the

Corporation. Instead of pursuing an aggressive policy and going out looking for business, they seem content to undertake the minimum services required of them and to find excuses for avoiding new work. It seems wrong that a national organisation with definite responsibilities to the public should have decided that the way to reduce their deficit was to curtail the air services provided. Their first stop should, I consider, have been not to cut their services, but to make a vigorous attempt to reduce their costs and to cut out any dead wood in their organisation.

Although Lord Douglas was sceptical as to whether many domestic routes could ever make a profit, he noted that the pre-war services of Channel Islands Airways had been profitable, and regarded the services to the islands as 'money spinners'. That they were not, he put down to a lack of local knowledge and an inability to delegate:

Channel Islands Airways, who did all their maintenance on the Islands, carried out the main overhauls of their aircraft in the winter and did most of the normal maintenance in the mid-week period in the summer. By this means, they were able to use all their aircraft at the time when they needed them most, viz., at the week-ends in the summer. BEA, on the other hand, spread their maintenance evenly throughout the year, so that the same number of aircraft are undergoing over-haul at any one time. This arrangement may be the best way of obtaining the maximum use from the maintenance base, but it completely ignores the traffic requirements. It also means that the Corporation's engineering staff in the Channel Islands are not fully employed in the winter.

The Channel Islands representatives told me that there had been a very considerable increase in staff when BEA took over the services, and that, because of over-specialisation of the duties of the ground crews and lack of personal interest, it appeared to the local people that BEA were getting much less work from their staff than Channel Islands Airways did in similar circumstances. It is probably worth recording that Commander Waters, who was managing director of Channel Islands Airways and is now General Manager (British Services) in BEA, was most embarrassed when I pressed him to explain (in front of his Chairman) the differences between the operation of the Channel Islands services by his old company and by BEA.

And in an admission that would seem to vindicate those recently sacked Scottish pioneers, Lord Douglas extracted the following information about BEA's air services in the Highlands and Islands of Scotland:

The Ministry prepared for me a statement comparing the cost of operating the Scottish services with DH89's by the AAJC[6] in 1944 with the cost of similar services by BEA in 1947/8. This showed that BEA's maintenance costs were three times those of AAJC and that the total operating costs were twice as high. BEA's explanation that the increase was due mainly to the higher cost of staff, because of the higher wages and shorter hours which now apply, is not very convincing. I suspect that the real reason is that their standards of operation are too lavish.

Lord Douglas suggested that the corporations might co-operate with each other more over such matters as passenger handling, airport coaches, booking offices, maintenance, even pooling of aircraft and crews, to cover weekend and seasonal peaks. That might lead to an amalgamation of all three corporations; as a first step, he thought BOAC and BSAA could be merged. He devoted much space in the report to considering the future development of air-freight services and facilities, allowing the charter airlines the right to continue tramping and fruit-importing, but urging the corporations to undertake a more proactive role in establishing their own services, possibly in co-operation with the Post Office: 'Here is an ideal way for two nationalised industries to co-operate with one another and to give the public a better service'.

Whatever his feelings may have been about BEA, he was not over-impressed by the charter companies either. He thought they too should co-operate with each other more, and criticised the decision of the two largest charter carriers, Skyways and Airwork, not to join BACA, which he said reduced its usefulness and made co-operation between the members all the more difficult, leading to cut-throat competition. Lord Douglas disapproved of competition, cut-throat or not, as his later record as BEA chairman shows. Tellingly, he also noted that very few of the main charter companies relied solely on the business of operating aircraft, boosting their revenues with other work, such as maintenance, aircraft conversion, coach building and airport services, which he took to indicate that, 'few of the companies have sufficient faith in the air charter business to trust their whole future to it'. The post-war boom in travel had dissipated, and in any case the corporations were now better able to meet the demand for individual travel; freight opportunities had also diminished, and the independents 'wanted some guidance about the field that would be left open for a good Charter Co. in the future'. Associate agreements were seen as a useful step, but the charter airlines wanted greater security of tenure and quicker approvals. BEA wanted them only to operate on routes that the corporation had given up, or in order to provide additional peak summer capacity; in any event, the corporation also wanted to be in a position to take back any routes that had been successfully developed by the charter airlines. As for inclusive tours, the government had already agreed that they could be offered by travel agents and charter airlines; their number was small, and the airlines concerned, Airwork and Skyways, drawn from the first tier of the independent airlines. It was a small foot in the door, a minor concession to the charter airlines, it would surely not lead to a deluge. BEA accepted that inclusive tours could be operated over routes in which they had no interest, but was reluctant to allow competing services, except when there was a demonstrable shortage of capacity, as happened at weekends on routes to the Channel Islands and Isle of Man. BEA was not alone in this. The most prolonged anti-charter policy in the post-war era was pursued by the insular authorities in the Channel Islands, which over the last half of the twentieth century has never deviated from the opinion they expressed to Lord Douglas, 'that they were strongly opposed to the "inclusive tour" type of Associate Agreement. They thought that the tours were being used as a blind to operate what amounted to scheduled services. They would much prefer, therefore, that if Associate Agreements are to be granted, they should be for the operation of straightforward regular services.'

LORD DOUGLAS'S CONCLUSIONS

Lord Douglas seemed to agree. In his conclusions, he specifically approved only two categories for consideration as associate agreements:

1)   So-called ferry services, that is short distance over-water routes, such as the Weston–Cardiff ferry, which he thought were 'beneath the notice of a large Corporation'.
2)   Additional seasonal services. However these latter should only be operated under associate agreements with BEA, and not as inclusive tours; he thought the case for inclusive tours was special pleading.

He did not think that the charter airlines should be allowed to develop trunk routes. He realised that the six-month period of any agreement was probably too short, but was reluctant to allow them for longer in case they denied BEA subsequent access to the routes. Finally, he reiterated that charter airlines would still be able to operate charter services, redefined, hopefully, by the Ministry.

The report is much less about the charter airlines and associate agreements, and much more about the short-comings of the corporations, than was generally supposed at the time. As it was never published, the government was able to stifle any discussion of the more unflattering disclosures about the airlines in its charge, preferring instead to limit its comments to those elements covered by its original, and narrow, terms of reference. When Lord Douglas came to summarise his conclusions, of the thirty-four set down in his last paragraph, only eight refer to charter airlines and the associate agreements. Most of them dealt with the corporations, and he reserved his harshest criticism for BEA: 'The management of BEA appears to lack drive and there is evidence that, in many respects, the Corporation is inefficient. I therefore recommend that there should be a strict and detailed investigation into the organisation and staff of BEA with a view to effecting drastic economies'. He got the job.

ASSOCIATE AGREEMENTS

The government, when it came to consider Lord Douglas's recommendations, was more sympathetic than he had been to the charter airlines. It accepted his recommendations on associate agreements, as far as they went, but did allow that the agreements should be for a longer period, up to two years initially.

In January 1949 the government announced its plans for the continuation of the 'Associate Agreement' scheme. The 1946 Act would not be amended; the government merely delegated the process of considering route applications to the recently constituted Air Transport Advisory Council (ATAC)[7] under the chairmanship of Lord Terrington, a barrister with a long record of public service as an arbitrator. The ATAC would make recommendations for approval to the minister and, of course, the minister would have the final say. Agreements would normally last two years, and the government envisaged that services would cover either 'ferry' and 'cross-country' routes, or holiday routes which had heavy seasonal traffic. The corporations still had the power to reclaim any route that they wanted. Although the services were operated under associate agreements with the corporations, which meant initially BEA, they did not appear in the BEA timetable.

Lord Pakenham warned that associate agreements were not to be regarded as the thin end of the wedge. Under the headline 'Small Mercies', *Flight* magazine was scathing about the concession, starting with an extract from the BACA press release:

> Although welcoming the new arrangement, the Association hopes, one day, to secure amendments in the Civil Aviation Act to give real freedom to the independent operators, but meanwhile the Association is grateful to the Minister of Civil Aviation for the action which he has taken.
>
> In a communication to the Press, the British Air Charter Association, Ltd., expressed in the very polite words quoted its thanks for small mercies to the Minister of Civil Aviation in connection with his written answer to a question in the House of Lords last week. In view of the fact that the Association is not only at the small mercies of the minister but entirely at his mercy, such politeness is understandable. We should have expressed it much less politely as 'Thank you for nothing'.[8]

But *Flight* was unduly pessimistic. The charter airlines, with their remarkable ability to exploit to the full any small opportunity extended to them, and to develop low-fare and leisure markets in a way that no one could have foreseen, did reap no little benefit from the associate agreements that they concluded over the following years, even if the routes they operated relegated them to the second division. Furthermore, the licensing authority was more independent and less doctrinaire about inclusive tours than anticipated. Helped in part by the shrewd chairmanship of Lord Terrington, who was able to gauge the limits of what was acceptable to the prevailing government and even push out the boundaries a little, charter airlines were able to develop scheduled services for special markets, cross-Channel car ferries, flying-boat services, domestic networks, low-fare services to colonial Africa and above all, together with the tour operators, holiday flights to Europe. The government had opened a small loophole; resourceful charter airlines made it much bigger.

In April 1949 the first approvals for associate agreement services were announced, with a high preponderance of over-water routes to the Isle of Man, Isle of Wight and Jersey, as well as some trunk routes from London, to Manchester, Birmingham and the West Country. For the record, these were the services operated under associate agreements in 1949:[9]

Air Enterprises	Croydon–Sandown, Isle of Wight
	Croydon–Birmingham
Aquila Airways	Southampton–Lisbon–Madeira (Funchal)
Brooklands Aviation	Shoreham–Isle of Wight–Southampton
	Shoreham–Southampton–Jersey
Cambrian	Cardiff–Weston, Barnstaple, Jersey and Guernsey
East Anglian Flying Services	Southend–Ostend
Hornton Airways	London–Exeter–St Just (Land's End)
Lancashire Aircraft Corporation	Blackpool–Isle of Man, Southport, Jersey and London (Northolt); Leeds/Bradford–Jersey, Isle of Man and London (Northolt)
North-West Airlines[10]	Isle of Man–Manchester, Birmingham, Blackpool, Glasgow, Leeds and Newcastle
Olley Air Service	Croydon–Le Touquet
Patrick Aviation	Birmingham–Jersey, Isle of Man
Scottish Airlines	Prestwick–Isle of Man
Silver City	Lympne–Le Touquet
Sivewright	Manchester–Isle of Man, Jersey
Somerton Airways	Southampton–Cowes, Isle of Wight
	Portsmouth–Cowes, Isle of Wight
Transair	London–Ostend, Blackpool

Aircraft operated were mostly Rapides and Consuls, but Wayfarers, Dakotas and a DH 86 were also used. North-West Airlines, Somerton Airways, Cambrian's Jersey service, Scottish Airlines and Aquila had licences that covered 1950 as well, the rest expired before the start of the summer 1950 season. Most services were suspended during the winter months. Patrick Aviation did so well with its Birmingham–Jersey service that even BEA noticed, and took over the service for the summer 1950 season. The corporation was perfectly entitled to take this action, and it was even in the spirit of the associate agreements, but it was a body blow to Patrick which pulled out of scheduled services after the 1950 season, and closed down a few years later.

In June 1949 Aquila Airways inaugurated its fortnightly service from Southampton to Funchal in Madeira, via Lisbon, with an additional weekly service between Funchal and Lisbon. The Southampton–Madeira service was particularly successful during the winter months, and by the winter season 1950-51 Aquila had increased its services to three times a week, with a reduced service during the summer months. The airline had experienced an early rush of work when it started operating Short Sunderland flying boats from Southampton at the beginning of August 1948 and immediately found employment for them on the Berlin Airlift. The airline then flew ad hoc passenger and freight charters, but spotted an early opportunity to fly scheduled services to the rocky island of Madeira, a popular holiday destination with no airport. The airline received full co-operation from the Portuguese authorities, who even gave the airline domestic pick-up rights between Lisbon and the island.

Meanwhile, Silver City resumed its car ferry services from Lympne to Le Touquet on 13 April 1949, now under an associate agreement with BEA, initially planning a minimum of three flights a day, increasing to six a day by July; in fact, the service proved so successful that the airline and its French partner SCAL – Société Commerciale Aerienne du Littoral, the initials were the same as for Silver City Airways Ltd – were operating sixteen flights daily in July and August, rising to twenty-three on the busiest day. The fare for a single journey for a small car and its four passengers was £27, which was slightly more than the first-class fare on a ferry. Over 2,500 cars were carried in 1949; Silver City had been thinking 'ambitiously' in terms of 1,000. Understanding price elasticity of demand, Silver City began to pursue a policy of reducing fares for cars and passengers over the next few years, and just watched the traffic grow.

CHARTER FLIGHTS

During the winter months, Silver City also used its Freighters on charters and found useful work for them carrying horses and livestock. Not all charter aircraft had joined the Berlin Airlift, but there was, nevertheless, a severe shortage of the larger four-engine types available for other work by the end of 1948. Operators of Halifaxes were involved in the Northern Ireland milk run during September and October, and as the aircraft came off, they were redeployed to Berlin. Late-season fruit flights were left to foreign operators, but the return of the Dakotas in November from the Berlin Airlift meant that some capacity once again became available. At the end of 1948 Hunting Air Travel, which had no involvement at all with the Airlift, won a significant one-year contract with the Overseas Food Corporation (OFC), manager of the Ground Nuts Scheme in Tanganyika, to carry its staff between London and three designated airfields in East Africa, Dar-es-Salaam, Nairobi and Tabora. The scheme was designed to provide a source of oil for margarine, cooking fats and soap for the British market, and was planned to cover 2 million acres, involving large-scale clearing of virgin bush for planting. BOAC had suggested that as a government agency, the OFC should use the 'chosen instrument', but the OFC resisted the pressure and put the bid out to tender. The Hunting flights left from Bovingdon, taking three days over the journey, with night stops at Malta and Khartoum. Passengers were OFC employees, their wives and families; return flights also took three days.

SKYWAYS

Not all flights were quite so leisurely. Crew duty limitations were at the discretion of the company and good sense, and the use of so-called heavy and double crews allowed long flights to be performed without night stops. The problem of crew hours affected scheduled airlines less; operating to a regular schedule, airlines like BOAC could have replacement crews, also known as slip crews, already positioned at an overseas station, ready to take over from the incoming crew. Charter airlines, which on occasion also had to operate lengthy sectors, did not have that advantage; they could either night stop the crews and passengers, or fly with extra crews on the aircraft, who could take over and allow the first crew to rest. The aircraft were converted to have bunks so that off-duty crew could sleep, but these reduced the number of seats available for fare-paying passengers. In the following account Captain Brice of Skyways describes the background to planning such a flight with a Douglas DC-4 Skymaster, in this case a special series of charters undertaken by Skyways during August 1948 to carry the Palestine Police Force from London to Singapore:

One moment no one was thinking much about the Far East, and the next moment a telephone bell rang and there we were, committed to fly the Palestine Police Force, some four hundred strong, to Singapore – and in a hurry.

Our normal schedule for previous flights had been in the neighbourhood of eight days, but with aircraft heavily committed elsewhere, this was too long. Moreover, Skymasters with thirty-six seats were not going to be of much value in such a mass exodus, so there were modifications to be carried out before we even started. We converted a Skymaster from thirty-six to fifty-three, and with two Yorks already equipped with forty seats, we were ready to go in a very short space of time.

Then arose the matter of schedules. With the Yorks we had to take it a bit easy, because of their limited crew quarters and lack of sleeping accommodation, but we did contrive to position a slip crew at Karachi, in itself no mean feat for a charter company, and this speeded things up a bit.

With the Skymaster, however we had a more ambitious idea. We decided to plan the flight non-stop there and back, except for refueling stops, which would mean an overall time of just over four days.

At first glance this looked formidable and even impossible, but, like most problems, there were ways around, and we did achieve a figure of 91 hours' flying out of 110 with the same aircraft, and with the same crew. And, moreover, we did so, not once, but four times with, of course, a crew change at home base.

Our idea was not new, but it worked. We carried a double crew and provided sufficient beds for the off-duty crew to sleep whilst their opposite numbers worked. Each crew consisted of a captain, a radio operator, a navigator, and these worked only one sector before being relieved. A first officer, flight engineer and steward worked with both crews, but shared two beds between them, and usually spent half the flight time of each sector off duty. We carried five beds.

To help the steward as much as possible we arranged hot meals on the ground at every refueling stop, and lunch boxes were to be found on every seat after take-off. Crockery and cutlery were cut down to a minimum, although we still retained our bar box.

We decided that the senior captain was to retain control of the flight as an overall operation, but that otherwise each captain should be in supreme charge of the aircraft over the sectors which it was agreed that he should operate. This would be so irrespective of what happened.

So much for the broad outline of the operation, which had not proved too difficult to work out. All we now had to do was to work out a schedule in detail, and this proved to be more difficult than one might imagine.

To begin with, night flying was prohibited over Syria and Iraq because of the state of war which existed there. The monsoon season was at its height in Burma and India, with a consequent deterrent effect on night operations. Tengah Airport, at Singapore, was not available for night flying, except to scheduled airlines, and no alternative airfield could be used. Rangoon was unfit for heavy aircraft. Ngombo, in Ceylon, was only available for scheduled airlines. Special permission had to be obtained for a flight from Karachi to Calcutta unless one was an airline, and there was some doubt as to whether we would qualify. In fact, there were a lot of snags, and once again the fact was forced upon us that unless one was fortunate enough to be a chosen instrument benefiting from government reciprocal agreements, international air transport is, at best, a heck of a problem, and at worst a pain in the neck.

In the end we managed to work out a schedule which went straight through to Singapore, bar refueling stops, with the exception of a ten-hour stop at Bangkok to await the daylight at Singapore.

Briefly, we were to leave London at 12.00Z[11] on the first day, arrive at 23.00Z on the third day, spend an hour and a half there, and arrive back at London Airport at 04.05Z on the fifth day.[12]

The operation was completed successfully, Captain Brice reporting at the end that they arrived back at London Airport at 03.07Z, fifty-eight minutes early. The refuelling stops were at Malta, Damascus, Basra, Karachi, Calcutta and Bangkok, where they had a twelve-hour layover, before continuing to Singapore. The return trip, with no passengers, was quicker as they could overfly Bangkok and go through to Calcutta. Skyways used its Skymasters mainly to fly on behalf of BOAC, hence the thirty-six-seat configuration. It was easy enough to adjust the seating capacity to accommodate the charterer's requirements, but the higher capacity seats had non-reclining backs, uncomfortable on a flight that took just under fifty hours flying time. Apart from the BOAC contract flying from London to Abadan, Bahrain and Baghdad, and its contribution to the Berlin Airlift, Skyways was devoting considerable time and effort to developing services overseas. Dakotas were based in East Africa operating services for the OFC and the local airline, East African Airways, as was a Lancastrian which was used for a service to Mauritius and Reunion. Other aircraft were based in Kuwait and India. The company remained confident about the future; when Air Contractors, a Dakota operator that had participated in both the Indian and Berlin Airlifts found itself in financial difficulties, Skyways bought it out early in 1949. The company employed around 2,000 people, 1,200 at its Dunsfold engineering base, and over 500 had been working on the Berlin Airlift.

AFTER THE AIRLIFT

But when the civil airlift came to an end, Skyways had no option other than to retrench, and made 400 flying and ground staff redundant. Worse was to follow. Now that BOAC had taken delivery of its Argonauts eight months ahead of contract, it was able to deploy them on routes to the Middle and Far East, replacing Yorks, Lancastrians and flying boats. As more Argonauts were delivered they were used to replace Skyways's Skymasters on services to Damascus, Abadan, Kuwait and Bahrain. General Critchley describes the end of Skyways in his autobiography:

We carried on Skyways for a year or so longer, but business became more and more difficult. By their Civil Aviation Act of 1946 and their Air Corporations Act of 1949, the Labour Government expressed its intention of crushing private enterprise aviation out of existence. One by one our licences were withdrawn and the business was handed over to the subsidized, nationalized air corporations. We were forbidden to continue flying between Singapore and Hong Kong because BOAC's flying-boat service was considered adequate. We were no longer permitted to operate from Nairobi to Mauritius because the government had given this traffic to Air France. Having done all the arduous development work on the coastal service from Nairobi to Durban, we were commanded to present the results of our labours to the East African Airways Corporation. Anglo–Iranian Oil was forced to use BOAC instead of our service to Persia. Questions were asked in the House about the enormity of a private company operating BOAC's routes to Pakistan, the Persian Gulf and West Africa, so we had to stop. The ground-nuts scheme collapsed and BOAC formed a contract charter department to undercut every one of our quotations, although they were at the time losing astronomic sums of the taxpayers' money.

Eric Rylands of the Lancashire Aircraft Corporation made an offer for part of our fleet and for the name Skyways. BOAC bought our private Middle East contracts and we sold our four Skymasters to a French company. This was certainly a mistake. We sold the Skymasters for £100,000 each. Within a year the Korean War had broken out and the Skymasters were selling at £250,000 each. It was a great tragedy that we were forced to close down and it was particularly sad that the devoted energy of our enthusiastic staff came in the end to nothing. The death of Skyways was due to nothing else but Socialist dogma practised by the Labour Government. All that is left is the glory of the pioneering work we did.[13]

The government read the situation differently:

Skyways Ltd has been the biggest and probably the most substantial of the British charter companies. There are grounds for thinking, however, that its promoters realised that the prospects for charter work in the three years immediately following the war would be good and that they were not seriously interested in long term prospects. Skyways are good employers and their standards of maintenance are high. They have concentrated in the main on operation of services, e.g. to West Africa and to the Persian Gulf where there was a substantial movement of traffic and BOAC were not in a position to provide the necessary capacity. Now that this phase is passing there is evidence that Skyways are attempting to sell their Skymasters and to reduce the size of their organisation.[14]

Other airlines were affected by the end of the civil airlift. There were about twenty Halifaxes and Haltons available and very little work for them; the Air Registration Board cancelled the aircraft's special landing weight increase, so payload was reduced by just under a ton. Spares had also become more expensive, especially spare engines. The government remained steadfast in its refusal to allow Tudor 4s to be used for carrying passengers, but relented towards the other marks of Tudor in service, the Tudor 2 and Tudor 5, which were licensed to carry up to seventy-two passengers. A.V.M. Bennett still had one of each, and his new company, Fairflight, took over the assets of Airflight and continued in the charter business, performing long-range flights to South Africa and Pakistan, before taking part in the airlifting of refugees from Aden to Israel. Although the big Tudor was not supposed to be able to perform economically over the South African routes, both Fairflight and William Dempster, another Tudor operator, were able to carry passenger loads in excess of sixty northbound from Johannesburg. Other charter operators began to throw in the towel. Westminster Airways, an airline that had been formed by British MPs and so could surely be described as well-connected, decided to wind up its flying operations, blaming 'the restrictive provisions of the Civil Aviation Act, 1946 and other restrictions on the activities of independent air charter companies'.[15] The remaining charter operators had to face another problem, quite apart from the shortage of work, and that was the increasing competition from the corporations; both of them were by now much feistier. BOAC maintained a fleet of Yorks for ad hoc charters; and BEA's Dakotas returning from Europe were able to pick up inbound loads such as textiles from France, which previously had been a staple of the charter airlines, by quoting low one-way rates.

THE CORPORATIONS

They still lost money; during the period 1948–49 the three corporations managed to lose over £11 million, bringing their total deficit to over £31 million, but the equipment situation was improving. By March 1950 BOAC's western routes were being operated by Constellations and Stratocruisers, and the Middle and Far Eastern routes were serviced by the Argonauts. Sir Miles Thomas was busy pruning the bloated workforce and improving productivity. Africa still had flying-boat service but these were replaced by Hermes landplanes towards the end of 1950. BEA, too, was newly enthused under Lord Douglas and Peter Masefield, and began to come to grips with its costs. The ever elusive break-even load factor, which had been around 130 per cent when the airline first started, that is, a fully loaded Viking with some extra passengers on the wings, began to approach a more reasonable 80 per cent. In August 1950 BEA finally ordered twenty-eight Viscount 701 turbo-props from

Vickers, an aircraft that was to transform both the airline's economics and passenger comfort standards when it entered service in 1953.

BSAA: A SHORT LIFE AND NOT EVEN A PARTICULARLY MERRY ONE

But all was not well with the third corporation. Following the unexplained loss of its second Tudor *Star Ariel* between Bermuda and Kingston, Jamaica, on 17 January 1949, BSAA's fleet of Tudors were again grounded, leaving this corporation to soldier on with its existing fleet of Yorks and Lancastrians. The Berlin Airlift was getting into its stride, and there were no spare four-engine aircraft available. The ban on Tudors was partially lifted and they were called on to play their part as freighters in the Airlift, but that was of no use to the developing scheduled passenger service routes to South America and the Caribbean. The government had long been concerned about BSAA's flight and operational standards and now found an excuse to act; BSAA was merged with BOAC on 31 July 1949, which transferred five twenty-one-seat Yorks to the new operation. Commentators at the time spoke warmly of the good team spirit and enthusiasm at BSAA, even as it laboured under a poor safety record and with outdated equipment. The corporation's vital contribution to the Berlin Airlift is often overlooked. After the take-over BOAC introduced Argonauts in 1950 but its stewardship of the South American services was patchy; they were suspended after the Comet crashes of 1954, and later resumed, only to be handed over to British United Airways in 1965.

One consequence of the take-over was the passing by the government of a Consolidation Bill – the Air Corporations Act of 1949 – which brought together under one Act the Civil Aviation Act of 1946, the Airways Corporations Act of 1949 amalgamating BOAC and BSAA, and any other orders and amendments dating from 1946.

THE DARKER SIDE

BSAA and the other corporations had their share of accidents; so too did the charter airlines. John Stroud, in his book *Annals of British and Commonwealth Air Transport*, lists twenty-three fatal accidents which occurred between 1946 and 1951, excluding aircraft on test, used in training or lost on the Berlin Airlift. The number for each airline is listed:

BEA	7
BOAC	5
BSAA	5
Railway Air Services	1
Scottish Airways	1

The accident involving the Mannin aircraft, a Rapide flying from Dublin to the Isle of Man on 11 November 1948 with two crew members and six passengers, seems needlessly tragic. The aircraft was unable to land at Ronaldsway because of weather conditions and, after holding over the island, the pilot decided to divert to Liverpool. About 3 miles out, the aircraft ran out of fuel and the pilot ditched in the buoyed channel north-west of Garston Docks. The passengers and crew climbed out of the cabin and clung to the plane, which sank after twenty-five minutes. Only one passenger managed to reach the shore. There was a misunderstanding as to where the pilot was landing which delayed the arrival of the lifeboat. After the aircraft was salvaged, nine unused life-saving waistcoats were found, one under each seat.

Because it involved a private charter flight, Stroud does not mention the accident to the Pullman Airways Consul G-AJGE, which happened on 27 February 1948. The Chief Inspector of Accidents blamed the pilot's 'irresponsible attitude' and it is difficult to disagree with him. The aircraft was coming back from Nairobi to the United Kingdom and *Flight* gives a full account of the report:

> On arrival at El Adem (the stop before Benina) the pilot had stated casually that his radio was not satisfactory, but omitted to mention the fact at debriefing. He appeared to regard flight planning purely as an 'irritating formality'. At Benina the unserviceable radio was reported to the ATCO and the pilot asked for his aircraft to be refuelled quickly as he was anxious to reach Castel Benito that day. As the Shell representative and his men were off-duty it was impossible to obtain a chamois-leather filter and, with the pilot's permission, the aircraft was refuelled to its capacity without a filter. One of the RAF party at the airfield pointed out to the pilot that his oil tanks were only half full, but he (the pilot) refused to allow them to be replenished, giving as his reason the hurry he was in.
>
> The ATCO advised a night stop at Benina in view of deteriorating weather in the Castel Benito area and the fact that the latter part of the proposed flight would be in darkness without radio. The navigator indicated that he would prefer not to continue the flight that day, that he was tired and that he doubted his ability to find destination in the circumstances. Moreover, he declared that he had no confidence in the pilot. The pilot enquired about accommodation for the night but, on finding that it could be arranged only in Benghazi, some 18 miles distant, he refused on the grounds of expense. At 1535 hr the aircraft was taxied rapidly on to a runway, which was not the one in use at that time, and immediately began its take-off run, downwind and without any preliminary ground testing, even though the starboard engine had been difficult to start.[16]

The pilot had 964 flying hours. One week later the body of one of the passengers, together with some of the aircraft wreckage, came ashore on the Tunisian coast.

Then on 12 March 1950 Britain suffered its worst aircraft accident when the Tudor 5 operated by Fairflight crashed at Llandow, a small airfield in Glamorgan, Wales. The accident happened as the Tudor was attempting to land after a charter flight from Dublin, carrying returning Welsh rugby supporters. Of the seventy-eight passengers and five crew, only three passengers survived. There was a court investigation which reached the conclusion that the most probable cause of the accident was to be found in the loading conditions of the aircraft, which gave a centre of gravity (c.g.) position considerably aft of that authorised in the Certificate of Airworthiness. This resulted in insufficient elevator control remaining when the pilot applied full power at a speed which, though well above the stalling point, was sufficiently low to cause serious instability. A.V.M. Bennett did not accept the findings, claiming that he had flown the aircraft as a test with the c.g. 12in outside the limit, with no problem. He speculated that the pilot's seat might have moved involuntarily, which was dismissed as 'inherently improbable' by the court investigation; he also thought that a bolt on the elevator hinge had broken.

INCLUSIVE TOURS

On a happier note, further inclusive tours were approved for the 1949 summer season. It comes as no surprise that one of the first series was operated by that trendsetter, Air Transport (Charter) (Channel Islands), flying thirty-two-seat Dakotas between Newcastle and Jersey on behalf of T.A. Bulmer & Co. During the fifteen-week period of its operation it achieved a 90 per cent load factor. Another interesting development was the international IT series from Lympne to Le Touquet operated by Air Kruise, which later developed into a significant coach-holiday operation. But there was a snag about the operation of inclusive tours under associate agreements, one that was to become a major issue and remain so for many years. In order to carry passengers on inclusive tours, charter airlines had to apply for an associate agreement with BEA and then charge the relevant scheduled service fare as part of the total cost; this requirement came to be interpreted as a provision that no inclusive tour could be sold for less than the equivalent air fare. Better known as Provision One (from its attachment to all-inclusive tour licences), it remained in force for many years. As a result, inclusive-tour prices were held artificially high because they were pegged to scheduled-service fares. *The Aeroplane* explained the problem and its somewhat ironic consequences:

> This pernicious arrangement is keeping the public out of the air. One of the great advantages to the public of the inclusive tour system is that through bulk purchase of transport and accommodation, tourist agencies are able to provide holidays on the Continent for people who would be unable to afford to go at all if they had to travel as individuals and pay full fares and hotel prices.
>
> The people for whom the charter companies are trying to cater have very modest incomes; none of them could afford to go by scheduled air service. So that the scheduled air lines

would not be losing customers if the charging of lower inclusive tour rates by the independent operators were permissible. Indeed, the charter companies would be building up a potential source of passenger traffic for the future when the Corporation's new aircraft come along and they are able, with the increased capacity, to offer lower fares than at present.

The paradoxical effect of the Civil Aviation Act of a Labour Government has been to reserve air transport for a privileged few at high fares, and to deny less affluent members of the community the chance to use air transport at the much lower charges which, again paradoxically, private enterprise operators are able to make available.[17]

During the dog-days of the first post-war Labour Government, it seems fitting that bringing air transport to the masses was no longer one of its goals. And in another change of direction, the government was about to stand on its head, and start giving more business to those mistrusted commercial venturers; it was time to look at how best to support Britain's considerable military presence overseas, from Hong Kong, Singapore and the islands of the Pacific in the East to the colonies in the Caribbean and Central America in the West.

SEVEN

RECOGNITION AT LAST?

THE FIGHT FOR THE TROOPING CONTRACTS
1950–51

GATHERING MOMENTUM

The government had shown itself willing, albeit in small measure, to ease the restrictions on private airlines in the matter of scheduled services, but it was not enough. The independents needed help and needed it soon. The ending of the Berlin Airlift deprived the operators of the larger four-engine aircraft of much of their business, and although many of the operators were able to withstand the blow, some did not. Skyways was the biggest company to fall to earth, followed by Bond Air Services; Flight Refuelling also faced difficulties, as did BSAA, which had just been taken over by BOAC.

The RAF needed help, too. Although the various RAF Commands were re-equipping with new Handley Page Hastings transports (around 140 of the C1 and C2 models were eventually to enter service with the RAF), there were insufficient resources to fly and maintain all of them.[1] Transport Command needed the aircraft for tactical purposes, such as paratroop dropping, as well as for emergency airlift operations; it also needed aircraft for its long-range squadrons operating on regular schedules to the Far East and round the Middle East with both passengers and freight. The Hastings was similar to the DC-4, unpressurised, but with a slightly wider cabin and a tail-wheel configuration, and was bigger than the Yorks and Dakotas it replaced; it had proved its potential value during the Airlift, but its use had been curtailed by the lack of crews. This factor, together with budgetary constraints and the dwindling number of acceptable troopships, were to lead the armed forces to look again at how to maintain their links with the considerable number of military bases that Britain maintained overseas. Experience with the civilian contribution to the Berlin Airlift had shown that, after some initial difficulties, co-operation between the civil and military operators could be made to work. Given that RAF Transport Command was being cut back in order to release funds for rearmament, the Air Ministry thought civil air transport might prove more cost-effective.

There was already a realisation that charter airlines could help provide air mobility for the forces in the same way that the Royal Navy relied on the Merchant Marine. *The Aeroplane* pointed this out in its leader of 18 November 1949:

> What time the Minister of Civil Aviation permits the screw to be tightened on the charter firms, the Royal Air Force seems to have reached a position where the availability of a healthy mercantile fleet when needed would be a solution to the problem of cutting its expenses.
>
> We do not believe that those who decry the utility of airborne forces will get their way – all experience shows the tremendous military importance of the mobility conferred by air – but we do believe that a strong charter fleet is essential to our security. How the availability of the aircraft and crews when needed by the RAF is to be secured we do not pretend to know. A solution can be worked out when the principle has been established.[2]

The Services recognised that there were limitations in using civil aircraft; they would not be able to handle all types of military cargo, especially vehicles, nor would they be available on standby for emergencies without the payment of expensive demurrage charges. But they clearly had their uses. A foretaste of what was to come occurred early in 1949 when Airwork, always an airline with very acute political antennae, was awarded a contract by the War Office to carry the wives and families of 5,000 Service personnel to the Middle East. The War Office already used chartered aircraft on occasion, and, finding it hard to secure sufficient shipping berths for service families, decided to contract Airwork to help clear the backlog. Using twenty-seven-seat Vikings the flights left several times a week for Cairo, and special fares, the same as troopship rates, were charged. The following year, 1950, Airwork was again awarded a similar contract to fly army personnel and their families out of Cairo, operating thirty such flights between June and November. In the meantime, troopships had been withdrawn from West Africa, and with surprisingly little fanfare Airwork was awarded another significant contract to carry forces and their families out to West Africa. The Vikings operated four to six times a month between January and June, the flights taking three days in each direction with night stops at Gibraltar and Kano, Nigeria. In July 1950 Hunting's Vikings took over the West Africa trooping contract.

The War Office was clearly satisfied with the civilian charter operators, and the Air Ministry, for different reasons, was also interested. The impetus for a change in policy, to switch from the accepted practice of trooping by sea to using air transport, came from a number of sources.

BOAC'S PROPOSALS

Even BOAC had ideas on the subject. Whitney Straight, the deputy chairman, looking ahead to the future delivery of the very large Brabazons and SR 45 Princess flying boat, thought that their size would be useful when moving soldiers, sailors and airmen between the United Kingdom and overseas posts. He was anxious to discuss his ideas with the military and the Ministry of Civil Aviation; the latter was not so enthusiastic. 'It is clear that important issues of policy are involved in the BOAC proposal', wrote Dunnett from the Ministry, 'I mentioned to Mr Straight that if the SR 45s were used extensively for trooping the problem of bases would require careful consideration. Mr Whitney Straight remarked somewhat airily that he did not think that this should cause any great difficulty.'[3] His boss, Sir George Cribbett, agreed to call a meeting, but wanted rather more detail:

> Before holding this meeting, however, I think we must ask Mr Straight to put his proposals in a rather more concrete, and less airy, form in a memorandum which the Ministry can consider in advance of the proposed meeting. It would be embarrassing to us to hear the BOAC proposals developed for the first time, on such an important issue of policy, at a meeting with the Directors of Movements of the Service departments.
>
> I think it might be as well to add that whilst we are only too ready to explore this possibility of securing full utilisation from the SR 45 and Brabazon 1, we will not be willing to entertain any substantial expenditure on ground facilities not otherwise required for regular air transport operations.
>
> I think we would be wise to make it clear to the Corporation that, even though we may be prepared to go ahead on the basis of their first firm statement, any subsequent request to augment the facilities would be their financial liability. It seems to me that it is only in this way that we can prevent irresponsible changes of mind by BOAC. We have suffered too much in the past through their whims not to be warned for the future.[4]

That was written on 17 October 1949. BOAC, however, was not prepared to be more specific and in the end Cribbett agreed to hold the meeting anyway. So on 22 November 1949 they met with representatives from the Armed Services and BOAC. Straight explained about the increase in capacity that BOAC was facing with the delivery of Comets, Hermes and ultimately SR 45s and Brabazons, and he made the good point, typically couched in airline jargon, that the Services would be able to obtain a 'higher utilisation of their available manpower' by substantially reducing the amount of time service personnel spent in transit if they were to go by air rather than more slowly by sea. The advantage was not solely due to reduced time spent in transit. Though travelling by sea obviously took more time, even more time was wasted on the ground at holding camps waiting for a passage. It was agreed that the service chiefs would prepare a statement of their requirements and then BOAC would prepare quotations to meet those requirements.

But events were to overtake this ad hoc committee. In other places and at more senior levels, serious thought was being given both to the plight of the charter airlines and the problems that the Services were facing.

THE MINISTRIES

It was not the Ministry of Civil Aviation which was to carry the torch on this issue, but the Air Ministry, the more senior Ministry, responsible for the RAF and which had, up until 1944, been responsible for civil aviation as well. Each of the main protagonists in the ensuing discussions had different goals. The Air Ministry wanted to derive the maximum fighting potential from its limited resources; money spent on air transport was money that could not be spent on warplanes, an important consideration as the Western Allies steeled themselves both for the Korean War and the continuing confrontation with the Soviet bloc. The Air Ministry saw civil air transport as complementary to, and less expensive in terms of manpower and cash than, its own RAF Transport Command. The RAF had co-operated with the charter operators during the Berlin Airlift, and the Air Ministry was aware that the Admiralty had a similar harmonious relationship with the Merchant Marine which was responsible for providing the troopships currently in use. The War Office, the biggest user of transport services, wanted to move its troops around its various bases as economically as possible. It saw some virtue in encouraging competition between sea and air; within the civil aviation sector, however, it was most anxious to promote competition between the corporations on the one hand and the independents on the other, recognising that competition would lead to lower rates. The Admiralty wanted to protect its Merchant Marine and ensure that the shipping companies still secured adequate business from trooping and the carriage of military cargo. The Admiralty had less leverage than the other two ministries as its movement requirements were smaller; but it succeeded in guaranteeing the future use of troopships for a time.

The Ministry of Civil Aviation did not have any such clear-cut goals, however. It suffered from being the most junior Ministry present, only established in 1944, and although it was responsible for the whole of civil aviation, it nevertheless considered its prime mission to support the corporations at whatever cost. This put it on a collision course with the two main Service ministries; they both wanted air transportation at the lowest possible cost, which they suspected the corporations were unable to deliver. The MCA was somewhat disparaging of the charter companies under its care, something that the other ministries found difficult to understand. Both the Air Ministry and the Admiralty were protective towards their charges and, in the end, the Air Ministry had to champion the charter carriers against the overt support that the MCA gave to the corporations. The MCA was poorly prepared and briefed: 'It is extremely difficult for the Ministry to provide any reliable information on this subject… In these circumstances, the only views the Ministry can express are based on such information as reaches it and must accordingly be treated with very considerable reserve… The Ministry has little information about the financial standing of these [charter] companies.' The Air Ministry had doubts, too, about the MCA's professionalism. 'It would be as well to draw attention to the safety factor and to the importance of using reputable firms', was the Air Ministry view in an internal minute, 'MCA will give guidance on this, but as a general principle the Air Staff should also be satisfied about operating standards (I doubt whether they would have agreed to the loading of the Tudor which crashed at Llandow, even though the aircraft had a Certificate of Airworthiness for the number of passengers actually carried)'. So the stage was set.

THE MELVILLE COMMITTEE[5]

As you know, the economies to be made in the Services are likely to include a substantial reduction in the size of Transport Command and there will in consequence be a decrease in the capacity available for the carriage of Service personnel and freight by air. The Air Charter Companies and the Corporations have got wind of the impending reduction and are keenly interested in securing business on behalf of the Services.

With the cessation of the Berlin Air Lift many of the Charter Companies in particular are beginning to 'feel the pinch', and if they are to be helped it is urgently necessary to let them know how much service traffic they can expect to get. BOAC also have problems in which they would like the Services to help them.

It seems to us most desirable that the position now developing should be considered with regard both to the immediate problems arising from the contraction of Transport Command, and to the broader consideration of the value of a healthy civil aviation as a war potential. I am sure you will agree that an examination of this kind must be on an inter-service basis.

We propose therefore, if you agree, to set up a small working party with the following terms of reference:

To consider the use to be made of civil air transport for Service purposes in the light of:

    (a) The reduction in size of Transport Command.
    (b) The value of a healthy civil aviation as a war potential.
    (c) Financial considerations.

The members would be representatives of the three Service Departments and of the Ministry of Civil Aviation. I propose that R.H. Melville (Assistant Under Secretary (Organisation)) should take the chair.

This letter was circulated by Sir James Barnes, permanent under-secretary[6] at the Air Ministry, to his colleagues at the Admiralty, War Office and the Ministry of Civil Aviation. The letter went out on 10 December 1949, but the rather touching references to charter companies 'feeling the pinch' were omitted from the letter sent to Sir Arnold Overton at the MCA. Maybe Sir James thought he was stating the obvious to his MCA colleague but, if so, he misunderstood the main thrust of that Ministry's policies. As becomes clear, the MCA, and its minister, Lord Pakenham, were more concerned about the well-being of BOAC than the fate of the charter companies. Since Ronald Melville was to chair the committee, it became known in time-honoured fashion as the Melville Committee.

The committee's first meeting was on 5 January 1950, at which various departments were asked to provide more detail of the requirements and the available resources. In the minutes of the first meeting, the MCA was somewhat dismissive of its charter airlines:

> From the Ministry of Civil Aviation point of view not all charter companies were satisfactory, but even the good ones might soon be obliged to go out of business if some regular work could not be found for them. This might be considered regrettable, but it was a logical consequence of the policy approved by the government. The government were concerned about the financial losses incurred by the Corporations.

In his own report of the meeting, the MCA's representative, Dunnett, notes:

> The Committee were particularly anxious that besides making an approach to BOAC we should make an approach to the charter industry. The Air Ministry are beginning to realise, partly due to the advent of the new Chief of Air Staff, that the charter industry constitutes a certain war potential and they would certainly be alarmed if any of the larger and better firms went out of existence without the Air Ministry being consulted. The War Office also favour the charter companies and in particular Airwork. They feel that Airwork have done them very well and that the existence of Airwork enables them to obtain competitive prices which they would not obtain if the Corporations had a monopoly.[7]

At least the charter companies, and Airwork in particular, had some friends in high places. Dunnett also noted that the Admiralty was less enthusiastic about air trooping, 'partly because they have a paternal interest in maintaining the mercantile marine at the highest figure possible'. In putting together a somewhat spurious list of available capacity for the committee, the MCA claimed that on 1 January 1950 there were 135 private air transport companies known to the Ministry, operating between them 634 aircraft: 280 of these were single-engine types, and 238 small twin-engine types (six to eight seats). There were then twenty-six companies which operated sixty-seven large four-engine and fifty-four large twin-engine aircraft. However, the figure for four-engine aircraft included twenty-five Halifaxes, eight Hythes (without Certificates of Airworthiness), Flight Refuelling's twelve Lancastrians and Scottish Aviation's two Liberators, also without Certificates of Airworthiness, so it clearly overstated the position; the Halifaxes and Lancastrians were in any case unsuitable for trooping purposes, a point recognised by the other participants on the committee. 'Lord Tedder in a recent speech… expressed the view there was nothing he would like better than to see a large number of civil aircraft maintained and operated as air tramps, thus constituting a military reserve. They were clearly, however, somewhat disappointed to see from the papers we put in how small the resources of the charter industry were at the present time. They expressed the view in this connection that to be worth while from the military angle the civil charter industry would have to be equipped with more suitable aircraft than, for example, Halifaxes.' Eventually the MCA compiled a list of approved contractors – Airwork, Huntings, Lancashire Aircraft Corporation, Silver City, Flight Refuelling, Skyways and Scottish Aviation (Fairflight was subsequently added) – which, together with the corporations, were considered for the next stage of the process.

At an early stage it was accepted that there would be sufficient airlift and troopship capacity for 1950, which inevitably took some of the pressure off the committee and partly explains why it took so long to make its recommendations and then see them implemented. The RAF was still flying at least nine sorties a month to Singapore, although each flight took around five to six days to get there, and the same amount of time to come back, a situation that was only improved when slip crews began to be provided en route. In certain cases, Transport Command charged the Services the full commercial rate for carrying passengers on its flights, although the following account in *The Aeroplane* suggests that there was a world of difference in standards:

> In the icy dawn, at the start of our journey, the backward facing seats in the Hastings resembled two rows of twin tombstones. In fact, the seat arrangement proved universally popular, and only the seats themselves came in for criticism on the grounds of comfort. The Hastings normally carries forty passengers… After several six-hour hops, most of our passengers had exhausted their reading material and, with nothing better to do, dozed, ate or wrote, or sat in introspective session like temporary hermits. One heard absolutely no criticism of the 'backs to the engine' conveyance, but the spartan qualities of the Hastings's interior do not make for luxury travel. In particular, the seats, without head or arm-rests, and with their rigidly vertical backs, not to mention the lack of leg space, seem to have been ingeniously devised to prevent the unfortunate occupants from enjoying a moment's rest.
>
> On this leg (Iraq to Pakistan), we once more had the unpleasant sensation of looking casually out of our window and having our attention riveted to the stiff, stark blades of the stationary starboard outer airscrew, standing out like a sore thumb. There is nothing quite so dead as a feathered power unit, and various unpleasant thoughts were common as we droned on over the endless wastes.[8]

The relative costs of trooping by air and by sea were to emerge as the main consideration. In the short to medium term, there was a general shortage of shipping; any available passenger ships were now heavily in demand for emigrant services to Canada, Australia and South Africa. The Services had access to sixteen troopships, but some of these were about to be withdrawn, whilst others needed to be converted to more acceptable peacetime standards. These converted ships would mean that carrying capacity would be reduced and the rate of hire increased. For ships equipped to war-time standards, the capitation rate per man-day (the rate that the Services were charged to carry one man for each day of the passage) was set at 30s (£1 10s), but on the converted ships it would rise to 45s (£2 5s), and the carrying capacity would be reduced by between one third and one half. These rates are the basis for calculating the cost of moving personnel by troopship in the following table:

Table 7.1: Capitation rates for a single journey from UK

To:	Average journey time in days	Uniformed personnel	
		War-time standard ships	Post-war standard ships
Malta	8	£12	£18
Egypt	12	£18	£27
E. Africa	26	£39	£58 10s
Ceylon	25	£37 10s	£56 5s
Singapore	31	£46 10s	£69 15s
Hong Kong	36	£54	£81

There were further rates for non-uniformed personnel, such as wives and families which, depending on the class of travel, could be between 10 per cent and 100 per cent more than the war-time standard rate.

As the committee proceeded with its work, initial assessments of a shortfall in regular trooping requirements began to emerge: around 22,000 to the Middle East in 1951, rising to 29,000 in 1952, and 8,000 to the Far East in 1951, rising to 10,500 in 1952. There were also proposals to build new troopships, but everybody recognised that that would take time and in the meantime the deficiency would have to be met by air transport. The MCA was, however, pursuing another agenda. It now had those ten Tudors on its hands that had been built speculatively to its order, when it was thought that the Berlin Airlift would continue into the winter of 1949–50.

> Mr Dunnett said that the Ministry of Civil Aviation was about to take delivery of 10 Tudors of different marks which had been completed as freighters and would need to be provided with seats… These aircraft were unpressurised and without heating and on this basis the ARB were prepared to give a full C. of A. for passenger carrying. A heating installation would be necessary before the aircraft were used for air trooping and this had yet to be developed. At the moment it was not possible to say what was involved in designing the installation which would be the responsibility of the purchaser.

It was hardly an alluring prospect, and encountered strong opposition from the Army:

> Major General Greaves said that the Tudor had a very bad name and should an accident occur
> when they were used for trooping awkward questions would be asked, particularly as women
> and children would be carried.

The War Office was supported in this by the Air Ministry, which shortly afterwards undertook its own review of the Tudor, and reached the conclusion that the economics of using the type for trooping were unfavourable. The Ministry of Civil Aviation was told that it could dispose of them, something the MCA was reluctant to do. For some time it continued to argue in favour of the Tudors despite the refusal of the other ministries to countenance them.

INTERIM REPORT

In March 1950 the committee sent out internally an interim report, estimating that there would be a shortfall in troopship capacity from 1951, and recommending that all the approved airlines should be invited to submit an estimate of costs to cover the trooping requirements to the Middle East and/or the Far East. At this stage it was not a formal tender; airlines were invited to submit estimates for the carriage of either 20,000 or 40,000 personnel and families to the Middle East (which meant Fayid in the Canal Zone) or, alternatively, either 10,000 or 20,000 personnel and families to the Far East (Singapore), with night stops at RAF staging posts. The scheme should be underway by 1951 but, as Melville noted wearily, 'We have been rather held up by uncertainty in the Ministry of Civil Aviation about policy in regard to Charter Companies'. The lack of loyalty shown by the MCA towards the independent airlines for which it was responsible is evident, and must have seemed especially shocking to the Air Ministry; before the war it had been the sponsoring department for civil aviation and again resumed this mantle when the Ministry of Civil Aviation championed its own narrower interests. In comparison, the Admiralty was always ready to defend the Merchant Marine, and did it almost too well.

The committee noted that there would be no additional business for the charter companies in 1950 as a result of its deliberations. But all three Service ministries were anxious to try and put at least some business in the way of the independents to tide them over until 1951. The War Office had already given a trooping contract to West Africa, and in addition there was some army co-operation flying. The Admiralty was using Airwork for twin conversion training, and the Air Ministry, which used charter companies for the Volunteer Reserve Schools, had a number of other proposals including intra-Mediterranean leave flights, summer weekend movements of whole units of the Reserve Commands and repair and maintenance work: 'In our view the most practical course to be immediately pursued in regard to the Charter Companies is to give them as much business as they can legitimately secure on a commercial basis within the framework of government policy, and to ask them to consider our proposals for air trooping in 1951'.

THE LOBBYING BEGINS

This course of action was taken by the Air Ministry, and in April Sir Folliott Sandford, the deputy under-secretary at the Air Ministry, was writing to his colleagues at the Admiralty and the War Office: 'The Air Council... consider it to be of importance that encouragement should be given to efficient Charter Companies. They would therefore be grateful for the co-operation of the Board of Admiralty and the Army Council in securing that, where work of a suitable nature exists, Charter Companies should be given an opportunity of tendering for it.' This attitude put the Service Ministries at loggerheads with the Ministry of Civil Aviation, which under Lord Pakenham followed a more doctrinaire line. At the next meeting of the committee in May, the minutes record that the MCA representative said:

> ...that on the question of competition between the Corporations and the charter companies, the MCA did not consider that it would be appropriate for a decision to be taken to place a contract with a charter company solely on the strength of competitive tenders. There were wider considerations of policy to be taken into account. Thus, although an air trooping service was not strictly a 'scheduled service' within the meaning of the Act, it was nevertheless a regular long-distance service and it might well be held that it ought, as a matter of government policy, to be reserved for the Corporations. Moreover, the latter would shortly have a certain amount of surplus capacity, and it might be impossible to justify giving a contract to a charter company which would involve it in having to purchase aircraft in order to carry out an operation which the Corporations were willing to carry out with existing machines.

The Service ministries wanted to support charter companies because they understood correctly that competitive tendering would ensure the lowest rates. They wondered, if the government insisted on the use of the corporations for air trooping at a price higher than that quoted by a charter company, would the MCA pay the difference? Fortunately for the charter companies, the committee was chaired by someone from the Air Ministry, for the Ministry of Civil Aviation saw its primary, if not its sole, duty as the protection of the corporations. Had the MCA been in the chair there would have been much greater pressure on the Service ministries to toe the government line and endorse the concept of a British 'Aeroflot', ultimately responsible for all aspects of civil aviation in the United Kingdom. As it was, the defence chiefs carried their ministers with them and were robust enough to stand up to Lord Pakenham and his successor. However, the struggle prolonged the whole process.

In the meantime the sparring went on. At the next meeting the Air Staff – the RAF component in the Air Ministry – was asked if it had a preference for charter companies as opposed to the corporations. Its response shows that planning for war now included a much more active role for the charter companies:

The Air Staff would prefer to use charter companies to the corporations for air trooping, not because they thought that the charter companies would produce more aircraft and crews than the corporations, but because present war plans envisaged a particular use for charter companies. Plans existed for the use of the corporations in war which were of less immediate value to the RAF on the outbreak of war than the plans for the charter companies. It was hoped to form, within certain charter companies, auxiliary squadrons and an organisation which could ensure on the outbreak of war the absorption within the RAF of these squadrons as front line squadrons. This was an organisational advantage favouring the use of charter companies and was of great value. Therefore, anything that encouraged the continued existence of the charter companies was desirable. It was indeed one of the objects of the Committee to keep the charter companies going.

The Air Staff had moved the argument on to a higher level. Now it was not just a question of cost; the RAF saw the charter companies as a front-line asset in time of war, organised into auxiliary squadrons and ready to be absorbed into the air force. The maintenance of charter companies therefore had a strategic value. Dunnett from the Ministry of Civil Aviation made the point in reply that a ministerial decision on charter companies versus corporations would be required. Lord Pakenham then wrote to his ministerial colleagues at the Service ministries on 17 July 1950 to plead the case for the corporations:

Whilst I fully appreciate the importance to the Defence Departments of fulfilling their trooping programme at the lowest cost in transport, there seems to me to be wider financial and general policy considerations… on the question whether the Corporations or the Charter Companies should be used for air trooping.

Is the employment of the Charter Companies on trooping desirable or financially justifiable, bearing in mind the size, suitability and efficiency of the resources of the Corporations and the cost to the tax-payer in subsidies if they are to maintain marginal capacity to which the SR 45 and Brabazon I will be added in the coming years?

The question whether the Charter Companies and/or the Corporations should be employed on air trooping raises, first, the policy consideration whether the tax payer should be required to support the Charter Companies, on war potential grounds, in addition to providing subsidy to maintain marginal capacity not fully utilised on the ordinary commercial services of the Corporation. BEA could obtain higher aircraft utilisation and, hence, increased revenues in reduction of subsidy if they secured Middle East trooping contracts. BOAC have the somewhat more difficult problem of fully using their aircraft and personnel resources on normal commercial services. Although BOAC have not categorically stated that they will have a surplus of capacity when the Hermes deliveries are completed, I think this will be so. This is due partly to falsification of forecasts of steady expansion of traffics and partly to the spread of protectionism overseas, which is restricting the Corporations' natural development. In addition to this marginal capacity which will shortly be seeking employment, the Corporation will be faced before long with the need for putting to useful purposes both the Brabazon I and SR 45, which as you know, are being produced as national experiments at great cost, with the approval of the Cabinet. Thus, with the early prospect of a surplus of aircraft and crews in BOAC, the issue may become whether the taxpayer can be asked to finance additional reserve capacity by placing trooping contracts with the Charter Companies, and, if so, whether BOAC will not have to undergo a surgical operation which must be costly in itself, lead to much labour unrest and reduce the war potential which they would otherwise provide. The additional immediate cost, if any, of Corporation contracts would comparatively be a very secondary consideration.

Lord Pakenham went on to explain that, if the corporations operated the trooping flights, government traffic would be carried by the nationalised airlines on work closely analogous to scheduled services which were reserved to them as a matter of government policy. As one would expect, Lord Pakenham's long letter, of which the above is only an extract, puts the corporations' case cogently. But one wonders if he or his staff actually knew the situation at BOAC. Under Sir Miles Thomas, the corporation had been pruning staff and cutting costs; it was a far leaner organisation than heretofore, and utilised its front-line fleet better. There was some capacity at the margin, mainly the by-now redundant fleet of Yorks and the soon to become redundant fleet of Hermes; BOAC was anxious to get shot of its newly delivered Hermes as soon as possible! Lord Pakenham was also arguing in favour of supporting the aircraft industry, coming back to Whitney Straight's initial musings. Was the fate of the airline industry to depend on the products of the aircraft industry?

Sir George Cribbett was sent off in turn to lobby his opposite number at the Air Ministry, Sir Folliott Sandford. On two occasions in August he tried to persuade Sandford to back down from promoting Air Ministry support for the charter airlines and go along with his Ministry in ensuring the trooping work was given to the corporations. He pointed out that the corporations had seventeen surplus Solent flying boats and that the MCA and BOAC together had up to sixteen surplus Tudors, albeit freighters. There were also some Yorks, but he accepted that the RAF was not interested in those. Now Cribbett was a doughty fighter and an intelligent man, but he cannot have believed that these proposals would have been in any way acceptable. Flying boats were uneconomical – that was why they were surplus to BOAC requirements – and the same economic criteria applied to the Air Ministry's requirements; indeed, earlier Cribbett had rather scoffed at BOAC's suggestion that the Princess flying boats could be used. As for the Tudors, both the Army and the Air Ministry had ruled them out as unacceptable and, a few months later, Lord Pakenham himself was to announce that no further passenger-carrying certificates would be granted to Tudors. Cribbett's scepticism is best summed up in his own words: 'I was merely the emissary of my Minister, acting on his instructions.'[9] Sandford was having none of it, however. He realised that the surplus resources of the corporations had a bearing on the question, but 'he considered that the charter companies having been asked for estimates, it would be morally difficult to refrain from inviting them to tender'.[10] He proposed to sit it out until the Melville Committee had submitted its full report. Privately, he reported on these meetings to his minister:

I gather from Sir George Cribbett that BOAC have considerably over-estimated the traffic potential in the immediate future; [and] that the loss on the Corporation's accounts this year will be considerably greater than last year.

The suggestion which Sir George Cribbett put forward was that the whole problem of the transport requirement of the RAF in war and the civil air transport potential required in peace for this purpose should be considered at high official level between the Air Ministry, MCA, Ministry of Defence and the Treasury. He admitted, however, that the Chancellor of the Exchequer had told his Minister [Lord Pakenham] that in his view the first step must be to discuss air trooping in the light of the Melville Report.

I said that I recognised that the points he had put to me about the spare capacity available in BOAC were relevant to Ministerial discussion on this subject, but that I could not see that discussion at a high official level would be profitable at this stage. In any case I was sure that it would be wrong to attempt to short circuit the Admiralty and War Office, as the MCA apparently wished to do.

Neither of his colleagues at the Air Ministry and the War Office was very accommodating to Lord Pakenham. Neither was prepared to accept the argument for the MCA position, at least until the Melville Committee had reported. The War Office went further and said that, given the financial circumstances of the government, it doubted the suggestion that air trooping contracts should no longer be put out to tender would be well received by the accounting officers of the Service departments – it foresaw 'grave difficulty'.

On 12 August 1950 the Secretary of State for Air, Arthur Henderson, announced at the Plymouth Air Display that the RAF would be using charter companies during the summer to move whole, mostly auxiliary, units by air. Nine tenders were issued for various short-term transport duties within the British Isles and to and from Germany; Scottish Airlines was an early beneficiary. With no publicity at all, Airwork was given a contract to fly service personnel between the various British bases within the Mediterranean area: Malta, Cyprus, Libya and Fayid in the Canal Zone. At the same time Cyprus Airways began using Fayid for Cyprus leave flights, allowing Canal Zone troops to spend their leave in the Troodos Mountains; the Egyptians were asked for, and granted, permission for these flights. In November the first Auxiliary Transport Squadron, No.622, was formed, incorporating Airwork; had there been a national emergency Airwork would have been incorporated into Transport Command (the experiment was relatively short-lived, and No.622 Squadron was the only Auxiliary Transport Squadron to be formed, being disbanded in September 1953).

THE MELVILLE COMMITTEE (CONTINUED)

Meanwhile, the committee continued to meet in order to thrash out a final report. But by the end of August 1950 the Army was having second thoughts about its numbers, having decided it did not need to move quite so many people around, and that, consequently, some of the conclusions of the interim report were no longer valid. In addition, the army now said it wanted to maintain a viable troopship capacity as a war potential, and went so far as to suggest that troopships might be able to accommodate the revised and reduced trooping totals. Obviously other ministries had been lobbying that summer as well, in this case the Admiralty and the Ministry of Transport, guardians of the Merchant Marine. The army's about-face undermined the work of the committee, as Melville noted sadly:

> A point which may strike you is the emphasis laid in the Report on considerations of the troopship potential... The fact is that we discussed the question fully at early meetings of the Committee and the Admiralty and the Ministry of Transport representatives accepted a reduction in the size of the troopship fleet. At our penultimate meeting, both these departments reversed their views.

He went on to say: '[I am] afraid I am by no means sure how the question of the conflict between the Corporations and the charter companies can best be tackled'.

THE MELVILLE REPORT

On 13 September the Melville Committee made its final report. The report started by repeating the clarion call from Lord Tedder, Chief of the Air Staff:

> Quite frankly, what the Services need is a counterpart in the air of the Mercantile Marine – scores, or rather hundreds, of economical load carriers, the tramps of the air. During the Berlin airlift we were fortunate in being able to get invaluable support from civil air transport, but that was largely fortuitous as an aftermath of the war. Efficient transport in adequate quantities is an essential part of our defences on land, sea and in the air, and the great bulk of that transport must, I suggest, in peacetime be a part of the economic productive effort of the nation. Until we are in the same position regarding air transport as we are as regards sea and land transport I do not think we can regard our position as sound.

The report went on to show how the assumptions the committee had made regarding trooping requirements were invalidated when at short notice the government extended National Service (compulsory military service) to two years, which it was thought would lead to a decline in trooping movements. The committee also considered that air trooping would be more expensive than by sea, by around 10–20 per cent to the Middle East, and rather more to the Far East, but that charter services would be a great deal less expensive than providing additional Hastings capacity for the RAF. The report discussed at length the relative merits of the corporations and the charter companies. The Air Staff still preferred the charter companies, both for their war potential as auxiliary squadrons and because all the Service ministries attached great importance to competitive tendering. The MCA had moved away from its previous championing of flying boats and Tudors, and suggested that BOAC might have surplus Hermes aircraft available. The Hermes, be it noted, had only just entered BOAC service that August. The MCA's position was well known, and potentially stronger, given that BOAC's new Hermes were now on offer. The Air Staff was able to counter most arguments:

> BOAC has more experience than the charter companies in moving large numbers of passengers. On the other hand, most of the air trooping which has been carried out by British Civil Aviation has fallen to charter companies and has been done satisfactorily. Moreover, BOAC's chief interest would still be its normal scheduled traffic, whereas if air trooping were given to one or more charter companies it would be by far their biggest concern. On balance, the advantage here seems to lie with the companies but it is clearly not a critical factor.
>
> As regards operating standards, the advantage lies with BOAC whose standards and record of safe flying are second to none. It does not follow that the charter companies would be unreliable. Companies such as Airwork and Hunting Air Travel also have good safety records and much experience of flying in the Mediterranean and Middle East.
>
> The Service Departments attach great importance to competitive tendering in the interests of economy and on the general principles of government contracting and, they further consider that opportunities to spend money provided for the Services to the best advantage should be preserved instead of being eliminated in the interests of a nationalised corporation. They consider that air trooping should not become a monopoly of a Corporation.

By now the Service chiefs were countering the arguments put forward by Lord Pakenham that it was a national duty to support the loss-making corporations. Many of the members of the Air Ministry would have remembered the experience of dealing with a monopoly during the war when BOAC was the main provider of air transport services to the RAF; that had led directly to the formation of its own Transport Command.

The report concluded that in view of the uncertainty over the future size of the troopship fleet, it was not able to present a trooping plan. But it recommended that either a direction should be given on policy grounds that a proportion of trooping should be conducted by air, preferably to the Middle East rather than the Far East, or alternatively it should be decided that the troopship fleet should be set at a certain minimum number, and any residual capacity could be provided by aircraft. It urged that a decision be made on the charter companies versus corporations issue.

COMMENTS AND THE AFTERMATH

The conclusions of the report were feeble and quite unable to give the clear direction that its authors, and the Service ministries, had wanted. The dispute over BOAC between the MCA and the Service ministries muddied the waters, the War Office was dealing in dwindling and increasingly fluid numbers, and the Admiralty wanted to preserve troopships as the main method of troop transport; all these contentious issues conspired to prevent a clear-cut decision. The appendices show to what extent the forces were supporting the charter companies: between £500,000 and £700,000 a year was being spent on Reserve Flying Schools, run by Birkett, Britavia, Airwork and Marshalls, amongst others; another £100,000 was being spent on Army Co-operation flights – Cambrian, Hunting, Lancashire and many others were the beneficiaries in that activity. Airwork operated a Communications Flight for the Air Ministry, and then there were the various War Office trooping contracts, to West Africa and within the Mediterranean, which accounted for over £250,000 per year.

The report came in for immediate criticism. The new Chief of the Air Staff, Sir John Slessor, thought not enough attention had been paid to the question of better utilisation of manpower and 'the value to the Service of having men at work on the jobs they are paid for instead of lying about on the deck of a troopship'. Field Marshall Sir William Slim, by now the Chief of the Imperial General Staff, made more or less the same point, although not so graphically, to the Chiefs of Staff Committee and did not think that this aspect had been covered in the Melville Report. Lord Pakenham wrote waspishly, 'I should like… to say that the Committee are to be congratulated on having produced so useful and clear a report even though, for reasons outside their control, they have not been able to present firm recommendations on the major points at issue'. He went to pick up his previous arguments as to the need to ensure BOAC was given the business as they now had so much surplus capacity – up to ten Hermes – 'for reasons which I need not enter here', and urged a ministerial meeting to resolve the matter. But Henderson at the Air Ministry was not biting; in his view there was no point in discussing whether BOAC or the charter companies should have the business until all had agreed that the business, air trooping, was to be had in the first place.

In the meantime, other Whitehall institutions were now examining the report, and emerging baffled. The Service Ministers' Committee, reporting in November, understood that in fact the total trooping requirement had increased again, 'in sharp contrast to the statement made by War Office representative on the Melville Committee that the introduction of 2 years National Service and other factors would greatly reduce the total volume of movement'. This strengthened the case for air trooping, particularly after another specialist committee, having studied the Melville Report, reported that air trooping would cost no more than sea trooping, 'The [specialist committee's] report states that it will cost no more to troop by air than by sea, and that during the period that obsolescent troopships are in operation, it will cost less to troop by air. This is almost the opposite of what the Melville Committee reported, after close examination.'

DECISIONS

But air trooping was back on the agenda, and that meant that the issue of BOAC had to be faced. The emerging view was that the charter airlines did not have suitable four-engine aircraft for the longer trips, mainly to the Canal Zone and the Far East, and so BOAC and its Hermes were favoured for those routes. The various ministries believed that twin-engine aircraft like the Viking could not operate to Fayid without a night stop, whereas the Hermes could. On the other hand, the independents were favoured for the shorter journeys, those to Malta and Libya. At this stage, the division of the contracts between BOAC and the charter companies along the above lines seemed to satisfy the Service ministries, although they were still anxious to maintain the benefits of competitive tendering. They were also aware of the political considerations: 'There is obviously a lot to be said in favour of giving as much government business to a State Corporation which is running at a loss and bought aircraft in excess of its needs. The arguments on the other side are also strong, and there is considerable pressure in the House of Commons on behalf of the Charter Companies.' Finally, after the Service ministers had met again on 28 November 1950 with Lord Pakenham, the Treasury and the Ministry of Transport, it was agreed to go ahead and request tenders for air trooping to the Middle East as an experiment. Lord Pakenham thought all the other ministers agreed with him, and understood that as only BOAC had suitable four-engine aircraft, it followed that BOAC would get the contract, 'as it had been ascertained that the Charter Companies were not in possession of suitable aircraft and could not therefore execute a contract, there appeared to be grounds for deciding now that all trooping should as a matter of policy be carried out by the Corporations'. But the other ministers urged that in order to avoid criticism, the contracts should all be put out to competitive tender regardless, and to this Lord Pakenham eventually agreed, secure in the knowledge that BOAC would win with its four-engine aircraft. Other decisions were made, too. There had been some doubt as to whether civil aircraft could use the airfield at Fayid in the Canal Zone under the terms of the 1936 Treaty, but it was decided that they could, after all. Melville wrote to his opposite number at the Foreign Office: 'We have reached the conclusion that the right course is to carry out this air trooping as an entirely military operation, using Fayid only, and say nothing to the Egyptians about it. The aircraft would be civil aircraft on contract, operated either by BOAC or one of the Charter Companies; but they would wear RAF roundels and the crews would be in uniform… Only those categories of personnel would be trooped who come within the definition of our rights under the Egyptian Treaty.'[11]

LORD PAKENHAM'S DILEMMA

But all was not well with the Minister of Civil Aviation. Early in the New Year, ugly rumours began to emerge that perhaps, after all, the charter companies could operate their twin-engine aircraft to Fayid without a night stop. He went back and reread the minutes of the meeting on 28 November and, on 23 February 1951, wrote a hurt letter to Manny Shinwell, the Minister of Defence:

> It was my clear impression that you had stated from the Chair that, although it was important on financial and general policy grounds to invite tenders, the use of four-engined aircraft on the work would be a specific requirement. It was on the strength of this statement, and in the

light of my knowledge that the private companies did not possess acceptable four-engined aircraft types that I refrained from pursuing at the meeting my strong plea that the surplus resources of the Corporation entitled them to prior consideration.

I now understand, however, that officials of the Air Ministry and War Office, who were present at the meeting, consider that the conclusions of the Committee, as recorded in the Minutes, allow of the invitation of tenders for twin-engined aircraft provided that the journey to the Middle East can be accomplished without an overnight stop. Although the conclusions, as recorded in the minutes, do not specifically mention the four-engine aircraft requirement, your remarks as recorded… seem to me clearly to imply that tenders would be invited only for four-engined aircraft.

You will appreciate that if the alternative interpretation is to be placed on the actual conclusion of the meeting, it may be necessary for me to re-open the question of placing the contracts with the private companies at a time when the taxpayer is called upon to subsidise the under-employed resources of BOAC.

He went on to say that he understood contracts for trooping flights to Malta were also now under consideration, and that he had no objection to those being offered to operators of twin-engine aircraft.

This is what the minutes, referred to in Lord Pakenham's letter, say:

In his [the Minister of Defence's] opinion the placing of contracts must be left open for competitive tender from both the Corporations and the Charter Companies. Naturally only those Charter Companies who possessed suitable four-engined aircraft and were otherwise able to meet the conditions would be in a position to carry out a contract. It would be quite indefensible, and lay the government open to considerable criticism, if it was decided to give the contracts for air trooping to the Corporations only.

The reader must decide whether Lord Pakenham was correct in his criticism. The Air Ministry, in the guise of Sir Folliott Sandford, was under no delusions on that score:

In my view the essence of the decision taken at the meeting on the 28th November was that we should place contracts for service to the Canal Zone after calling for tenders from any firm which was in a position to do the job properly. Admittedly, there was reference at the meeting to the use of 4-engined aircraft, because it was assumed at that date that the only way of doing the job without a night stop was by the use of such aircraft. I do not, however, consider that Lord Pakenham can claim that the Committee decided that 4-engined aircraft should be used…

He continued, quoting Shinwell's views:

… as a matter of principle the invitations to tender must be made open to all. That was the main point which the meeting endorsed. The Minister [of Defence] said that if the requirement was for four-engined aircraft, and the charter companies could not meet it, then

BOAC would get the job. It was definitely not agreed that we should fix the requirement on four-engined aircraft in order to ensure BOAC did get the job!

Shinwell wrote to Lord Pakenham accordingly, restating his belief that the main point on which he had insisted was that contracts had to be open to competitive tender. He pointed out:

It is quite true that in the course of the discussion, I mentioned that 'only those companies who possessed four-engined aircraft and were otherwise able to meet the conditions would be in a position to carry out a contract'. That was the position as I understood it at the time of the Service Ministers' Committee meeting. But it now transpires that the essential 'condition', namely, that the journey from the United Kingdom to the Middle East can be made without a night stop, can be met – and is currently being met – by the employment of twin-engined aircraft.

Lord Pakenham wrote back, saying all this placed him 'in a dilemma', and that the use of twin-engine aircraft was a subsequent development which was not present in his mind at the meeting; it should have been, however. Had he been better briefed he would have known, as his Service colleagues undoubtedly knew, that Airwork already operated its Viking flights to Egypt without a night stop en route. But we shall never know how he would have resolved this dilemma, for on 1 June he was moved to the Admiralty, and Lord Ogmore took over at the Ministry of Civil Aviation, for what was to be a very short tenure. The Admiralty was the least enthusiastic supporter of air trooping, so at least Lord Pakenham did not have to eat his words in any subsequent discussions on air trooping plans.

TENDER SKIRMISHES

The Air Ministry did not get around to issuing the tender documents for the Mediterranean and Middle East trooping tasks until June 1951, some eighteen months after the Melville Committee had first met. Sir Arnold Overton at the MCA had to write a little sharply to his colleague, Sir James Barnes, at the Air Ministry, 'I had assumed that you would consult us at the tender examination stage, but it appears… that this is not your intention'. He went on to reiterate BOAC's special claims for consideration, adding, 'I hope that the Corporations' tenders will be sufficiently competitive to gain a fair share of the contracts without any need for argument, but this may not be the case'. Sir James placated him, saying they would talk personally as to how the matter should be handled.

The Aeroplane mused on the possible outcome:

It seems unlikely that the Corporations will make any great effort to get the traffic. BOAC appears relatively indifferent to comparatively short-haul flights of about 2,000 miles single journey, and as the contract will start during midsummer when the scheduled traffic is at its heaviest, it seems unlikely that this Corporation will have many aircraft to spare for charter work. In addition a good deal of engine trouble on one of the Corporation's types has taken a heavy toll on the number of aircraft which might have been made available for non-scheduled flying.

BEA is hardly likely to want to tender for the Service traffic as its fleet is already below the numbers required to meet its scheduled service commitments.[12]

The magazine was close to the mark. After all the roaring and stamping by the Ministry of Civil Aviation over policy issues, when the time came the corporations were unable, and perhaps unwilling, to submit tenders that were even remotely competitive; that did not stop BOAC from propagating the myth in later years that it had been prevented by government from tendering for trooping contracts and as a consequence had been forced to dispose of its Hermes at knock-down prices. For the three tasks – Malta, Gibraltar and Fayid – the lowest tenders came from Hunting in all cases. On the UK/Malta task, Hunting was bidding just over £20 per passenger per round-trip, while BEA bid £26, and BOAC over £38. The difference on the Fayid tender was just as embarrassing. Hunting's bid was £36 11s per passenger, and BOAC and its Hermes came in at just under £66 per passenger. The Director of Contracts said, somewhat sniffily, that quite apart from price differences, the corporations' tenders were so hedged with reservations that they were virtually 'cost plus' contracts, and totally unacceptable. There were two other issues to consider. First, Hunting really did not have enough aircraft to complete all three contracts; if all three were awarded, Hunting would have to procure additional capacity, most likely RAF Valettas.[13] Secondly, Airwork had put in a bid for the Fayid task using Hermes acquired from BOAC. The Airwork bid, at £46 13s a seat, was some £19 cheaper than BOAC, even though Airwork proposed using BOAC aircraft, but that was still more expensive than Hunting.

Barnes and Overton had their little talk. Barnes came away feeling that the MCA was not going to press the issue of preferential treatment for the corporations in view of their uncompetitive bids. So ended the major argument, not with a bang but a whimper. In any case, the MCA was now pressing the case of Airwork and the Hermes contract. Airwork, always a favourite with government agencies, had judged its bid astutely; BOAC was anxious to dispose of its surplus aircraft, the government was anxious for BOAC to lose some, if not all, of its excess capacity, even the use of four-engine aircraft accorded with the Ministry view.

The problem for the Air Ministry was that it wanted trooping flights to Fayid to start immediately, whereas neither BOAC nor Airwork could guarantee starting before the New Year. Also, the Airwork bid still worked out at over £107,000 more than the Hunting tender. Which Ministry was going to pay the difference, if the accounting officers began to grumble? Having lost out all along the way so far, the Ministry of Civil Aviation was not prepared to concede this final point. Furthermore, it had some scores to settle with Hunting.

LORD OGMORE'S REARGUARD ACTION; IS IT APPROPRIATE FOR SERVICE VOTES TO BE BURDENED WITH, WHAT IS IN ESSENCE, A LARGE SUBSIDY FOR CIVIL AVIATION?

The lobbying started again. Lord Ogmore wrote to the newly appointed Chancellor, Hugh Gaitskell, on 16 July 1951, 'My predecessor wrote to yours on the 20th July, 1950' he started, rather unpromisingly, 'At that time my predecessor was anxious that, even if private companies submitted lower tenders than the corporations, the saving to Service Department Votes by the acceptance of such tenders might well be more than offset from the Exchequer standpoint by the cost to BOAC of maintaining surplus resources'. He did concede the point on BOAC, 'BOAC's tender [for the UK–Fayid contract] is much higher and the excess annual cost as compared with the Hunting Air Travel tender is estimated by the Air Ministry to be in the region of £270,000. I would agree that we could not sustain the claim of BOAC against a difference of expenditure of this order.' He went on to press the claims of Airwork, pointing out that the higher cost of the Airwork tender should be offset against the saving to BOAC of maintaining surplus Hermes. He also objected to the use of Huntings, which had recently scored a victory in the courts against the government:

> This company [Hunting] is associated with an aircraft maintenance organisation [Field Aircraft Services Ltd] which undertakes all its maintenance. The latter company, until recently described themselves as engaged inter alia in air transport work and on a wages claim from the Trades Unions for payment of the appropriate air transport industry rates in uniformity with the Civil Aviation Act had an award made against them in the Industrial Court. In order to set aside this award they amended their Articles of Association in such a way as to take the company outside the reach of the provisions of the Civil Aviation Act relating to terms and conditions of employment and the case came again before the Industrial Court. The Court had no option in the changed circumstances but to deal with the case as not being subject to the requirements of the Civil Aviation Act… In my view, government Departments should not give encouragement to contractors who seek to evade the intentions of government policy.

The so-called 'fair wages' issue was a red herring. The Service departments rightly observed that it had never been raised before, and that anyway Huntings was on the list of government-approved airline contractors. In rebuttal, Sir James Barnes said:

> The remaining arguments in Lord Ogmore's letter seem to me to be special pleading of the worst kind. We have never received any adverse reports of Field Aircraft Services either from the Ministry of Labour or the Ministry of Civil Aviation, and if, as appears to be the case, the firm are complying with the fair wages resolution, I should not have thought we need take any cognizance of what is said in Lord Ogmore's letter. As regards Huntings, they are on the MCA's fair list of charter operators… The further argument that the company has only twin-engined aircraft cuts no ice at all, as it is not for the Ministry of Civil Aviation to tell us what our operational requirements are.

BRITISH BASES I

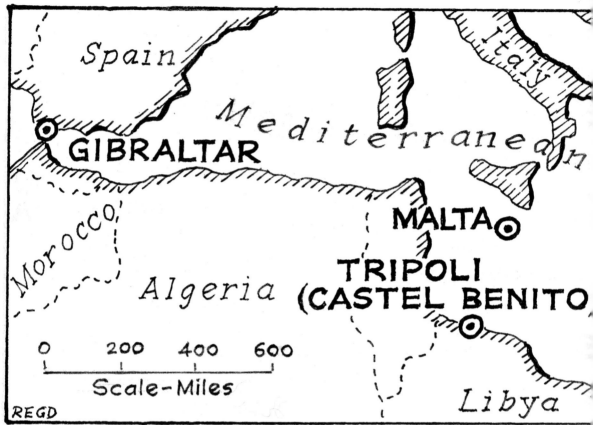

But this time Barnes was less successful. Despite the delay that would ensue, the ministers decided to request new tenders for the United Kingdom–Fayid task, specifying four-engine aircraft, after BOAC had agreed that Hermes would be made available 'at a price to be stipulated to the tenderer in advance on application to the Corporations.' Barnes had no option but to accept this decision taken over his head, but being a good civil servant he had already worked out how to use this setback to his advantage. The exclusion of Huntings from the Fayid tender left the company free for the other two major tasks, Malta and Gibraltar, for which it had already submitted the lowest tender. Barnes's parting shot was to award these contracts to Hunting, and the Intra-Med (air trooping within the Mediterranean area) contract to Airwork, 'on the normal contractual basis without prior consultation with the Ministry of Civil Aviation. I should be glad, however, if the Ministry of Civil Aviation could be informed of what we are doing without going into too much detail as to why we are excluding the Corporations.'

THE MEDITERRANEAN

BRITISH BASES IN THE MIDDLE EAST

By the end of the war, there were over 200,000 British and Indian servicemen based in the Middle East, but their numbers had declined after the British left the Palestine and the Indians left the Empire. Nevertheless, there were still around 80,000 troops just in the Canal Zone as this volume draws to an end. The Canal Zone, the world's biggest military base, 120 miles long and 30 miles wide, was the hub of British military activity in the Middle East, and head-quarters of the British Middle East Office. From there it supervised a whole complex of military establishments, garrisons, aerodromes, and naval bases in Malta, Libya, Cyprus, Jordan, Iraq, the Persian Gulf and Aden. Malta, Cyprus and Gibraltar were all British colonies, Aden a protectorate. The British had been involved militarily in Egypt since 1882, and in 1936 had concluded the Anglo-Egyptian Treaty which confirmed their control of the Canal Zone and gave them the right to reoccupy Egypt in the event of war. Libya had been colonized by the

Italians, but the British, from their bases in Egypt, had driven them and their German allies out during the Second World War, and then remained there as a garrison. British influence in Iraq and Jordan were as a consequence of the First World War, which had led to the collapse of the Ottoman Empire; the British had long had treaties of friendship with many of the states in the Persian Gulf, and had commercial interests, especially vital oil interests, there and in Iran.

THE FIRST OF THE NEW CONTRACTS

And so it was that Hunting, by now well experienced in negotiating for and winning large-scale contracts, was the first airline to be awarded major trooping contracts under the new policy: Task 1, covering Malta, and Task 2, Gibraltar. The airline would carry around 30,000 passengers a year between the United Kingdom, Malta and Gibraltar; the contracts ran for two years from 15 August 1951 and involved forty to fifty flights a month. Airwork was the other successful airline in the first round of the trooping contracts, receiving in September a two-year continuation of its contract for the Medair (also known as Intra-Med) service, shuttling 20,000 service personnel each year between the main British defence areas in the Mediterranean, the Canal Zone and Malta in its Vikings. Airwork was also successful in the next major contract, Task 3, known as Canzair, flying between the United Kingdom and Fayid in the Canal Zone, and undertook to buy four of the surplus Hermes from BOAC. The earliest Airwork hoped to have the aircraft in service was by March 1952; in fact it was to be June before the first Hermes operated a trooping flight. When the service eventually started, Airwork flew a daily frequency, year round, to Fayid. Malta, with its central location in the Mediterranean, became an important transit point for service personnel and their families; an army movement control and trooping centre was established at Imtarfa and was soon processing 250 troops per day.

But the delay in redelivering the ex-BOAC Hermes to Airwork had a severe impact on the implementation of the Canzair contract. So the Air Ministry began chartering in Yorks from Lancashire Aircraft Corporation for the thirteen-hour flight from the United Kingdom to the Canal Zone. During the twelve-month period from July 1951 to June 1952, Lancashire carried around 10,000 Service personnel into the Canal Zone. The Air Ministry adopted a pragmatic approach to equipment shortages in the airlines' fleets; if the contracted carrier was unable to fulfil its allotted task, another carrier would be chartered in to provide supplementary capacity. Although the independents fought hard for the major contracts, the award of these to specific carriers was not necessarily detrimental to the rest, as in practice the Air Ministry awarded many supplemental contracts to run alongside the main contractor.

When the supplementary Canal Zone contract came up for renewal in September 1952, the Ministry of Civil Aviation had a new proposal to put forward. Now that BOAC had withdrawn all its flying boats, and given that the RAF still had Sunderlands operating in the Far East, would it not be a good idea to retain the operational knowledge and skills required for flying-boat operation by awarding the additional task to Aquila Airways? That way, a flying-boat capability could be retained which would be beneficial in the long run; many Service officers believed that there was a future for flying boats, and the SR 45 Princess was still seen as a future prospect for the British airline and aircraft manufacturing industry. Aquila even came in with the lowest bid, but Barnes was always ready to resist pressure from the MCA to back its pet projects, and this case was to be no different. Citing a number of factors, such as the cost of maintaining facilities at the seaplane base at Fanara, complications with immigration and health controls there, and the lack of flexibility of flying boats, he was remorseless and recommended instead that the contract be awarded to the incumbent Lancashire, whose tender was around £34,000 more. He noted:

> A further important financial factor is that Aquila's will have to buy and convert Solent flying boats in order to carry out the job. This will take a minimum of three months, but I should mention here that when the original Canzair contract was awarded, the contractors, Airwork Limited, took over Hermes aircraft from BOAC which it was estimated would take six weeks to modify to an operational state. In the event, it took some seven or eight months and the excess cost falling on the Air Ministry was heavy.[14]

Lancashire successfully tendered for Task 4, the Caribbean service. Lancashire's Yorks, down-seated to thirty-six, were used twice a month to carry personnel to the British garrisons in Bermuda and Jamaica, starting on 2 July. The aircraft had to fly the long way round, via Iceland and Newfoundland, taking twenty-seven hours, and was payload restricted on the Keflavik–Gander sector, a distance of 1,370 miles.

WITH A LITTLE HELP FROM YOUR FRIENDS

A Labour Government awarded the first major trooping contracts to the independents. After they regained power, the Conservative Government effectively reserved the trooping contracts for the independents by not permitting the corporations, BOAC in particular, to hold aircraft available specifically for charter operations. To that extent, the government did perpetuate the mixed economy model in civil aviation, helping the independents on the one hand, propping up the corporations with the other. The trooping contracts sustained the private sector, but the alternatives would have been more costly; the government would either have had to invest in equipment and manpower to beef up RAF Transport Command, or accept the corporations' cost plus contracts. The corporations, however, could and did tender successfully for many of the ad hoc trooping requirements which arose from time to time, but thanks to the support given them by the Service ministries, and the Air Ministry in particular, the charter companies were able to tender for the longer-term government contracts in the years to come. Trooping contracts were to become the core business for many of the major charter airlines over the next fifteen years. They offered year-round work; charter operators could just about get by on summer work, but the prospect of bread-and-butter work during the winter months put them on a firmer financial footing. Now that the freight boom of the early post-war years was just a memory, and passenger work in the ascendancy, the industry was much more susceptible to the peaks and troughs of demand. The developing inclusive-tour market merely exacerbated the problem; British holidaymakers usually wanted to go on holiday during the summer months, and mostly at weekends. Year-round government contracts seemed like a real life-line. Nevertheless, the government still hedged its bets, and ordered two new troopships.

EIGHT

FEELING THE PINCH
1950-51

THE BROADER PICTURE

The Labour Party had won an overwhelming victory in 1945 but, as 1950 approached and with it the prospect of an election, the government seemed to have achieved its main objectives with no very clear idea as to what to do next. The economic situation had deteriorated again. Britain was still having difficulty balancing its accounts with the dollar area, and there was a further drain on the gold and dollar reserves in the second half of 1949. This was rectified in the short term by a massive devaluation of the pound in September 1949, 30.5 per cent, bringing the pound down from $4.03 to $2.80. Professor Aldcroft explains why the structural problems of Britain's trading position did not improve in the immediate after-war years:

> Britain continued to concentrate on the downstream markets of the sterling area and the third world to the neglect of the rich and expanding markets of North America and later Western Europe... it was found considerably easier to push exports to these markets than to North America or Western Europe. The missed opportunity in Western Europe was even more ironic given the fact that until the middle of 1949 at least Britain had it within her grasp to participate in the reshaping of Europe and its recovery... Unfortunately the Labour Government eventually turned its back on Europe in favour of the time-honoured Imperial connections. Consequently Britain failed to participate in the trade boom within Western Europe between 1948–51, which helped to insulate the latter from the main effects of the US recession of 1949 and the payments crisis which hit Britain.[1]

The election, held on 23 February 1950, saw Labour's overall majority reduced to six. When the new Parliament met again, the Chancellor announced that he would keep the overseas travel allowance at £50 per adult (increased to £100 in December), and motorists would receive an additional £10. In June 1950 the Korean War began, bringing the United States and its United Nations allies, including Britain, into conflict with North Korea and later the newly constituted People's Republic of

China. Britain had to start rearming, and to pay for it a whole raft of unpopular measures were taken, including higher income taxes and higher purchase tax on cars, television sets and radios. Things did not get much better in 1951. It rained in London for sixty-three of the first eighty-eight days of the year, although, fortunately, the weather cleared up enough for people to enjoy the Festival of Britain when it opened that summer. Prime Minister Attlee recognised the country's dissatisfaction and called an election for 25 October 1951.

1950

The New Year started promisingly for some; Airwork had its Sudan Government leave contract renewed for another year, providing two to three Viking services a week. But for many, the post-Airlift slump continued. Kearsley Airways, veteran of the Airlift, was just one of a number of airlines that decided to quit the aircraft-operating business and sell its Dakotas profitably when demand for them was high; it continued, and indeed continues, in business as an aircraft overhaul and repair contractor. But as ever, when one airline left the scene, there was always another ready to take its place. Crewsair acquired Dakotas and began flying in March 1950, quickly making its mark as an operator of ad hoc charter flights; its founders included Messrs Barnby, Keegan and Stevens who were later to lend the initials of their respective surnames to one of Britain's best known independent airlines, BKS Air Transport. Crewsair was involved in African operations from the start, using the Dakotas to fly out missionaries to East Africa, returning with passengers homeward bound from South Africa; later it began operating closed group flights on a regular basis to and from Rhodesia, much to the annoyance of the Ministry. As 1950 progressed, and the demands of the Korean War took up some of the slack in the market, there was more charter business to be picked up by those airlines which remained in the business, but price competition was intense. *The Aeroplane* highlighted a problem that never goes away. How does a new entrant secure business in the market? By offering cut-price rates as an incentive:

> Wild cat operators are still inclined to quote uneconomically low prices in their anxiety to attract custom and, for the established companies, this is ruining business in certain sections of the market by needlessly depressing charges.
>
> Once a rate on a commodity which normally goes by air is lowered it is almost impossible to get it back to an economic level. Shippers will not entertain increases on the lowest charge that they have paid previously. A recent example is the rate for shipments of penicillin which used to pay about 1s 6d a kilo, but a few flights were fixed at 5d a kilo. And now, if any operator can carry at this price the commodity will have to be shipped at the new low cost.
>
> Some rates have never before in the post-war period been quite so low, as aircraft owners with an imperfect knowledge and an incomplete picture of the market quote almost any price often direct to the shipper in order to get the business.[2]

The Korean War had some impact on charter services and charter rates. The RAF was able to airlift a brigade out to Korea using its own resources, but Eagle's Yorks were used for ad hoc services to Singapore, Hong Kong and Iwakuni in Japan, and the War Office also chartered BOAC's Yorks and Skyways's Dakotas. Likewise, shippers found that space on ships was harder to secure, so more urgent freight was sent by air, providing work for the remaining Halifaxes of Lancashire and Eagle.

One of the most notable increases was that seen in the number of charters concluded for the movement of ships' crews. This is thought to have resulted partly from shipowners' ready appreciation of the great saving in time and money which the use of the air transport can effect and also from the close contact which the Baltic Exchange makes possible between the charterer and the broker.

There was no lack of short-haul business, and in this sphere the charter companies were at their greatest advantage, as the numbers of seamen to be moved were usually suitable for machines such as Vikings and Dakotas. In particular, Scandinavian buyers of new British ships sent their delivery crews by chartered aircraft.

Deliveries by air of essential spare parts – of which carriage by surface transport might have meant that a ship was out of commission for some weeks – included such heavy loads as a seven-ton tail-shaft from Amsterdam to Mauritius, a 4½ ton rotor from Abadan to Amsterdam for re-winding (after which it was re-delivered to the Persian Gulf) and a 4½ ton rudder stock from Prestwick to Singapore.

During the year, also, a number of chartered companies were engaged on contract work which involved the movement of servicemen and civilians, with their families, to posts overseas.

Pilgrim flights to Rome and a number of inclusive tours to – among other places – Austria, the South of France and Corsica, also contributed to the overall increase seen in the charter business.

Freight operators found that some of their most common loads were textiles, flown from France to the United Kingdom. There was also a steady traffic in chemicals from this country to Northern Italy. During the latter part of the year the Corporations made use of their larger charter aircraft to augment their freight services to Singapore and Hong Kong and to fulfil certain government commitments.[3]

MORE OF THE SAME

In 1950 there was a large increase in the number of proposed associate agreements with BEA, although as many were denied as were granted. Airlines were refused any flights between the Channel Islands and London and, for that matter, Birmingham. BEA also took over the developing passenger services from London to Le Touquet. Morton Air Services entered the scheduled market with services from Bristol. Eagle and Starways were also new names; Starways started its long association with Liverpool, Eagle was granted West Country routes from Bovingdon, which it did not take up.

When applications were granted, some routes, on closer inspection, did not warrant the investment needed to develop them. Many of these secondary and third-level routes were inherently thin, and undercapitalised airlines were not in a good position to stand initial losses while the traffic on the routes built up. A subsequent anomaly that arose from the grant to the corporations of their exclusive rights was that private airlines ended up competing with each other on feeder routes that manifestly did not warrant and could not withstand two or more competing airlines. The trunk routes with the densest traffic flows remained a monopoly of BEA.

One change that did come about in time for the 1951 season was the decision to extend the period of the agreements to five years, and even longer in some cases. BACA had lobbied for the change, saying that it was difficult for airlines to make expensive investment decisions over such a short time-scale, and BEA and the minister agreed. Perhaps because he had been intimately connected with the start of the scheme and was anxious for it to succeed, Lord Douglas took matters further, and invited the charter airlines to discuss their plans with BEA. The corporation was able to indicate which proposals would not sustain an objection, and even invited some airlines to operate alongside it on peak Saturdays to the Channel Islands; Olley and Morton were awarded agreements out of London, and Jersey Airlines out of Southampton.

HORIZON HOLIDAYS

In its issue of 23 June 1950, *The Aeroplane* reported: 'Another low-cost air movement of students and teachers to Corsica began a few weeks back. They are accommodated

Avro Anson 1 G-AIRN of Starways. (MAP)

there in special camps. No other details are at present available.' From such modest beginnings did a former journalist launch the modern inclusive-tour industry.

Vladimir Raitz, born in Moscow, spent his childhood in Berlin, Paris and Warsaw, before going to school in England. Graduating from the London School of Economics and Cambridge, he became a journalist with United Press and then with Reuters. A Russian friend invited Raitz to join him in Calvi, where some Russian colleagues had organised a holiday camp; accommodation was in tents with twin beds. They asked him to help them find clients in England. If he could organise cheap air transport to Corsica, Raitz realised that he could sell inexpensive holidays in the sun, at a time when the British were beginning to hanker for some relief from the post-war austerity that they had endured for five long years.

There was the small matter of chartering suitable aircraft and coming to some arrangement with the MCA and BEA. Fortunately, BEA did not serve Calvi and so in time were prepared to grant the carrier an associate agreement. But initially Raitz had to rely on closed groups, and after some delay he was told he could market the holidays to nurses and schoolteachers. He turned to Lambert Brothers, brokers at the Baltic Exchange, and they suggested that icon of the charter airline industry, Air Transport (Charter) (CI), which duly provided him with a thirty-two-seat Dakota to operate fifteen return trips between Blackbushe and Calvi on Sundays, taking 5½ hours each way. With a legacy of £3,000 from his grandmother, he was able to finance the start-up costs.

The MCA's procrastination over the permit meant that arrangements were completed too late in the season, and the advertisements in *Teacher's World* and the *Nursing Mirror* in the spring of 1950, and the duplicated brochure sent off to potential clients, only drew in 300 holidaymakers. With 480 round-trip seats to sell, this was not enough to break even in spite of the attractions offered. 'Holidaymakers live in large tents fitted with beds and mattresses, two to a tent – the best sanitation – meals are taken out of doors.' There was a special inducement to Britons still living with food rationing: 'English visitors will be pleased to find that they are served twice daily with a meat dish.' The cost of the holiday was just £35 10s for a fortnight, the novelty of flying as a means of going on holiday was a powerful inducement, and days in the more or less guaranteed sun were an attraction but, even so, Raitz managed to lose money in his first year. 'The chief reasons for the disappointing sales', he later said, 'were probably that the advertising was placed too late in the year and that I had priced the holiday too low. People just couldn't believe that a good holiday in Corsica could be had for the price quoted.'[4] Undeterred, next year Raitz went to the bank and borrowed £2,000 to finance Horizon's 1951 holiday programme. This time an additional 100 passengers set off for Corsica; Horizon was over the break-even point and the package tour industry was launched. The next year, 1952, armed with a seven-year associate agreement with BEA, Raitz was able to cast his net wider as he was no longer limited to the closed group. Still using Air Transport Charter (CI), he charged £39 10s for a fortnight's holiday, but only £13 of this came from the personal tourist allowance, a good selling point. In 1952 Horizon pioneered a second destination, using the newly opened airport at Palma to fly holidaymakers to Majorca in the Balearics, establishing a pattern of developing new holiday destinations further afield in the Mediterranean. Within the next few years Raitz was introducing inclusive tours to Sardinia (1954), Perpignan and Malaga, for the Spanish Costa Blanca and Costa del Sol respectively (1956), and Minorca (1957).

BOAC, OFC AND 'A SQUALID DEAL'

The corporations, in particular BOAC with its large fleet of under-utilised Yorks, were now much more active in the charter market, greatly to the dismay of the charter airlines. Charter airlines were always very nervous about incursions into their market by the corporations, a situation that did not resolve itself until much later, when the economics of specialisation and vertical integration secured the inclusive tour leisure market for charter carriers. Of course, all small airlines have to expect some competition from large, well-financed, government-backed corporations, and anticipate some bruising in the process; but if the charter airlines back then occasionally sounded whiny, and whinged about their own need for protection from external pressures, they had few other resources to fall back on. There were no multi-million pound deficit grants if things went wrong.

And things could go very wrong. The biggest blow was dealt to Hunting, which after a year's successful operation of the Overseas Food Corporation's contract to East Africa, tendered for renewal at £63 18s per head, having completed sixty round trips: it lost the contract to BOAC. The Hunting service had been flown by Vikings which could operate to any of the three designated OFC airports. The BOAC service was less convenient as the passengers had to use its regular services to East Africa, which were by flying boat to Lake Naivasha, about 60 miles from Nairobi; OFC personnel then had to transfer by coach to Nairobi where they joined flights operated by East African Airways to their final destination. There was some indignation that loss-making BOAC was encroaching on the charter airlines' market share, with BACA ready to take up the cudgels, proclaiming that this was 'a deliberate attempt to harm the Independent Companies at any cost, and this cost comes from the taxpayer'.[5] During the subsequent debate in the House of Commons, the details of the arrangement began to emerge. BOAC had had discussions with the OFC at the very highest level and it had been agreed that BOAC would tender at the Hunting rate, based on 85 per cent load factor and then adding 10 per cent. The BOAC offer was set at £72 10s and was accepted. The BOAC rate was some £50 below the normal airfare, and the apparent discrepancy was justified on the grounds that the OFC passengers would be fill-up traffic, using otherwise empty seats, and boosting load factors to 100 per cent; at such high load factors BOAC would have been turning away high-revenue passengers in order to carry the OFC passengers. When challenged, the Parliamentary Secretary, Lindgren, did not deny that BOAC was aware of the Hunting tender. The affair aroused some Parliamentary passion, as it was thought that the government and BOAC were taking advantage of the financial backing of the Treasury (the Exchequer was covering the bulk of the corporation's losses through deficiency grants) to undercut the private airlines. For once, Lindgren, usually so ready to defend the corporations, appeared at a loss for words. He accepted many of the statements made by the opposition MPs who had been well briefed, and even left them with the last word. In fine Parliamentary style, Alan Lennox-Boyd, Conservative MP for Bedford, summed up: 'It is not only the case that the Civil Aviation Act has been broken – for it has been broken in the most monstrous way – since the Parliamentary Secretary said that the Exchequer grant would not be used for the purpose of undercutting private operators and we believe that it has been used to break the Act. However our charge tonight is much more than that. It is that a squalid deal has been arrived at between two government Corporations which has driven out of this business a highly reputable firm whose members pay taxes to the State to enable us to carry out these risky experiments.'[6]

The loss of the contract was a serious blow for Hunting, representing around 45 per cent of its business and providing work for up to six Vikings. However, BOAC's triumph was short-lived, for by 1950 the Ground Nuts Scheme had turned into a fiasco, bogged down by technical problems, maladministration and an almost complete lack of transport infrastructure, and by early 1951 had failed, without ever having sold a single ground nut.

GOVERNMENT CONTRACTING

The Hunting episode had highlighted one of the main concerns about government tenders – that the corporations, in this case BOAC, had full access to the tenders submitted by the charter airlines and could adjust their own submissions accordingly. The government finally recognised these concerns, and decided that in future, all such civilian tenders should be handled by the Ministry of Civil Aviation. Under the new arrangement, MCA acted as the 'impartial' arbitrator, and government departments submitted their requirements to the Ministry's Air Services (Charter) section, which then simultaneously issued them for tender to both the corporations and to approved independent operators.[7]

The growing trickle of government contracts were not confined exclusively to the military. In 1950 the government gave British Nederland Airservices (BNA) a contract to provide a leave service for the British Administration in Tripolitania, one of the constituent provinces in what was about to become the Kingdom of Libya. BNA bought a Viking to supplement its Dakota fleet, and operated a round-trip once every twenty-one days, rotating fifteen to twenty administration staff at a time through the posting. The benefits to the government were clear; instead of having to allow an additional twenty days' leave for the sea passage, the trip by air to and from England only took one day. When BNA closed down at the end of 1950, the contract was taken over by Scottish Airlines.

CLOSED GROUPS

If the government was at last beginning to recognise the value of the charter airlines in the longer term, the charter airlines were still determined to exploit whatever openings were available to them. As Lord Pakenham ruefully remarked in a debate in the House of Lords on 6 December 1949, there was one field of activity – that of 'regular services offered by private companies to particular classes of the community' – which had not been envisaged at the time the Civil Aviation Act was drawn up. Closed groups and travel clubs, or 'affinity groups' as they were later known, were organisations and clubs that chartered aircraft for their own use; they then resold the seats individually to their own members. The flights did not require a licence, as they were not systematic and not available to the general public; this saved much fuss and bother. Vladimir Raitz had advertised his first inclusive tours only to nurses and teachers because initially he was not able to obtain a licence, not the first and certainly not the last occasion when a tour operator and an airline would use this method to circumvent the licensing requirements. Closed group flights were the main vehicle for the operation of unlicensed flights, but non-systematic flights, that is, occasional flights not operated on a regular or scheduled basis, had their uses, too. For the historian the main difficulty is that being unlicensed, such flights were also unrecorded. Some of the larger charter airlines did report passengers carried on charter flights, but many of the smaller airlines did not.

Although anxious to choke off this activity, the government found it could do little by way of prosecution in the courts; the Act was too loosely worded, and did not sufficiently define terms such as 'member of the public'. In discussing an alleged breach by Airwork early in 1950, James Dunnett of the Ministry pointed out the difficulties:

> The fact is that it is extremely difficult to draw the line and to say on which side of the line each case falls. I would agree that if a substantial section of the public is involved, an offence is committed; but what is a substantial section of the public? The benefits of the service clearly need not be necessarily available to all members of the public but it is not easy to say what is such a class or section as can properly be described as 'the public' for the purposes of the Section. I do not believe that a Court would convict on these facts. That is, of course, a matter of opinion, and I may well be wrong, but what is clear to me is that an unsuccessful prosecution would certainly be regarded as a major triumph by Airwork and the other Charter Companies.[8]

In the 1950s there were plenty of quite legitimate organisations which did offer cheap flights to their members. The Roman Catholic Church was an early exponent, quickly understanding the advantages to its members of being able to make pilgrimages inexpensively. Forces' and veterans' associations were charterers in the early post-war days; the Boy Scouts and student associations catered for somewhat younger members. Perhaps the most famous of all, ironically, was Whitehall Travel, which drew its membership from the British Civil Service. With refreshing candour, its founder, George Wenger, explained in his first brochure how Whitehall Travel could offer charter facilities to its members:

> Whitehall Travel has been formed by a group of Civil Service staff associations with the aim of providing holidays abroad at the lowest possible cost to their members. By keeping the overheads to a minimum, by private charter of aircraft, and by fullest use of bulk facilities it has been possible to offer members better value for their money than they could obtain through any commercial agency. The only means of reducing the cost of air travel is by chartering complete aircraft, but the Civil Aviation Act forbids members of the general public to take advantage of such facilities. The various organizations of the National Staff Side of the Civil Service are considered closed societies for the purpose of the Act and permission has consequently been received to make private arrangements with one of the best-known charter companies. The terms agreed upon are extremely favourable.[9]

Airwork was the main beneficiary of Whitehall Travel's contracts.

Over time, special organisations developed which did nothing else but organise charter flights for their members. Being closed, information about such groups is scarce; no passenger returns were ever made and the organisations have long since disappeared. Travel clubs were especially effective in the colonial markets where demand was strong for cheaper air links back to the United Kingdom. Hunting Air Travel went so far as to create the East African Club to which employees of British firms based in East Africa could belong. Because the traffic originated in East Africa in a more benign regulatory climate, the British Government was powerless to take any action, much to Lord Pakenham's chagrin. Instead, the flights were finally made legitimate by the next Conservative Government, and formed the basis of the original Colonial Coach Class services to East and Central Africa.

OUTPOSTS: MALTA

Closer to home, but another example of overseas business developed by the charter airlines, was the development of air services in Malta. Strategically located in the middle of the Mediterranean, Malta was always going to be an important hub for airlines in the region, and charter airlines were quick to spot the opportunity. By early 1947 British Aviation Services, parent company of Silver City, had formed a local company in partnership with Cassar and Cooper, and based Airspeed Consuls on the island. Other companies followed suit, The Instone Airline and Chartair both establishing local companies; soon all three companies merged to form the first Air Malta, with a 50 per cent shareholding in Maltese hands. Scheduled flights were operated to Libya, Rome and Sicily. In 1949 two Doves were introduced, followed by the first of three Dakotas, which were more suitable for some of the longer sectors like Malta–Cairo; the Dakotas were leased in from Eagle and Ciro's. Considering

Airspeed Consul G-AIKZ of Air Malta. (MAP)

the Silver City ancestry, it comes as no surprise that late in 1950 a Bristol Freighter was also introduced experimentally on Air Malta's routes. But the pioneering airline was snuffed out in January 1951 when all its shares were acquired by Malta Airways, a subsidiary of BEA, which took over its operations. It was to be twenty-three years before the name Air Malta was revived.[10]

A NEW ERA?

As 1950 drew to a close, the charter airlines might have derived some comfort from remarks made by Lord Pakenham. In a debate in the House of Lords on 6 December, his old rival and former Tory predecessor Lord Swinton joked about claims then being made by BEA that a new era had opened to the private operators – BEA's press release referred to the future of Associate Agreements.[11] In one sense, he said, it would be true to say that a new era was opened to the early Christians when they were introduced to the lions, and went on the criticise the corporations for muscling in on charter work. Lord Pakenham was forced to reply, 'My feelings towards the charter companies are those of goodwill. I entertain towards them nothing but feelings which are entirely Christian and humane', although he spoiled the effect by then going on to say, 'but I can never forget my responsibilities as watchdog to the taxpayer'. Despite that, the corporations still managed to lose almost as much in 1949–50 as in the previous year.

Indeed, his support for the corporations was all-embracing. He turned his back on his predecessor's more indulgent attitude towards the charter airlines and, as we saw in the previous chapter, tried to create a Soviet-style 'Aeroflot', with the Ministry and corporations responsible for all aspects of civil aviation. He accepted that charter flights were no longer limited to taxi operations; aircraft were just too big now. But he still wanted to control what he regarded as 'pirate bus' operations. Charter airlines would be tolerated insofar as their commercial activities could be regulated by the government, so he wanted all business to be offered to the corporations in the first instance; it would then be at their discretion whether it was shared with the charter airlines. Associate agreements were but a first step in this process.

He was duly taken up by 'Commentator' in *The Aeroplane* who had a clearer understanding of the issues:

> As I see it, the real issue for the Minister of Civil Aviation is not the narrow one: 'How can I see that my Corporations have the best possible chance of making a success?' but the much broader view: 'What must I do to achieve the most substantial and healthy expansion of Britain's air transport industry?'
>
> It does not at all necessarily follow that if charter companies obtain air transport contracts for large-scale carriage in various parts of the World, that the Corporations' scheduled services will suffer. Indeed, the majority of, if not all, the contracts that the independent operators have sought to conclude have involved entirely new fields of air transport traffic. The conditions of the Air Corporations Act have compelled them to develop the non-schedule side of the business. The generation of new traffic by the charter companies need have no ill-effect on the financial position of the Corporations. BOAC and BEA's problem all along has not been a lack of revenue-producing traffic but a high cost of production.
>
> In combating strenuously the efforts of the charter companies to build up new overseas business, the Minister and the national air line monopoly are begging the question... Here is an opportunity for statesmanship on the part of the government rather than the lopsided party political attitude. One is constantly driven back in this context to the obvious analogy between this industry and the growth of Britain's sea-carrying trade in the past. Little imagination is required to visualize how our sea-going trade would have fared had it been in the hands of a single government-controlled corporation with a mandate to prevent all other British shipping enterprise.[12]

To put the last remark into context, although in decline, British shipping in 1950 still accounted for over 21 per cent of the world fleet.[13]

AVIATION TRADERS LTD

While opportunities still existed for charter airlines, at least one enthusiastic entrepreneur saw more rewarding possibilities on the ground. Freddie Laker had formed Aviation Traders in 1947 at Southend and used the company to overhaul, rebuild or scrap the aircraft which he went out and bought. He had taken over BOAC's fleet of Haltons in time for them to be operated by Bond Air Services throughout the Berlin Airlift. Now that the Airlift was over, he began turning ploughshares back into swords; he purchased a number of Halifax A Mk9s, the transport version, and converted them into bombers for the Royal Egyptian Air Force, arming them with Vickers guns in the nose, Browning machine-guns in the tail turret and a full bomb-bay. He overhauled three ex-BEA Vikings for BOAC, which passed them on to British West Indian Airways. If he was not converting or overhauling aircraft, he was scrapping them:

> Laker went to government surplus sales and bought everything and anything. He bought aircraft in batches of fifty and sixty and engines by the hundreds. At one sale he bought ninety-nine Halifaxes and six thousand engines. He paid prices as low as £50 per plane. He bought armoured trucks, radios, US war surplus planes, weapons, ammunition, crates of equipment that had never been opened, job lots that could contain anything. The government departments hardly knew and cared less what they were getting rid of as long as they could sweep their vast stockpiles clean. Freddie was prepared to buy anything provided it was cheap enough. Cheap enough meant that he could guarantee to make a profit from melting down the metal of which the planes were made, mostly aluminium.
>
> Laker organised his men into teams. After he had bought a job lot of war surplus planes they flew up to the aerodromes where the auctions had been held and cut the planes to pieces on the spot with hacksaws and oxyacetylene cutters. The teams built brick melting pots, big tanks with oil-injected heating like glorified blowlamps. Then they threw the bits of fuselage and wings into the pot and tapped off the molten metal into aluminium bricks.
>
> When they had nothing else to do Laker's men broke up aero engines, salvaging the brass and copper scrap.[14]

LIVING WITH GULLIVER

Airwork was again able to start 1951 with good news, having successfully tendered for the contract to operate the air-cargo service across the Cook Strait for the New Zealand Railways, beating off competition from Silver City Airways. Airwork established a subsidiary, Straits Air Freight Express, to operate a fleet of Bristol Freighters over the 70-mile sectors and used mechanical handling to speed up the turn-round times. If Airwork could not find sufficient business opportunities in the United Kingdom, it went abroad and looked for more. But the airline also looked after its interests closer to home, and was prepared to take up the cudgels on behalf of the independents in the growing dispute with the corporations over the increasing volume of charter traffic that the latter were now carrying. With an eye to a wider audience, its commercial manager, Sir Archibald Hope, set out the arguments clearly for more commercial honesty on the part of the corporations in a letter to *Flight* magazine:

The case presented by the non-scheduled operators is based on the claim that the Corporations are using their subsidy, paid with tax-payers' money, to assist their quotations for non-scheduled services. It has been argued by the protagonists of nationalization that, because the Corporations' non-scheduled activities reduce the subsidy, the subsidy is not being used. This, of course, is illogical nonsense.

If this argument is carried to its ultimate conclusion, it would mean that the Corporations could undertake non-scheduled or charter work at prices which covered their basic operating costs, plus one penny of contribution to their overheads, this reducing their subsidy by that amount. The private enterprise operators, however efficient they may be, obviously cannot reduce their overheads beyond the true amount, and it follows inevitably that, if the Corporations are allowed to persist in their present policy, the non-scheduled operators must be forced of business.

The non-scheduled operators, therefore, contend that the Corporations' present policy is contrary to public policy for at least three reasons. First, the non-scheduled operators acquired their aircraft and built up their business on the strength of numerous Ministerial pronouncements, both inside and outside Parliament, that the Corporations would not be allowed to use public money to compete against them. These protestations are now lightly thrust aside, on the grounds that it is necessary to protect the tax-payer's pocket. This argument was just as valid when the promises were made, and surely the non-scheduled operators are entitled to point out the breach of good faith by a government whose promises encouraged them to invest large sums of money. Secondly, if the Corporations persist in their present policy, for the reasons outlined above, the non-scheduled operators must be forced out of business. From the point of view of national defence, it is at least also arguable that this would be unfortunate. Thirdly, a better way to reduce the taxpayers' loss – and no one denies the desirability of doing so – would be for the Corporations to get rid of their surplus aircraft and surplus staff, rather than operate non-scheduled services with them at prices which are economically indefensible. The Corporations will doubtless deny that they have surplus aircraft, but examination of their published figures for the past five years shows that their utilization is far below that of many other international operators, and even of some of the British non-scheduled operators. Only when they actually achieve really high utilization can they justifiably claim that they have no surplus aircraft and are merely using spare capacity for non-scheduled services. [15]

Part of the subtext here was that Airwork wanted some of those surplus aircraft! Modern four-engine airliners which did not have to be paid for in dollars were very desirable, and it was time to move on from the trusty, but venerable, Avro York.

YORKS

One airline that had faced up to the post-Airlift depression was Eagle, which invested in three Yorks bought second-hand from BOAC. They could seat up to forty-six passengers as well as being fully convertible for freight, and were used on ad hoc

Avro York G-AGNZ of Eagle Aircraft Services. (A.J. Jackson Collection)

charter work. In April 1950 a York lifted one of the largest single loads ever when it carried a ship's propeller shaft, weighing over 9 tons and measuring 18ft 8in, from RAF Thornaby to Amsterdam for the *John Chandris* in dry dock at Rotterdam. Just loading such a big piece of equipment through the side door of the York required some ingenuity. The airline also bought a Dakota which, as we have just seen, was chartered to Air Malta for the summer, flying to Cairo, Catania and Rome. After Bamberg bought the Luton Flying Club, he moved the airline's base there early in 1950. On 1 September Eagle took over Trent Valley Aviation, based at Nottingham, bringing another Dakota into the fleet. Three more Yorks were added at the end of 1950, bought from the liquidators of the Argentine airline FAMA for a reported £9,000 each, together with a very large stock of spares, and the two Dakotas were then disposed of. During 1951 Eagle's Yorks were active in support of the Korean War effort, flying for the War Office to Hong Kong, Singapore and Iwakumi in Japan; more peaceably, they also undertook a number of Hadj flights carrying pilgrims from Kano in Nigeria to Jeddah and back.

Indeed, by mid-1951 Eagle was the only independent operator of large four-engine transport aircraft, barring five Halifaxes still in Lancashire's inventory, and the remaining three big Tudors. Together with BOAC, Eagle benefited whenever there was any long-haul work to be done, such as trooping flights to Japan in connection with the Korean War. Eagle became a major contractor for the government and operated fifteen round-trip flights to the Far East for the various Service departments in the period July 1950 to June 1951. Then, in August, the airline operated seven more flights carrying casualties from Singapore to the United Kingdom, with yet more in September and October; the Yorks were modified to carry twelve stretchers and a number of sitting cases. With rumours of impending large trooping contracts, the need for more heavy lift was becoming clear. Surrey Flying Services was resuscitated; it was taken over by Laker's Aviation Traders and bought two of Eagle's six Yorks, which it started operating in October. More spectacular, however, were the actions of Lancashire Aircraft Corporation, which relieved BOAC of much of its stock of Yorks in May 1951; some twenty-three were bought for £135,000, leaving BOAC with the remaining ten to be used as freighters. Another landmark in the long and mutually beneficial relationship between BOAC and Lancashire, it allowed BOAC to side-step adroitly those competition issues about which Sir Archibald Hope had been complaining. Lancashire installed fifty folding seats and quickly signed up contracts with the Air Ministry to carry Royal Auxiliary Air Force ground personnel to summer camps at home and overseas, as well as securing other ad hoc business; it rebranded its long-haul operations 'Skyways of London', retaining 'Lancashire' for its domestic services. The increasing demand for long-haul charter flights is illustrated in one of *The Aeroplane*'s typical weekly reports in June 1951 on 'The Charter Business':

A BOAC York left Tokyo for London on June 14 with 40 seamen. Five days later one of Lancashire's new fleet of Yorks left Stavanger for Melbourne with an auxiliary engine for the 6,300 ton Norwegian ship Arena. This was the first long-distance flight completed by Lancashire's Yorks since it took over 23 of them from BOAC recently. The first charter completed about two weeks ago was to Germany. Lancashire is overhauling a number of the Yorks and hopes to have three in service by the end of [June].

Another BOAC York left London for Melbourne on June 20 chartered by Sir William Seager and Co., Cardiff shipowners. It took 31 seamen out to Australia and returned with 28.

On June 26, Crewsair's Viking left London with passengers for Johannesburg and on the return flight was due to collect another group of passengers at N'Dola. They were employees of mines in Northern Rhodesia's copper-belt region, returning to this country for leave. This was the second trip of this nature undertaken by Crewsair.

Lancashire's Halifaxes completed two flights recently, one carrying BEA cargo to Malta and one from Prestwick to Malta on June 19 with a load of 10ft steel tubes.

Eagle's Yorks made two flights to Baghdad with freight, and two flights for the Air Ministry to the Canal Zone.

A good example of fast liaison between a broker and operator occurred recently when Lambert Bros. were requested by a shipowner to rush a spare part for a vessel to Belfast. The call came in at 16.30. One hour later the part was being loaded into a Transair Anson and two hours later was delivered in Northern Ireland.[16]

Avro York G-AMGL of Surrey Flying Services. (A.J. Jackson Collection)

ASSOCIATE AGREEMENTS IN 1951 AND BEYOND

Towards the end of 1950, new associate agreements for the following years were announced. What was noticeable this time round was that BEA was calling in more of the services to the Channel Islands and Isle of Man, so that many of those remaining were granted for one year only. First, Patrick Aviation had lost the Birmingham route, then Sivewright lost its Manchester–Jersey services when BEA took them back. Now Sivewright also lost its Manchester–Isle of Man service, as did Lancashire and North-West Airlines. BEA announced its intention of taking back the Glasgow–Isle of Man services, another blow for Lancashire and North-West, as well as Scottish Airlines. Sivewright stopped operations early in 1951; North-West sold its Dakotas early in 1951 and operated its residual services with Rapides and an Aerovan, before ceasing operations at the end of the season.

There were some winners, however. Silver City was awarded the first ten-year agreement for its vehicle ferry service, and Cambrian was awarded five-year permits for its growing network of services from Cardiff. Air Enterprises was allowed to continue to develop its services from the Isle of Wight for another five years, but in the event ceased operations by the end of 1953. Lancashire was developing a sizeable network to the Isle of Man, with services from London, Leeds, Blackpool and Liverpool. Scottish Airlines reopened its Prestwick–Isle of Man service and launched a promising new daily service from Prestwick to London, Northolt, via Burtonwood, the former American base situated between Manchester and Liverpool. Timings were geared to Scottish and Manchester demand, and the fares were set at the same level as BEA's own services to Renfrew and Manchester; BEA only ran a once-weekly service to Manchester from London. Another Manchester-based airline was the charmingly named Melba Airways, operating Rapides to Sandown on the Isle of Wight. *Aeronautics* commented approvingly:

In May this year, the first scheduled air service from Manchester to Sandown was inaugurated. Melba Airways, in association with British European Airways, operate the service with eight-seat DH Rapides, a two-hour journey for £9 5s 0d return. It is a Saturday and Sunday service. This airport is a busy place at week-ends, for in addition to the Melba service, Air Enterprises Limited run seven flights in each direction on Saturdays between

De Havilland Rapide G-ALGE of Manchester-based Melba Airways, seen at Newcastle. (MAP)

Croydon and Sandown, a 35 minute journey for 88s return. As many as 250 passengers arrive here each week. The reception lounge at Sandown is small, but very luxurious. The cocktail bar is up to the highest standard in appearance and service.[17]

Elsewhere in the article, the writer, Squadron Leader David West, enthuses about the lobster lunches at the Flying Club for 4s, and notes two young pioneers in the making, John Britten and Desmond Norman, putting the finishing touches to their BN-1F monoplane. The two were later to achieve great success with the Britten-Norman Islander.

By this stage, a sparse network of associate agreement services was developing. No routes in Scotland, but Scottish Airlines had its service from Prestwick–Northolt via Burtonwood. The Isle of Man was well served from northern points, in part due to the efforts of Lancashire Aircraft Corporation. Cambrian was specialising in services from Liverpool and Wales; East Anglian Flying Services had its interests at Southend. In 1951, the independents carried 91,000 scheduled passengers, nearly half of them on the two main international routes, Silver City's vehicle ferry flights and the Aquila service to Madeira. Around 24,000 passengers were carried to the Isle of Man, but traffic to this destination was down, largely because BEA had taken over the Manchester route. To put matters into perspective, by this time BEA was carrying over 1 million passengers a year.

PROBLEM AREAS

Typically, it was either feast or famine. After the problems of 1950, a capacity shortage began to develop in the charter market by mid-1951. A number of airlines had ceased trading, taking advantage of the demand for Dakotas to sell up. Those that remained suddenly found that they had more business than they could cope with. First of all, the Air Ministry, in the middle of the complicated negotiations over air trooping which have been recounted in the previous chapter, let it be known that it was interested in putting out to tender various trooping tasks; airlines that were anxious to secure this business were unwilling to allow their aircraft to be committed elsewhere. But the rumoured deadline of 1 July came and went with no contracts placed. This coincided with a crisis in Iran where the new government of Dr Mossadeq in Teheran had nationalised the assets of the Anglo–Iranian Oil Co.[18] in May. The British Government, convinced that the Iranians would not be able to run the refineries successfully, beat a strategic retreat, imposed an embargo on Iranian oil and began to evacuate all 4,500 British personnel from Abadan, the main refinery. Initially, RAF Transport Command and BOAC were used to transfer staff back to the United Kingdom. Later, between ten and fifteen civil Yorks were held on standby as back-up during the crisis, which lasted most of the summer; the government paid BOAC and Lancashire demurrage rates when they were not flying and so denied them to other charterers. The evacuation was finally completed with the help of a number of other charter airlines. Even Aquila was brought in, flying staff out from the Shatt-al-Arab waterway in its Hythe flying boats; and the big Tudors of William Dempster were also used during the last days. The final act was played out at the beginning of October when the few remaining Anglo–Iranian personnel left Abadan on board the cruiser HMS *Mauritius* while the Royal Marines band played *Colonel Bogey*. But even as the last notes were sounding off, the government faced another crisis in the Middle East, this time in the Canal Zone, where British troops were stationed under the terms of the Anglo–Egyptian Treaty. The War Office had to charter in Yorks and Vikings to fly in reinforcements to boost the British garrison, an airlift that was to last over two months. Then a marked shortage of Dakotas developed. Those airlines which still had Dakotas, like Air Transport Charter (CI), Crewsair, Starways and Scottish, found they were in demand by BEA which was suffering a severe equipment shortage, partly due to delays in the delivery of the new Airspeed Ambassadors. Airspeed should have delivered six Ambassadors by 15 March 1951 but, after a number of mishaps, was somewhat behind schedule. The first Ambassador for BEA was not handed over until 21 August, and entry into scheduled service was not until 13 March 1952, only one year ahead of the first entry into service of the Viscount. BEA had also decided to modernise its Dakota fleet, renaming the class Pionair, and needed to charter in more capacity from the independents as its own aircraft were temporarily withdrawn; it was then further affected when the new Pionairs were redelivered late. Some services had to be cancelled or curtailed, and others contracted out to the independents; for example, Hunting operated the London–Amsterdam night excursion service in June. To make matters worse, BEA then suffered from a work-to-rule by some of its employees causing further shortages. The Dakota operators were inundated with work, both Scottish Airlines and Air Transport Charter (CI) using their aircraft to fly services for BEA as well as their regular charter commitments, which were not inconsiderable; Scottish had just picked up a six-month contract to fly oil workers for the Iraq Petroleum Co. from Northolt to points in the Middle East and Persian Gulf. The lack of availability in the United Kingdom is apparent in the number of fixtures given to foreign airlines. Prominent amongst these was the Norwegian airline Fred Olsen, whose Dakotas visited British airports almost on a daily basis during the summer.

Meanwhile, back in Berlin, the Russians were causing problems again. This time they were refusing to grant transit visas for certain items manufactured in West Berlin, so that by mid-August, £6 million worth of goods had accumulated in West Berlin. A second minor airlift between Berlin and Hamburg was started in August, using aircraft from Pan American, Air France and BEA. The difference in cost between ground transport and the airlift was borne by the Berlin Senate and the Allied High Commission. Remembering, perhaps, the lessons of the previous Airlift, the last remaining Tudor of A.V.M. Bennett's Fairflight was chartered in by the British Foreign Office; it was soon carrying 50 tons a day out of Berlin. At the end of the year the Russians suddenly and, as it turned out, temporarily, began granting export clearance again to most Berlin-manufactured goods. But the Tudor was retained in Berlin for the time being, a decision that was to benefit Laker when his company took over Fairflight late in 1951.

INDUSTRY AFFAIRS

Reflecting the growing importance of other forms of activity, the British Air Charter Association (BACA) changed its name, in August 1951, to the British Independent Air Transport Association (BIATA), following claims that the word 'charter is too limited and no longer embraces all roles which private companies are called upon to perform'. The association also took the opportunity to expel the two corporations from among its ranks. Its first chairman was Eric Rylands of the Lancashire Aircraft Corporation, and he quickly instituted an annual dinner for its members to which prominent guests were invited, usually including a government minister. The speeches at the dinner allowed the chairman to sum up the year's achievements and were an occasion for special pleadings; it was a useful forum for the independent airlines, and a conduit to the government. Other early members of the BIATA Council were Air Commodore Powell of Silver City and British Aviation Services, Captain Morton and Captain Olley, Group Captain McIntyre of Scottish Aviation, Wing Commander Elwin of Cambrian and Harold Bamberg of Eagle.

One sector of the industry that was seriously affected by the shortage of aircraft available for charter was the Baltic Exchange. The Baltic Exchange had a long history of arranging freights by sea, and entered the aviation market after the war. Lambert Brothers struck the first deal when it arranged a shipment of flowers from Nice for LEP Transport on 29 December 1947. With fewer and fewer aircraft in the market, brokers were unable to fix business, especially freight charters. Their plight was made more difficult by the fact that the government was contracting the bulk of the long-haul aircraft capacity, and dealt directly with the airlines concerned, so that no brokerage fees were payable. The following comment from *The Aeroplane* neatly describes the somewhat uneasy relationship between the brokers and the charter airlines:

> Although no one could pretend that private operators would shed many tears at a possible decimation of the brokering organizations while this current boom in business continues they might have second thoughts about it when things became normal.
>
> Brokers are backed by organizations of overseas agents, some of them of considerable size, which most charter operators would find impossible to arrange themselves, and without these agents' help finding charter work overseas would not be easy.[19]

Crewsair, meanwhile, was metamorphosing itself after three of its directors, Messrs Barnby, Keegan and Stevens, quit and went on to form Crewsair (Engineering) at Southend Airport, taking with them the Dakota in settlement for their shares. They quickly renamed their company Aero Charters. Crewsair's managing director, Edward Haley, retained the existing aircraft operating company, and shortly afterwards, on 3 December, took over Trans-World Charter, adding its four Vikings to his remaining Viking and Anson. He was to use them on a short-term Air Ministry contract to Bulawayo in Southern Rhodesia, carrying RAF personnel.

SOUTH AFRICAN AFFAIRS

On 18 March 1951 a Dakota charter flight arrived in London, operated by Tropic Airways. This was the first flight of a new South African airline, two of whose directors were named as Captain Meredith and Captain Creed. They asked Davies & Newman, shipping brokers, to represent them on the Baltic. Tropic also operated out of Hamburg and Amsterdam, carrying German and Dutch immigrants, and by late 1952 had bought a York from the South African Air Force, equipping it with sixty seats.

William Dempster specialised in the South African market, too. In April 1950 the company had bought a Tudor 5 and converted it to carry fifty-two passengers; a second was delivered in September 1950 and converted to carry sixty passengers. These aircraft were used on semi-regular services to and from South Africa under charter to Pan African Air Charter, a Johannesburg-based company; they were also used to carry cargo, operating latterly from Stansted. The company called them 'Avrocruisers' and was able to operate them over precisely those routes for which BOAC had found the aircraft unsuitable. In a related development, Lord Pakenham decided on 3 March 1951 not to grant any further passenger-carrying certificates to Avro Tudor aircraft. Only those Tudor 2s and 5s which already had passenger-carrying certificates would be permitted to retain them; that meant that if the Tudor 1s and 4s were ever to fly again, they would only do so as freighters. By this stage there were only three of the long-bodied Tudor 2s and 5s flying, one with William Dempster (the other was lost in a landing accident in October 1951) and the two which Laker had acquired when he took over Fairflight.

Avro Tudor 5 G-AKCD of William Dempster. The larger Tudor 2 and 5 variants looked different from the other Tudors, being wider as well as longer. (MAP)

THE CHARTER YEAR

The passing of each year was usually marked by one or other of the aviation journals:

Looking back on 1951, most of the European charter companies (or 'independent operators', as some now prefer to be called) would probably agree that the year was one of the most difficult in their history. Although the amount of business circulating was generally firmer than in previous years, for most of the time there was an acute shortage of aircraft, caused entirely by political disturbances in various parts of the world. Many of the smaller British companies went out of action altogether, leaving only a few operators with four-engined aircraft and an even smaller number with medium types such as Dakotas and Vikings. Despite the difficult situation, a very large amount of chartering for ordinary purposes was done in the first six months of the year. The latter half, however, saw the almost complete disappearance of 'independent' aircraft from the market – caused by heavy government commitments and the blocking of all flights to the Far East because of fuel shortage.

The high-intensity airlift in the Pacific caused serious aircraft shortages in the United States, as most operators had had to commit their fleets for indefinite periods on Korean duties. American buyers came to Europe in order to purchase every available American-built machine; in some instances they bought second-hand Dakotas at treble their normal value. Many of the smaller companies were tempted to dispose of their fleets at what was obviously the peak of the market, and this led to the closing down of certain well-known British and French concerns.

By early spring the number of available medium-range aircraft in the United Kingdom had sunk to a critical level, the remainder being made up of Vikings which, in view of their higher operating costs, had previously been unable to compete with Dakotas on the open market. The unavoidable use of Vikings caused charter rates to rise very sharply. Towards the end of spring several companies acquired a number of ex-BOAC Yorks, and for the first time were able to operate fleets that were more or less suitable for world-wide duties. They were thus able to recapture to some extent the exceptionally heavy traffic to Australia and the Far East which had previously been carried by the charter sections of foreign airlines. The Yorks, in fact, now form the basis of British charter fleets. It is not very suitable for westbound Atlantic traffic, although flights have been made with reduced payloads. For eastbound routes, however, the York is comparable with the DC–4. Prior to 1951 the number of charter aircraft in Europe had been evenly spread over several countries, but by last summer the balance of owning-power had again reverted to this country. A few companies are still operating in France and Scandinavia, using aircraft of the short- and medium-range variety.

Of the types of loads carried it can probably be said that the British Government, using medium and heavy aircraft for the transfer of troops and freight to Middle and Far East destinations, were the most active charterers on the market. The heaviest freight loads, however, were transported between the UK and Sweden; outward flights were made with machinery and very heavy consignments of reindeer meat were lifted for the return journey. Until the opening of the government trooping contracts in the summer, passenger movements were in a minority. The shortage of medium-range aircraft left very little at the disposal of the tourist, and loads were mainly confined to ships' crews.

Most suitably equipped operators were only too willing to commit their aircraft for long periods on the high-density trooping contracts which the Air Ministry offered in the summer. Some of these, however, terminated at the end of the year and, so far as aircraft availability is concerned, the market is now enjoying a short breathing space. Though it constituted a serious blow to the charter companies at the time, the Persian oil situation has now ceased to affect operations.[20]

The Persian crisis, following the seizure of Anglo–Iranian's assets, including the refinery at Abadan, had two significant consequences, both of which are referred to in the above extract. First, the supply of oil was cut off as the British effectively embargoed the distribution and sale of any oil that came out of Abadan (that was not much anyway as the refinery ground to a halt). The loss of this supply affected India and Pakistan, and for four months fuel supplies at their airports were cut. Secondly, for much of the summer and autumn, the British Government froze the use of the Yorks that BOAC and Lancashire were operating, retaining them for the evacuation of the staff from Abadan and the emergency airlift to the Canal Zone. As a final note on the Persian crisis, the Iranian economy did indeed suffer severely from the loss of its oil production, and Dr Mossadeq was in turn overthrown two years later when the Shah reaffirmed his authority. A consortium of oil companies, including Anglo–Iranian,[21] then took over the running of the Abadan refineries on behalf of the Iranian National Oil Corporation, and the oil began to flow again.

LABOUR FINALE

As Prime Minister Attlee approached the coming election, what had been his achievements in the restless world of civil aviation? His government had nationalised most of the existing airlines, but not all. The few that remained out of its clutches, and the eager newcomers, had proved to be an asset at times, a nuisance otherwise (in Appendix 5 there is a guide to the British independent airlines, those that had survived to the end of 1951). Some of his ministries supported them enthusiastically; others, including the sponsoring Ministry of Civil Aviation, found them unmanageable and troublesome. The charter airlines had outgrown their intended status of air-taxi operators, and had even reclaimed some of their old scheduled service routes. They had begun to build up the three pillars of their future existence: limited scheduled services; government trooping contracts; and the nascent inclusive-tour holiday business. They thought they could look forward to even better things if the Tories came back to power, for the Conservatives had promised:

We are determined, when the opportunity comes again, to restore a wide measure of private enterprise in the air, to throw the lines open to private competition under proper regulation, and to have some system analogous to the Civil Aeronautics Board in the United States, which has given the benefit of co-ordination and the benefit of competition as well.[22]

The corporations may have been alarmed at the prospect of a new government regarding competition as a benefit, or maybe they were just too busy getting their respective houses in order. They had indeed made enormous strides, but it was not until 1950–51 that the deficits of both corporations finally show signs of diminishing. Table 2 shows the corporations' financial fortunes over these early years; expressed in 2002 sterling values on the GDP index, the combined deficits of the two corporations between 1946–47 to 1951–52 were equivalent to almost £4 billion. Table 1 gives passenger figures that include a breakdown for the independents of the source of their passengers. Both corporations could take credit for some significant technical advances. BEA had started experimental helicopter services in 1948, and on 29 July 1950 operated the world's first scheduled passenger service by a turbine-engine airliner, when a Viscount flew from Northolt to Paris Le Bourget; the service continued for two weeks, but BEA's Viscounts did not enter regular service until 1953. The corporation was still operating a mixed fleet of Vikings, Dakotas and Rapides as this volume draws to a close. By contrast, BOAC had almost resolved its equipment problems, withdrawn its last flying boats and started Comet development flying, prior to its introduction into service in 1952.

John Longhurst shall have the last word; he thought that the time had come to move on from 'overruling principles' and find a better economic model:

> Those who support the present policy of monopoly seem automatically to assume that the introduction of competition will undermine the industry and that the word competition implies, ipso facto, uneconomic competition.
>
> Lord Pakenham said in the House of Lords… 'One overwhelming lesson from the study of the history of British civil aviation stands out a mile – if I may be forgiven the colloquialism – and that is the impossibility, gradually recognised by all who had had to handle these questions at first hand, of allowing within our own aviation effort unfettered freedom to compete, of permitting full licence of the air. We must recognise the necessity of rationalizing or regulating to a very great extent the number and size of the units concerned'.
>
> Nobody has ever suggested that we should indulge in 'unfettered freedom to compete'. No other country does this. Always there is a non-political licensing board that considers each application to operate a service, from the dual points of view (a) 'would the competition involved by the operations of this new service create an uneconomic situation for the operators on the route as a whole', and (b) 'is the granting of this licence likely to weaken or to encourage and strengthen the nation's transport industry?'
>
> The raison d'être of a route licensing board is to see that the competition is healthy, not unfettered and accordingly unhealthy, and undermining the industry. As has been pointed out so often before, things are very seldom black and white, they are usually grey. The extremities of political doctrine, e.g. unfettered free enterprise and State monopoly, have now been experienced. The one has been found to undermine the financial strength of the industry, while the other inhibits a large amount of potential enterprise. It might now be worth trying mixed enterprise, especially because the indications are that in other countries this is working very well.[23]

APPENDIX ONE

AIRCRAFT TYPES[1]
EARLY POST-WAR

AIRSPEED COURIER

The Courier was the first British retractable-undercarriage type to go into quantity production, and flew in April 1932. Powered by a single Armstrong Siddeley Lynx engine and able to carry five passengers, it was used by two significant airlines pre-war, North Eastern Airways and Portsmouth, Southsea & Isle of Wight Airways (PSIOWA). After the war, the sole remaining survivor was used by East Anglian Flying Services, later Channel Airways, in 1947 for a season's joy-riding.

Delightful atmospheric shot of Airspeed Courier G-ACVF of North Eastern Airways, taken in 1937. (MAP)

Another atmospheric shot, against a background of camouflaged hangars, of Airspeed Consul G-AJGA belonging to Northern Air Charter, later taken over by Lancashire Aircraft Corporation. (MAP)

AIRSPEED ENVOY/CONSUL

The Envoy was built in the mid-1930s as a successor to the Courier, still constructed of wood, but with two engines. Over 8,550 were built as the Oxford twin-engine advance trainer for the RAF. After the war Airspeed bought back many of these Oxfords and converted them inexpensively into five/six-passenger light transports, calling the type Consul, and selling for around £5,500. Airspeed appointed Airwork as distributors, and seventy were delivered to British firms alone. In all, Airspeed sold 161 together with an additional forty-six which were converted to civil standards for special purposes, for organisations like the MCA Flying Unit. The airliner needed a crew of two and had a range of 600 miles with an 800lb payload. The British charter airlines with the biggest fleets were Chartair (nine), Morton Air Services (eight), Westminster Airways (seven), and Air Enterprises (seven), and they also saw service with Lancashire Aircraft Corporation, Olley Air Service and Transair, among others.

AIRSPEED (LATER DE HAVILLAND) AMBASSADOR

The Ambassador was built to the Brabazon Committee's Type 2 recommendation for a short-haul aircraft. BEA ordered twenty of the piston-engine aircraft in 1948 when it was having cold feet about the turbo-prop Viscount. It finally entered service over a year late, in 1952, four years after KLM had introduced the similarly specified Convair 240, and only one year before the Viscount. Airspeed did not have the resources to develop the aircraft, and after the firm was taken over by de Havilland, production was abandoned after the completion of BEA's order.

ARGONAUT

See Douglas DC-4 Skymaster/Canadair C4 (DC-4M).

AUSTER

Produced in large numbers for the military, the civil versions included the Autocrat and Aiglet. With three to four seats, this single-engine, high-wing monoplane had a range of about 500 miles and was used by flying clubs, training establishments and charter companies. The first post-war flight by a charter airline, on 1 January 1946, whose operation is claimed by Cambrian Airways, was flown by an Auster Autocrat between Cardiff and Filton.

Auster Autocar G-AJYK of Airviews, a Manchester-based company that undertook aerial photography as well as general charter work. (MAP)

AVRO ANSON

The Anson first flew in 1935 and over 11,000 of these twin-engine, low-wing monoplanes were built, mainly as trainers for the RAF; after the war, ninety-eight were registered in the United Kingdom and no fewer than 140 saw service in Australia. Transair operated up to eleven as freighters, carrying morning newspapers and mail, and other more specialist uses were as survey aircraft.

The Avro 19 was developed after the war as a small airliner, seating up to nine passengers with a range of 350 miles. This variant of the Anson had a higher cabin ceiling and the luxury of hydraulically operated flaps and undercarriage. Railway Air Services introduced the type in 1945, and its aircraft subsequently went to BEA. Hunting, Sivewright and Westminster flew them on passenger charters.

British European Airways inherited Avro 19 G-AHIC from Railway Air Services, but all the Ansons were soon replaced by Dakotas. (A.J. Jackson Collection)

AVRO LANCASTRIAN

A straightforward conversion of the Lancaster bomber, this very interim airliner entered service with BOAC during the war, and opened up the Kangaroo route to Australia. Seating nine passengers, it was not an economical proposition nor a very comfortable one; passengers sat on top of a 500-gallon fuel tank, with four Merlins bellowing away

Avro Lancastrian G-AGLF of the British Overseas Airways Corporation. A war-time photograph, note the censor's determined attempt to obliterate the nose of the Avro Lincoln in the background. (MAP)

nearby, for hours on end. On the other hand, it did dramatically reduce the journey time to Australia, to three days. BSAA operated them too, but with thirteen seats. Of the independents, only Skyways and Silver City flew them on charter services although Flight Refuelling was to use a number of them to carry fuel during the Berlin Airlift. The Lancastrian had a range of over 4,000 miles and flew at 230mph.

AVRO TUDOR

The unhappy story of the Tudor is related in Chapter 5, but this development of the Lincoln bomber, powered by Rolls-Royce Merlins and with a pressurised fuselage, was built in a number of marks, of which those that are relevant to this story are as follows:

Tudor 1   The original short fuselage version, seating twelve to twenty-four passengers. Not accepted by BOAC and most were subsequently rebuilt as Mk4s for BSAA.

Tudor 2   The longer fuselage version, seating up to sixty passengers, of which only four were built. One was used by Airflight as a tanker during the Berlin Airlift.

Avro Tudor 4 G-AHNJ in very plain British South American Airways' markings. (MAP)

Tudor 3	A nine-seat government VIP version based on the Tudor 1. I can find no record that these aircraft were ever used in their intended role.
Tudor 4	Seating thirty-two passengers and with a fuselage 5ft longer than the Tudor 1, this was the version used by BSAA and later converted by Air Charter. It had a range of 4,000 miles.
Tudor 5	With the same fuselage length as the Tudor 2, the six aircraft built were used on the Berlin Airlift as fuel carriers by BSAA and Air-flight.

AVRO YORK

Basically a Lancaster bomber with a new large-capacity, square-section fuselage, 258 Yorks were built between 1942 and 1948. The backbone of the RAF's transport capability immediately after the war, Yorks also entered service with BOAC, BSAA and Skyways. Carrying thirty passengers, or up to 9 tons of freight over 1,000 miles, Yorks were used extensively by British charter airlines in the 1950s. The largest fleet by far was that of Skyways, which after its take-over by Lancashire Aircraft Corporation, bought twenty-three from BOAC.

Not what it seems! This is Lancashire Aircraft Corporation's Avro York G-AGOB with the company's crest on its nose, but otherwise sporting Royal Air Force roundels and serial number WW501, to allow it to operate to airfields in the Suez Canal Zone. (MAP)

Boeing Stratocruiser G-AKGJ *Cambria* of British Overseas Airways Corporation. (MAP)

BOEING STRATOCRUISER

A development of the C-97 military transport, the Stratocruiser had a capacious 'double-bubble' two-deck fuselage, with seating in BOAC service for fifty-two passengers together with a number of sleeping berths on the upper deck, and a lounge-bar and freight holds below. BOAC pioneered its luxurious 'Monarch' service with Stratocruisers in the early 1950s.

Bristol Brabazon G-AGPW at Filton, Bristol. (A.J. Jackson Collection)

BRISTOL TYPE 167 BRABAZON

A very large airliner by the standards of the day, it was designed to carry 100 passengers over ranges of 5,500 miles at a cruising speed of 250mph with four pairs of coupled 2,500hp Bristol Centaurus engines buried in the wing, driving contra-rotating propellers, although production aircraft were planned to use Proteus turbine engines, which would have given a cruising speed of 330mph. One prototype was built of this awe-inspiring airliner: 'I will fly the cockpit', said Bristol's chief test pilot 'Bill' Pegg, 'and I imagine the rest of the aeroplane will follow'.[2] The Brabazon duly appeared at the Farnborough Air Show in 1950 but it never went into commercial service, a victim of financial and political pressures as well as some unresolved technical issues. 'The size of the project seems to have overawed the authorities. Like Brunel's *Great Eastern* steamship, the Brabazon was a pioneer on the grand scale born a generation too soon for its environment.'[3]

BRISTOL TYPE 170 FREIGHTER/WAYFARER

Owing much to the pre-war design of the company's Bombay, the Type 170 was to have been used to carry vehicles and supplies to jungle airstrips during the Burma campaign, but the war ended before this could be realised. Bristol adapted the design to have a stronger floor and large opening nose-doors, calling it the Freighter; the Wayfarer was a passenger-carrying version without the nose doors. Tough and very reliable, the aircraft was sold to air forces and airlines throughout the world but is perhaps best remembered for its role in the 1950s as a vehicle ferry with Silver City, Channel Air Bridge and British United Air Ferries (later British Air Ferries). The Freighter could carry two cars and up to fifteen passengers; the later and larger Mk32 could carry three cars and up to twenty-three passengers.

Bristol Aeroplane's sales demonstrator Bristol 170 Freighter G-AGVC in 1949. (MAP)

CONSOLIDATED LIBERATOR

More Liberator bombers were produced in the United States during the war than any other warplane. The British bought a small number, and they were used mainly by Coastal Command, which exploited their excellent long-range capability to the full. A number were transferred to BOAC for the Return Ferry Service, and after the war BOAC continued to use the type as freighters. Scottish Aviation acquired five Liberators and used them on passenger services and as fuel carriers during the Berlin Airlift.

Consolidated Liberator G–AHYB was still being used by British Overseas Airways Corporation in 1949 as a freighter in support of its maintenance organisation at Dorval in Canada. (MAP)

CONSUL

See Airspeed Envoy/Consul.

DAKOTA, DC-3, DC-4

See under Douglas.

DE HAVILLAND

Not only did de Havilland build airliners that allowed for economical and profitable operation, it also exported them in significant numbers. Over 1,100 of the four major pre-war types – the DH83, DH84 Dragon, DH86 and DH89 Rapide – were built:

DH83

The four-seat Fox Moth, powered by a single 130hp Gipsy Major, launched many a domestic service after its first flight in January 1932. Bought by a number of aspiring airlines, it was good value at £1,045 and was to be found in the fleets of Hillman's Airways, PSIOWA, Norman Edgar's Western Airways and Olley Air Service, amongst others. It flew at 105mph and had a range of just over 400 miles.

DH84 DRAGON

Edward Hillman was so impressed by his Fox Moths that he ordered four of its twin-engine successor, the Dragon, straight off the drawing board; the design was originally conceived as a double Fox Moth, to meet a requirement from the Royal Iraqi Air Force for a multi-purpose, twin-engine aircraft. With a cruising speed of 109mph, and carrying eight passengers, its economics were superior to the Fox Moth, combined with the extra safety of twin-engine operation. Hillman's Airways had six in service for the summer of 1933 and was followed by most of the pioneering airlines in Great Britain and further afield, including Canada and Australia. The total number built in England was 115, and a further eighty-seven were built for the Royal Australian Air Force during the war.

DH86

Originally built to an Australian specification, this handsome four-engine, ten-seat airliner was used by a number of British airlines, as well as Qantas, before the war, in

A tribute to a great Scottish pioneer, Captain E.E. Fresson, who flew de Havilland Dragon G-ACIT on services throughout the Northern Isles before and during the war. After nationalisation, the aircraft was used by the Airways Aero Association, pleasingly named *Orcadian*. (MAP)

De Havilland DH86B G-ADYH of Captain Olley's West Coast Air Services, which linked Dublin with Croydon, Bristol and the Isle of Man. (MAP)

particular Railway Air Services, British Airways, Imperial Airways and Jersey Airways. After the war, the few remaining continued in service for a while with RAS.

DH89 RAPIDE

The Dragon Rapide was built as a faster successor to the DH84, and first flew in 1934; it was a scaled-down version of the DH86. From 1937, the type was fitted with flaps and re-designated DH89A. Over 700 Rapides, as they came to be known, were built, including the Dominie trainer for the RAF. Carrying six to eight passengers on two Gipsy Queen engines of 200hp each, the Rapide flew at 115mph and had a range of 400 miles. Rapides were the mainstay of British airlines before, during and immediately after the war; indeed, BEA had the largest fleet, when it took over thirty-nine from the railway companies in 1947 and a further six from Channel Islands Airways.

DH95 FLAMINGO

De Havilland's first all-metal stressed skin aircraft, it entered service briefly with Guernsey and Jersey Airways in the summer of 1939. Not dissimilar to the Douglas DC-5, but with a tail-wheel, it had two engines and could carry up to twenty passengers over 1,000 miles. The war put paid to any ideas of further development, and those that had been ordered

A pair of de Havilland Rapides bearing the red rose of Lancashire Aircraft Corporation, including G-AKNV. (MAP)

Only one de Havilland Flamingo returned to commercial service, British Air Transport's G-AYFH, after war-time service with the Fleet Air Arm's No.782 (Transport) Squadron. (A.J. Jackson Collection)

were finished and delivered to the RAF. British Air Transport operated one example after the war, G-AFYH.

DH104 DOVE

First flown in 1945, the Dove resulted from a Brabazon Committee recommendation – Type 5B – to replace the Rapide, and proved very successful for de Havilland, with over 500 built. Most were sold as executive aircraft or to the military, but a small number were used by British charter airlines, both for charter and scheduled services, seating up to eleven passengers. Its high purchase price and 50 per cent greater operating costs than the Rapide ruled it out for most charter airlines, though.

DH106 COMET

Designed to meet the Brabazon Committee's Type 4 specification for a jet-propelled mail carrier, the first prototype Comet was built under conditions of some secrecy, and amazed the world when it was first rolled out in 1949; personally, I think it was inauspicious that the aircraft was rolled out backwards. It first flew on 27 July 1949 and went on to break

Morton Air Services bought de Havilland Dove G-AJDP from Melba Airways, which had in turn bought it from Hunting Air Travel. It was to spend much of its life chartered to the Burmah Oil Co. (MAP)

world records, flying at over 450mph and cutting journey times in half. Comets had not yet entered service with BOAC by the end of this volume.

DOUGLAS DC-3 DAKOTA

Most Dakotas operated by British airlines came from RAF stocks after the war, and so are conversions of the C-47, the military designation of this fabulous twin-engine workhorse airliner. Around 10,600 were built in the Western world, just under 500 by the Japanese, and possibly up to 6,000 more in the Soviet Union. It could carry up to thirty-two passengers or 3½ tons of freight over 1,500 miles at a speed of around 170mph. In BEA service it outlasted the Vickers Viking which had been introduced to replace the Dakota after the war. Most early post-war charter airlines operated the Dakota, which had excellent airfield performance and was supremely versatile. More than 300 have been registered at various times in the United Kingdom, and it has been used by no fewer than sixty-five British airlines, including BOAC, BEA and Railway Air Services.

DOUGLAS DC-4 SKYMASTER/CANADAIR C4 (DC-4M)

The DC-4 entered service with Skyways in 1947, but they were sold off in 1950. Able to carry up to eighty-eight passengers, or around 8 tons of freight, the DC-4 had a range of some 2,500 miles. The Canadians built a version that was powered by Rolls-Royce Merlins, known by BOAC as the Argonaut, which was pressurised and somewhat noisy. Unlike British built interim types, the Argonaut had a long innings with BOAC, remaining in service for eleven years until 1960.

Converted by Scottish Aviation, Douglas DC-3 Dakota G-AJAY was used by Westminster Airways on the Berlin Airlift. (A.J. Jackson Collection)

Douglas DC-4 Skymasters were rare on the British register. Skymaster G-ALEP was owned by Mining and Exploration Air Services and operated on their behalf by Silver City. (MAP)

HANDLEY PAGE HALIFAX/HALTON

More than 6,000 Halifax bombers were built during the war, but early in 1945 Handley Page manufactured 100 Halifax C.VIII transports, capable of carrying up to 8 tons of freight using an under-belly pannier, or eleven passengers in its slender fuselage. After the end of the war, these almost brand-new aircraft could be purchased for around £2,000. BOAC bought twelve of them and had them converted by Short Brothers into ten-seat airliners, naming the type Halton. They were used mainly on West African services for about eighteen months, before being sold to Laker's company, Aviation Traders; these

Handley Page Halifax G-AIHU of Lancashire Aircraft Corporation. (MAP)

were the aircraft used by Bond Air Services during the Berlin Airlift. Many of the others found their way into British charter fleets and were used extensively on fruit and other freight charters. Tony Merton Jones notes that in December 1947 there were forty-five Halifaxes and Haltons in operation, more than any other type of heavy transport aircraft, with the DC-3 coming second with thirty-seven in service. Both Lancashire Aircraft Corporation and LAMS operated sizeable fleets. It was the first aircraft type in the Eagle fleet; Lancashire was the last operator, running down its fleet in 1951.

The first production Handley Page Hermes 4, G-ALDA, seen here during the 1949 Farnborough show. This aircraft never entered service with BOAC, but was used by Airwork from 1952 onwards. (MAP)

HANDLEY PAGE HERMES

The Hermes was a development of the HP64 proposal, itself a development of the Halifax. Powered by four Bristol Hercules engines, with a pressurised fuselage and a new tail with single fin and rudder, the Hermes shared the engines and wing design of the Halifax and was produced in a military variant, the Hastings, still with a tail-wheel, while the handsome passenger carrying Hermes 4 boasted a tricycle undercarriage and was some 13ft longer. The Hastings went on to give many years of service to the RAF, participating in the Berlin Airlift and only finally being withdrawn in 1977. The Hermes 1 had an inauspicious start when the prototype G-AGSS crashed shortly after taking off on its first flight on 2 December 1945. The Hermes 4 was selected by the Ministry of Supply and BOAC for the Empire routes, replacing Yorks and the flying boats on African services, but had a very brief career with the corporation, between 1950-53, before being replaced in turn by the Comet[5] and the Argonaut. The fairest description of the Hermes is as an enhanced interim design, because it still used the basic Halifax wing, eleven years old by this time, and this penalised the aircraft's range, as did its propensity to fly tail-down. With a full payload, its range was not much more than 1,400 miles.

HANDLEY PAGE/MILES MARATHON

The original Brabazon Type 5 specified a small feederliner intended to replace the DH Rapide. Miles Aircraft persuaded the committee to recommend a larger, four-engine feederliner as a replacement for the four-engine DH86, and proposed the M.60 Marathon, powered by four Gipsy Queen engines, an all-metal, high-wing aeroplane which would carry fourteen passengers. The Brabazon Committee duly changed its Type 5 proposal, so that the Marathon became the Type 5A, and the eight-seat DH Dove the Type 5B. By the time Miles was looking for a production order, the company was in serious financial trouble and receivers were appointed in 1948, but the MoS was not anxious to lose the design team and so persuaded Handley Page to take over the project. Handley Page increased the capacity to eighteen passengers and secured an order from the MCA for fifty aircraft, thirty for BEA and twenty for BOAC. However, BEA refused to take delivery, preferring to stay with Rapides for the Scottish services, and BOAC had very limited success in persuading its associated companies to take the type. The RAF received twenty-eight for use as navigational trainers, and Handley Page closed down production after forty aircraft. De Havilland built a successful four-engine, fourteen-seat feederliner themselves, the Heron, so the idea was not misconceived but seems to have lost its way in the execution, not helped by the financial failure of the original designer and manufacturer.

HERMES

See under Handley Page Hermes.

LOCKHEED 10 AND 14

British Airways used these two variants of Lockheed's pre-war twin-engine all-metal airliners on European services. The ten-seat Lockheed 10s were twice as fast as the biplanes used by Imperial Airways on the route from Croydon to Paris, but their small size meant that they were relatively expensive to operate. Amelia Earhart was flying a Lockheed 10-E when she disappeared on her round-the-world flight in 1937. British Airways bought the larger fourteen-seat Lockheed 14 for its projected route to West Africa and South America, but they were deployed mainly on the route to Stockholm, and during the war BOAC used them in Africa.

LOCKHEED CONSTELLATION

The Constellation started life in 1943 as the American C-69 military transport, although the majority were completed after the war as civil aircraft. BOAC was allowed to buy the

Lockheed Constellation G-ALAM was bought from the Irish airline, Aerlinte Eireann, by British Overseas Airways Corporation in 1948, mainly for use on the services to Australia. (MAP)

earliest model, the L049, immediately after the war ended, in order to start transatlantic services. The corporation subsequently also bought the developed, longer-range L749 version, which could carry up to sixty-four passengers.

MILES MESSENGER/GEMINI

The Gemini was a small twin-engine four-seater, with a retractable undercarriage, developed from the single-engine Messenger. With a full load of three passengers and pilot, it had a range of about 150 miles, but this could be extended to 600 miles with auxiliary tanks. An attractive looking aircraft, immortalised in Cecil Lewis's book *Gemini to Jo'burg*.

MILES AEROVAN

This unusual box-like small freighter was developed and built by Miles in the immediate post-war years as a private venture. Selling for around £5,500, over fifty were built, but twenty-three crashed and a further five were lost in gales, so the type probably holds the record for being the most accident-prone aircraft. It was used by a number of the smaller British charter airlines and could carry up to ten passengers or a ton of freight over 350 miles; at a pinch, it could carry a very small Fiat car. Air Contractors and Beirut-based

Arab Contract and Trading both had six, while Ulster Aviation had five, mostly used to ferry Miles Messenger and Gemini parts from the factory in Ulster to the Miles factory at Woodley. John Stroud commented on flying in the Aerovan, 'My main impression was that, with the floor only 2ft off the grass, one appeared to be taking off on one's bottom.'[6]

Miles Gemini G-AGUS in flight. (MAP)

Miles Aerovan G-AILC somewhere over England. (MAP)

MILES MARATHON

See under Handley Page/Miles Marathon.

PERCIVAL PROCTOR

A development of the 1935 Vega Gull, the Proctor was built and used in large numbers for military communications during the war, and some were subsequently adapted for civil use, including BSAA, Western Airways, Cambrian, Air Taxis (Croydon) and Hunting Air Travel. It was a three-seater, powered by a single 210hp Gipsy Queen engine. After the war, production resumed of a four-seater, the Proctor 5, and many saw service with British charter airlines, such as Island Air Services, Kenning Aviation and Kearsley Airways.

SAUNDERS-ROE SR.45 PRINCESS

Saunders-Roe, or Saro, with its tradition of building flying boats, naturally wanted to continue building them after the war, and proposed the big SR.45 after studying the development of the turbine engine, which promised a much higher power/weight ratio

Percival Proctor 4 G–ALEO of Birkett Air Service, at Croydon. (MAP)

than had previously been available. The aircraft was to have carried up to 200 passengers over 3,000 miles at 350mph, allowing a non-stop England–New York service. Peter London, in the Putnam series *Saunders Roe and Saro aircraft since 1917*, describes pithily what happened next:

> During the spring of 1945, Saro made proposals for the building of SR.45 to the Ministry of Supply (MoS), and the Minister, George Strauss, was most enthusiastic over the proposals. He regarded SR.45 as an important part of BOAC's future service. BOAC indicated some interest (though at no time firm commitment) to both the MoS and the Ministry of Civil Aviation. An order was placed for three SR.45s in May 1946. Total contract price was £2.8 million. The Ministry of Civil Aviation was deemed the 'contracting authority' in the May 1946 development but soon afterwards the MoS asserted that it was the sole authority for the purchase of new British civil aircraft. It was generally taken for granted by the government, the MoS, and in particular George Strauss, that BOAC would want SR.45, especially for its trans-Atlantic routes. Only BOAC appeared to query this.[7]

But development and building of the first aircraft was fitful and slow, and by the time the first aircraft was ready to fly, in August 1952, the costs had risen to £10.8 million, about half attributable to the coupled Proteus engines which were being used on the Brabazon landplane project. The prototype made an appearance at the Farnborough Air Show of 1952, but was disastrously underpowered. BOAC kept on sending out mixed messages, indicating continuing if tentative interest in the aircraft, configured for only 105 passengers in BOAC service, but refusing to commit itself. Work on the other two partially built aircraft was suspended, and after the government rejected an offer from Aquila Airways, the entire programme had ceased by June 1954 and all the aircraft were cocooned. There were many attempts to revive interest in the Princess flying boats, some still involving BOAC, but by the end of the 1960s all three hulls had finally been broken up.

SHORT SUNDERLAND/BOAC HYTHE CLASS

The mighty Sunderland was one of the exceptional aircraft of the Second World War, and 749 were built. Similar to the 'C' Class flying boats of Imperial Airways, with its capacious hull it proved suitable for transport work, and a number were made available to BOAC during the war, mainly for use on the Poole–Cairo–Karachi–Calcutta service. After the war, BOAC modified the aircraft by fairing in the gun turrets at the nose and tail, and upgrading the passenger accommodation. Named the Hythe Class, and carrying up to twenty-two passengers, they were used to reopen routes to the Far East and Australia. Withdrawn from service in 1949, twelve were eventually sold on to Aquila Airways, which operated them successfully on its services to Lisbon and Madeira.

Short Sunderland 3 G-AGJJ showing its forward gun turret fairing which was slid back when mooring. (MAP)

VICKERS VIKING

The most successful of the post-war 'interim' airliners, the Viking was a development of the war-time Wellington bomber with a new fuselage that could seat up to thirty-six passengers; Airwork and Hunting bought them as soon as they became available. Including RAF versions, the Valetta and Varsity, over 600 were sold, and many Vikings saw service with British charter airlines, flying well into the 1960s. The Viking was significantly faster than the Dakota although it had slightly higher operating costs and needed longer runways.

VICKERS VISCOUNT

Development of the Viscount, the world's first turbo-prop airliner, was helped by the experience that Vickers gained in the commercial market through building the Viking. One of the Brabazon recommended designs, the project languished for a while and the piston-engined Ambassador, built in parallel, might have assumed the mantle of Britain's contribution as medium-range passenger airliner. But Vickers persisted and with the help both of BEA and Trans-Canada Airlines, produced a truly world-class airliner bought by many significant airlines. Its entry into service with BEA was awaited as this volume ends.

This Vickers Viking was built originally as a sales demonstrator for the manufacturer, in whose colours it is seen, before passing to British European Airways in 1950. (MAP)

The prototype Vickers Viscount G-AHRF first flew on 10 July 1948. Test flying continued throughout 1949, and early in 1950, BEA markings were applied for a demonstration tour of European capitals. This was followed by the world's first scheduled turbo-prop airliner passenger flight, on 29 July 1950, from London's Northolt airport to Paris Le Bourget. (MAP)

WESTLAND

In 1947, Westland signed an agreement with United Aircraft to build Sikorsky helicopters under licence. The agreement allowed Westland to incorporate British components, to develop the helicopters, and to sell them world-wide except in North America. BEA used the Westland S-51 Dragonfly for its experimental cross-country scheduled and mail services between 1948 and 1951.

BIOGRAPHICAL DETAILS
WHO'S WHO[1]

AIKMAN, BARRY THOMSON
Director and general manager, Lancashire Aircraft Corporation, 1945-47; managing director, Aquila Airways, 1948-56; chairman, Barry Aikman Travel.

ASHLEY, CAPTAIN RONALD JOHN
Air display pilot with Sir Alan Cobham, 1934-45; with Olley Air Service, 1937-40; served in RAF, 1940-46, seconded to Associated Airways Joint Committee, 1941-42, and BOAC, 1942-46; managing director, Skyways, 1946-52.

BAMBERG, HAROLD ROLF
Chairman and managing director, Eagle Aviation, Cunard Eagle and British Eagle International Airlines, 1948-68; chairman, Sir Henry Lunn, Poly Travel, Everyman Travel and Rickards Coach.

BARNES, SIR JAMES
Permanent Under-Secretary of State, Air Ministry, 1947-55; director, Short Bros and Harland, 1955-63.

BEBB, CHARLES WILLIAM HENRY 'CECIL'
Toured S. Africa with Alan Cobham Aviation, 1933; with Olley Air Service, 1936-23; chief test pilot, Cunliffe-Owen Aircraft, 1939-43; chief test pilot, A.W. Hawkesley, 1943-24; chief test pilot, Dunlop Aviation Research Dept., 1944-24; chief pilot, Olley Air Service, 1946-53; operations manager, Transair, 1953-60; operations manager, British United Airways, 1960

BENNETT, AIR VICE MARSHAL DONALD CLIFFORD TYNDALL
Imperial Airways, 1935; co-founder of Atlantic Ferry Service, 1940; founded RAF Pathfinder Force, 1942; AOC until May, 1945; director and general manager, BSAA, 1945-48; chairman, Airflight, 1948; Fairflight, 1949

BIRKETT, FLIGHT LIEUTENANT GEORGE

Managing director, Birkett Air Service, 1932-53; director, Tipsy Aircraft.

BOOTH, JOHN WELLS

Chairman, The Booth Steamship Co., formerly director, Cunard White Star Line; chairman, BSAA, 1945-49; director, BOAC, BOAC Associated Companies, 1949-65; director and chairman, Aden Airways.

BRABAZON OF TARA, LORD (LT-COL. JOHN THEODORE CUTHBERT MOORE-BRABAZON)

First English pilot to fly, holder of Aviation certificate No.1; Assessor, R101 Inquiry, 1930-31; Minister of Transport, 1940-41; Minister of Aircraft Production, 1941-2; president, Brabazon Committee, 1942-43; chairman, Air Registration Board, 1946-64; owner of number plate FLY 1.

BRICE, CAPTAIN DAVID ALLEN

Joined Imperial Airways on Empire Routes, 1939; served with RAF Coastal Command and Atlantic Ferry Organisation, 1939-41; joined BOAC 1941 chief pilot, BSAA, 1946-47; operations manager, Silver City, 1947; director of training, Skyways, 1948-49; Senior Captain, Stratocruisers, BOAC, 1949-54; managing director, Sir Henry Lunn, 1955-57; managing director, Milbanke Travel, 1958.

BRUCE, THE HON. MRS VICTOR

Born Mary Petre in 1895, she became an inveterate record breaker, sometimes with her husband, when they drove an AC car round the track at Montlhéry for ten days and nights, sometimes on her own, as when she later drove a Bentley round the same track continuously for twenty-four hours. She learned to fly in 1930, after she had bought a Blackburn Bluebird IV more or less on a whim, and with just forty hours in her logbook, flew it solo to Japan, and then across the United States, a voyage referred to by *The Aeroplane* as a '19,000-mile solo jaunt across three continents'. She also pioneered in-flight refuelling, staying aloft in a Saro Windhover for sixty-three hours in 1932. She formed Air Dispatch in 1934, which moved to Cardiff during the war. The company switched to building bus bodies after the war and changed its name to Bruce Coachworks. She achieved another personal best in 1973 when she drove a Ford Capri around Thruxton at 110mph, aged seventy-eight.

COBHAM, SIR ALAN JOHN

Aviation pioneer, performed many long-distance survey flights in the 1920s; promoted National Aviation Day, Ltd, which toured British Isles, 1932-33; National Aviation Displays, Ltd, 1934-35; pioneer of refuelling in the air, experimental and development work, 1936-46; reconstituted Flight Refuelling Ltd, 1948, chairman and managing director, 1948-69.

CRIBBETT, SIR GEORGE

Deputy Secretary, Ministry of Civil Aviation, 1946-56 (Director of Civil Aviation); deputy chairman, BOAC, 1956-60; director, BOAC Associated Companies, 1957-63.

CRITCHLEY, BRIG.-GENERAL ALFRED CECIL

Born in Canada, he was a General by the time he was twenty-seven, serving in the 1st Canadian Division in the First World War; appointed Air Commodore, RAFVR, 1939; organised and commanded initial training for RAF air crews, 1939-43; director-general of BOAC 1943, resigned 1946; chairman, Skyways, 1946-54.

DADE, CAPTAIN JOHN

Pilot, Jersey Airways, 1935; senior pilot, Straight Corporation, 1938-39; RAF, 1939-45; director and operations manager, Morton Air Services, 1946-48; joint managing director, Air Enterprises, 1948-53.

DAVIES, S. KENNETH

Formed Cambrian Air Services 1935, managing director until 1951; managing director, British Parachute Co., 1939-45; board member, BEA, 1951-67.

D'ERLANGER, SIR GERARD JOHN REGIS LEO

Member of London Stock Exchange, 1935-39, at that time associated first with Hillman's Airways, then British Airways; Commanding Officer, ATA, 1939-45; member of board, BOAC, 1940-46; chairman, BEA, 1947-49; chairman, BOAC, 1956-60.

DOUGLAS OF KIRTLESIDE, LORD (MARSHAL OF THE ROYAL AIR FORCE WILLIAM SHOLTO DOUGLAS)

AOC-in C, Fighter Command, 1940-42; AOC-in C, Middle East Command, 1943-44; AOC-in C Coastal Command, 1944-45; Air C-in C, British Air Forces of Occupation, Germany, 1945-46; C-in C, British Forces in Germany, British Military Governor, 1946-47; director, BOAC, 1948-49; chairman, BEA 1949-1964; chairman, Horizon Travel, 1964.

FRESSON, CAPTAIN ERNEST EDMUND

Promoted North British Aviation, 1929, and Highland Airways, 1933; Highland Airways amalgamated with Northern and Scottish Airways, 1937, and became Scottish Airways; he continued as director until Scottish Airways was absorbed into BEA, 1947; area manager, Scottish Division, BEA, 1947-48.

GANDAR DOWER, ERIC LESLIE

Actor and aviation enthusiast, in 1934 he established Aberdeen Airways and developed Dyce airport; first services from Aberdeen (Dyce) to the Northern Isles in 1935; airline's name changed to Allied Airways (Gandar Dower) 1937; elected Unionist MP for Caithness and Sutherland, 1945; sat as Independent, 1948; lost his seat, 1950. He resisted the nationalisation of his airline and the appropriation of his airport vigorously, finally settling all claims against Ministry of Aviation, Board of Trade and BEA regarding both the airline and airport in 1973.

GUINNESS, GROUP CAPTAIN THOMAS LOEL EVELYN BULKELEY
Together with Lord Cowdray's Whitehall Securities, he was an early investor in Airwork. Member of Parliament for City of Bath, 1931-45; chairman, Airwork, 1943-51; then, president, Airwork and from 1960, president, British United Airways.

HARTLEY, BRIG.-GENERAL SIR HAROLD
Vice-president, LMS Railway, and director of scientific research, 1930-45; chairman, Railway Air Services, 1934-45; chairman, BEA, 1946-47; chairman, BOAC, 1947-49.

HOPE, SIR ARCHIBALD PHILIP, BT.
Joined Airwork, 1945; managing director, Airwork, 1952-56; chairman, BIATA, 1956; chief executive, Napier Aero Engines, 1962-63.

HUNTING, SIR PERCY LLEWELLYN
Chairman, Hunting Group of Companies, which included Percival Aircraft, Field Aircraft Services, Hunting Aviation, Hunting Aerosurveys, 1927-60.

HUNTING, WING COMMANDER GERALD LINDSAY
Governing director, Hunting Group of Companies. Brother of Sir Percy, father of Lindsay Clive Hunting.

HUNTING, LINDSAY CLIVE
Joined Hunting Group, 1950; director, Hunting Group, 1952; vice-chairman, 1962; chairman, 1975-91; director, British United Airways, 1960; president, BIATA, 1960-62; president, SBAC, 1985-86.

JONES, SQUADRON LEADER R. J. 'JACK'
Pleasure flying from Herne Bay Holiday Camp, summer 1946; registered East Anglian Flying Services (later Channel Airways), 16 August, 1946; first post-war operator out of Southend, 1947; managing director, and later chairman, Channel Airways, until 1972.

KENNARD, WING COMMANDER HUGH CHARLES
Served throughout Second World War in Fighter Command; formed Air Kruise (Kent) 1946, managing director and chairman, 1946-54; director, Skyfotos, 1948-59; director, Luxembourg Airlines 1947-51; joint managing director, Silver City Airways 1957-60; director, Air Ferry, 1962-64; managing director, Invicta Airways, 1964.

LAKER, FREDERICK ALFRED

Managing director, Aviation Traders, Aviation Traders (Engineering), and Air Charter, to 1960; managing director, British United Airways, British United Air Ferries and Aviation Traders (Engineering), 1960-65; director, Air Holdings, 1961-65; chairman and managing director, Laker Airways, 1966-82.

LINDGREN, GEORGE SAMUEL

MP (Labour) for Wellingborough 1945-59; Parliamentary Secretary to Ministry of Civil Aviation, 1946-50; Joint Parliamentary Secretary, Ministry of Transport, 1964-66. Created Life Peer 1961.

LONGHURST, JOHN

Served with Imperial Airways and BOAC 1935-43; editor *Air Transport and Airport Engineering*, 1945-48; air transport editor, *The Aeroplane*, 1943-51, also wrote under the pseudonym 'Commentator'.

MCCRINDLE, MAJOR JOHN RONALD

Commanded London–Paris Communication Squadron during Peace Conference, 1919; managing director, Hillman's Airways, then managing director, British Airways, 1935-40; deputy director-general, BOAC, 1940-47; board member, BOAC, 1946-58; adviser on external affairs, BOAC, 1948-58; director, East African Airways, British West Indian Airways and Bahamas Airways; adviser, UK Delegation, Chicago Civil Aviation Conference, 1944 and Civil Aviation Conference, 1946.

MCINTYRE, WING COMMANDER DAVID FOWLER

Pilot to Houston Mount Everest Flight Expedition, 1933; founder, with the Duke of Hamilton, Scottish Aviation, 1935; managing director, Scottish Aviation and Scottish Airlines, 1946; died 8 December 1957 in a Scottish Aviation Twin Pioneer which crashed during a demonstration flight in Libya.

MASEFIELD, SIR PETER GORDON

Joined editorial staff *The Aeroplane*, 1937; chairman, Editorial Committee, *Inter-Services Journal on Aircraft recognition*, 1942-45; Personal Adviser Civil Aviation to Lord Privy Seal, and Secretary War Cabinet Committee on Air Transport, (Brabazon Committee), 1943-45; British Civil Air Attaché to USA, 1945-46; director general, Long Term Planning and Projects, MCA 1946-48; chief executive, BEA, 1949-55; managing director, Bristol Aircraft, 1955-60; managing director, BEAGLE and Beagle Aircraft, 1960; chairman, British Airports Authority, 1965.

MEASURES, WING COMMANDER ARTHUR HAROLD

Joined Imperial Airways, 1932; superintendent, Railway Air Services, 1934; manager, Associated Airways Joint Committee, 1940-46; operating manager, West Coast Air Services, 1941-46; managing director, Scottish Airways, 1937-46; board member, BEA, 1946-56.

MEKIE, EOIN CAMERON

Secretary, legal adviser and joint general manager to the Edmundsons Electricity Supply Group of Companies, 1941 until nationalisation in 1948; chairman British Aviation Services and its subsidiaries, including Britavia, Silver City 1949-62.

MELVILLE, SIR RONALD

Entered Air Ministry, 1934; Assistant Under-Secretary, 1946; chairman, Committee on Air Trooping, 1950; Deputy Under-Secretary, War Office, 1960-63; Ministry of Defence, 1963-66; Secretary (Aviation), Ministry of Technology, 1966-71. Knighted 1957.

MORTON, THEODORE WILLIAM 'SAMMY'

Civil aviation 1931-40, with Hillman's, then with British Air Navigation (Banco) and latterly as chief pilot, Olley Air Service; chief test pilot, London Aircraft Production, 1940-45; chairman and managing director, Morton Air Services, 1946-68; chairman and managing director, Olley Air Service, 1953; director, British United Airways, 1960-68.

MUNTZ, ALAN

British Petroleum, 1922-6, and Anglo–Iranian Oil, 1926-28; with Sir Nigel Norman founded Airwork and Heston Airport, 1928; with Banque Misr, Cairo, founded Misr Airwork, 1932; with RE Grant Govan, Delhi, helped found Indian National Airways, 1933; became vice chairman of Airwork, after Whitehall Securities and TLEB Guinness (who became chairman) acquired an interest in Airwork; founded Alan Muntz & Co., 1937; with L. E. Baynes, founded Baynes Aircraft Interiors, 1954.

NATHAN, LORD

Minister of Civil Aviation, 1946-48.

NORWAY, NEVIL SHUTE

Chief Calculator to Airship Guarantee Co., on construction of Rigid Airship R.100; founded Airspeed Ltd, 1931; joint managing director, 1931–38; commissioned RNVR 1940; retired 1945. Author of many novels under the name 'Nevil Shute' and autobiography *Slide Rule*.

OGMORE, LORD (FORMERLY DAVID REES REES-WILLIAMS)

MP (Labour) Croydon South, 1945-50; Minister of Civil Aviation, June-October 1951; President, Liberal Party 1963-64.

OLLEY, GORDON PERCY

Joined Handley Page Transport on first Continental air services, 1919; with Handley Page Air Transport, 1922-24; pilot with Imperial Airways, 1924-33; formed Olley Air Service, 1934-39; deputy manager and operations manager, Associated Airways Joint Committee, 1939-46; managing director, Olley Air Service, Air Commerce and Air Booking, 1946-58. Author, *A Million Miles in the Air*.

OVERTON, SIR ARNOLD EDERSHEIM
Permanent Secretary, MCA, 1947-53; board member, BEA, 1953-63; director, Cambrian Airways, 1955.

PAKENHAM, LORD
Conservative Party Economic Research Department, 1930-32; personal assistant to Sir William Beveridge, 1941-4; Chancellor of the Duchy of Lancaster, 1947-48; Minister of Civil Aviation, 1948-51; First Lord of the Admiralty, 1951. Became Earl of Longford, 1961.

PEARSON, THE HON. (BERNARD) CLIVE
Second son of Lord Cowdray, he was chairman of S. Pearson & Son, 1927-54, and also responsible for the family's aviation interests through its holding company, Whitehall Securities Corporation; chairman, British Airways, 1936-39; chairman, BOAC, 1940-43; director, Southern Railway, 1936-47.

POWELL, AIR COMMODORE GRIFFITH JAMES
Imperial Airways, 1929-39, as pilot Empire routes and Atlantic experimental flights, later operations manager in Bermuda; senior air staff officer, RAF Ferry Command, 1942-43; Senior Air Staff Officer, No.45 Group, RAF, 1944-45; managing director, Britavia, Silver City, British Aviation Services, 1946-57; director, British West Indian Airways, 1958-61; chairman and managing director, Bahamas Airways, and resident BOAC manager, 1961-65; European director, Invicta Airways, 1966.

RAITZ, VLADIMIR
Journalist, United Press, then Reuters, 1943-50; established Horizon Holidays, 1949; established Pilgrim Tours (with Transair), 1953; bought Quo Vadis Travel, 1957; launched Club 18-30, 1970; Horizon in receivership, 1974, bought by Clarksons; managing director, Medallion Holidays, 1975.

REITH, LORD
First general manager, BBC, 1922; managing director, 1923; director-general, 1927-38; chairman, Imperial Airways, 1938-39; and first chairman of BOAC, 1939-40; Minister of Information, 1940; Minister of Transport, 1940; first Minister of Works, 1940-42, leading to Ministry of Works and Planning; Captain, RNVR, director of Combined Operations Material Dept., Admiralty 1943-45.

RUNCIMAN OF DOXFORD, 2ND VISCOUNT, (WALTER LESLIE RUNCIMAN)
Director, Short Bros. 1935-39; director-general of BOAC, 1940-43; Air Cdre. and Air Attaché, Tehran, 1943-46; member, Air Transport Advisory Council, 1946-54.

RYLANDS, J. ERIC
Chairman, Skyways; chairman and managing director, Eric Rylands Ltd; Samlesbury Engineering, later Skyways Engineering; director, Lancashire Aircraft; Skyways de France;

Skyways Coach Air; Bahamas Airways; Middle East Airlines; chairman BIATA, 1949-52 and president 1958-59.

SANDFORD, SIR FOLLIOTT HERBERT
Entered Air Ministry, 1930; PPS to successive Secretaries of State, 1937-40; attached to RAF Ferry Command, Montreal, 1941-42; Secretary, Office of Resident Minister, West Africa (See Lord Swinton), 1942-44; Assistant Under-Secretary of State, Air Ministry, 1944-47; Deputy Under-Secretary of State, Air Ministry, 1947-58.

SILSOE, LORD (ARTHUR MALCOLM TRUSTRAM EVE, KC THEN QC)
Chairman, Air Transport Licensing Authority, 1938-39.

STARLING, CAPTAIN ERIC ALLEN
Chief pilot, Aberdeen Airways (later Allied Airways (Gandar Dower)), 1934-39; RAF Coastal Command to 1946; joined Scottish Airways, 1947 until absorbed by BEA; flight manager, Scotland, BEA, 1949-68.

STRAIGHT, AIR COMMODORE WHITNEY WILLARD
Entered civil aviation 1934, having started in motorcar racing; formed Straight Corporation, which, before the war, controlled twenty-one associated companies operating airlines, flying clubs and aerodromes throughout Great Britain, and continued after the war, being renamed Airways Union in 1949; served RAF 1939-45 as fighter pilot and later commanded Nos 216 and 46 Groups, Transport Command; Additional Air ADC to King George VI, 1944; deputy chairman, BEA, 1946-47; managing director and chief executive, BOAC, 1947-49; deputy chairman, BOAC, 1949-55; executive vice-chairman, Rolls-Royce, 1956; deputy chairman, Rolls-Royce, 1957-71; chairman, Rolls-Royce, 1971-76.

SWINTON, VISCOUNT, LATER FIRST EARL OF (PHILIP CUNLIFFE-LISTER)
MP (Unionist) for Hendon, 1918-35; held many offices of state from 1921, including: Secretary of State for Air, 1935-38; Cabinet Minister Resident in West Africa, 1942-44; First Minister for Civil Aviation, 1944-45.

TERRINGTON, LORD
Chairman, Industrial Disputes Tribunal 1944-59; chairman, Air Transport Advisory Council, 1947-60; first chairman, Air Transport Licensing Board, 1960; Deputy Speaker, House of Lords, 1949-61.

THOMAS, MALDWYN LEWIS
Founded Jersey Airlines in 1948, although the registered name was Airlines (Jersey) Ltd, to avoid confusion with Jersey Airways, recently nationalised and now part of BEA. managing director, 1948-62; director, British United Airways and managing director, British United (CI) Airways, 1962-65.

THOMAS, SIR MILES, LATER LORD THOMAS OF REMENHAM

Technical editor of *The Motor*, then editor of *The Light Car*, until 1924; with Lord Nuffield from 1924, finally vice-chairman and managing director, Morris Motors Group, 1940-47; deputy chairman, BOAC, 1948; chairman, BOAC, 1949-56; chairman, Monsanto Chemicals, 1956-63; chairman, Britannia Airways, 1967; director, Thomson Organisation, Thomson Travel.

WILCOCK, GROUP CAPTAIN CLIFFORD ARTHUR BOWMAN

Deputy director Manning, Air Ministry and Senior Personnel Staff Officer, Transport Command, 1939-45; chairman, Air Schools, Derby Aviation, Wolverhampton Aviation, Derby Airways; MP (Labour) Derby since 1945, Derby North since 1950.

WINSTER, LORD (REGINALD THOMAS HERBERT FLETCHER, CREATED BARON WINSTER 1942)

MP (Labour) for Nuneaton, 1935-41; Minister of Civil Aviation, 1945-46; Governor of Cyprus 1947-49.

WOODS HUMPHERY, MAJOR GEORGE EDWARD

General manager, Daimler Airway and Daimler Hire, 1922-24; managing director and/or general manager, Imperial Airways, 1924-38. In a tribute to him in 1962, Lord Brabazon said, 'He is the best airline operator this country has ever had, which is why I suppose he got the sack.'[2]

WYATT, SIR MYLES DERMOT NORRIS

Assistant and later deputy secretary to the Commissioners for Port of Calcutta, 1925-33; joined Airwork as general manager, 1934; managing director, 1938; chairman and managing director, 1951-60; chairman and managing director, British United Airways, 1960; chairman, Air Holdings, 1961. Knighted 1963.

APPENDIX THREE

LIST OF ABBREVIATIONS

AOC-in C	Air Officer Commanding-in-Chief
ARB	Air Registration Board
ATA	Air Transport Auxiliary
ATAC	Air Transport Advisory Council
ATCO	Air Traffic Control Officer
ATLA	Air Transport Licensing Authority
AVM	Air Vice-Marshal
BACA	British Air Charter Association
BEA	British European Airways (Corporation)
BNA	British Nederland Airservices
BOAC	British Overseas Airways Corporation
BSAA	British South American Airways (Corporation)
CAB	Civil Aeronautics Board
CI	Channel Islands
DUS	Deputy Under-Secretary
Hp	Horse power
IATA	International Air Transport Association
ICAO	International Civil Aviation Organisation
IRO	International Refugee Organisation
IT	Inclusive Tour
KLM	Royal Dutch Airlines
LAMS	London Aero and Motor Services
lb	pound (weight)

MAP	Ministry of Aircraft Production
MCA	Ministry of Civil Aviation
MoS	Ministry of Supply (formerly Ministry of Aircraft Production)
Mph	Miles per hour
MTCA	Ministry of Transport and Civil Aviation
OFC	Overseas Food Corporation
PRO	Public Records Office
PS	Permanent Secretary
PSIOWA	Portsmouth, Southsea and Isle of Wight Aviation
PUS	Permanent Under-Secretary
RAF	Royal Air Force
RAuxAF	Royal Auxiliary Air Force
RAS	Railway Air Services
SBAC	Society of British Aircraft Constructors
STOL	Short Take-off and Landing
TCA	Trans Canada Airlines
TNA	The National Archives (formerly Public Records Office)

APPENDIX FOUR

AIRWORK AND THE IRO

AIRWORK AND THE INTERNATIONAL REFUGEE ORGANISATION

On 28 May 1948, Airwork announced the following major contract:

> One of the largest charter contracts ever placed has been secured by Airwork Ltd., in the
> face of keen competition from foreign companies. The contract is worth £1,200,000 and is
> for the time charter of five DC-4 Skymasters to carry refugees for the International Refugee
> Organization of Geneva. During the first year 17,500 displaced persons, whose relatives
> and sponsors in Canada are paying their passages, which will cost $260, will be flown from
> Hamburg to Montreal. The DC-4s, which will be operated by Airwork, will start making the
> first flights at the beginning of June.[1]

But Airwork never operated its own DC-4s throughout its entire existence. No other
aircraft suitable for the long transatlantic journey would have been available; Airwork
never operated Yorks either, and in any case they would have been less than ideal as
Airwork was bidding against other operators of modern American built aircraft. So what
happened? It is a sad story, and none of the participants come out of it well. Airwork
was at best over-optimistic, if not naïve, in thinking it could put together a complex
programme of flights across the Atlantic at short notice. Because Airwork did not own
any DC-4s, it would have had to lease in aircraft and operating crew from a third party
initially, which detracted from the more obvious benefits of the contract to a British
enterprise. The British Government was shown to be half-hearted and ineffectual in its
support. There was outright hostility from Lindgren, the Parliamentary Secretary, and
the lines of communication to the Canadians through the High Commission in Ottawa
were weak and prone to misunderstanding. No representative from the Ministry of
Civil Aviation went out to Canada to try and help a British airline pursue a worthwhile
and long-term contract. But the real villain of the piece is the Canadian Government,
implacable in its opposition to charter airlines and holding most of the best cards; it
had the final word and was always able to disregard the low-key representations from
the British, imposing its own blue print from start to finish and, indeed, achieving its
goal at the end.

On being awarded the contract, Airwork tried to clear its lines as best it could, with the British Government, and asked for support in obtaining permission from the Canadians. Strictly speaking the flights were fifth freedom, that is to say, they were to operate between two countries (Germany and Canada), neither of which was the country of the airline's domicile or aircraft registration (United Kingdom); the flights were, therefore, not covered by the licensing restrictions of the 1946 Act. Approval would have to be obtained from Canada, but the flights would originate in the British Zone of Germany and, as there was a total prohibition on the operation of any German airlines, Airwork must have thought on balance it had a reasonable case and legitimate aspirations. The first flights were due to start in June. Airwork had some experience of transatlantic operations, having delivered aircraft to North and South America, but would need to acquire the aircraft and train the crews, all of which would take time. It proposed subchartering the initial flights to an American charter airline, Seaboard & Western, whilst its aircraft were brought up to United Kingdom standards and the crews trained. The Ministry appeared ambivalent over this contract, with hostility at the parliamentary level, particularly from Lindgren, whereas his civil servants were generally more supportive. Inter-departmental tensions were as nothing to the next obstacle, however: the Canadians. They were determined to view the matter from their own unique perspective and were in any case opposed to charter airlines. Why did not BOAC operate the flights? As they were to be so regular they amounted to a scheduled service, and so had to be covered by the bilateral agreement on air services between Canada and the United Kingdom, did they not? Would the British Government sponsor the operation? The answer was no, it would not, and it thought the Canadians misunderstood the bilateral issues, as the flights were from Germany not the United Kingdom. As for BOAC's position, that was up to Airwork and whatever agreement it could negotiate with the corporation. However, the British Government did try and tell the Canadians that it supported the application from the commercial point of view, but even that was misunderstood by the Canadians, who assumed therefore that the British Government did not support it politically. Dialogue with the Canadians, never easy at the best of times, was further hampered by the need to transmit all messages through the British High Commission in Ottawa, relying on non-expert staff to pass on specialised technical information and opinions to the Canadian authorities. Then the men from the Ministry had to deal with the British Foreign Secretary, the redoubtable Ernie Bevin, when the IRO complained to him about the slow progress. He pointed out how politically important the resettlement programme was, and also that it would save dollars if Airwork were to do the work rather than a Canadian airline, in this case Trans-Canada Airlines (TCA). With a fine sense of timing, BOAC then started to make unhelpful noises. Lord Hartley, the chairman, possibly with another agenda on his mind, complained that charter companies were being allowed to buy American aircraft, which were denied to 'the chosen instrument'. The response from Mr Dunnett, the under-secretary, betrays some exasperation with the whining from BOAC:

> I am getting a little tired of these complaints from the Corporations to the effect that charter companies can get American aircraft more easily than they can. The short answer is that the charter companies are subject to the same Exchange Control rules as the Corporations but go out into the world and find American aircraft which can be purchased for other than dollars… (BOAC) had no grounds for [the] suggestion that a drain on sterling was necessarily involved. Airwork had managed to secure a contract which provided that their dollar costs would be met by the International Refugee Organisation in dollars.[2]

But then Airwork drew down the wrath of the British as well when it approached the Canadians directly, causing irritation at the British High Commission. The May deadline had come and gone, and Airwork was no nearer obtaining approval from the Canadians, so Sir Archibald Hope went to see them. This action displeased the High Commissioner, who felt that all contact should go through the proper channels, and worked himself up into a rage over it: 'Chief need at the moment is to prevent (Airwork) from queering the pitch further, but we hope to ensure this'.[3] Actually, the chief need was to process the not unreasonable application from Airwork, but the High Commission was dealing with the Canadians on a day-to-day basis and, inevitably, took on board their concerns and prejudices. The Canadians especially disliked independent charter operations on the Atlantic route, which they regarded as the preserve of TCA, and by extension, BOAC. Furthermore, they remembered that the previous year, the British Government had forced TCA to take over commercial responsibility for the Ontario Immigration Scheme by refusing to give fifth freedom rights between the United Kingdom and Canada to an American charter airline; in the end, Trans Ocean Airlines had had to operate the flights as subcharters for TCA. The Canadians were determined that the British would be forced to operate the flights under the aegis of BOAC, if at all.

In the meantime, the MCA had to placate Mr Bevin and the Foreign Office, so it wrote his under-secretary a letter. The style is masterly and the communication stands as a superb example of one government department pulling the wool over the eyes of another, without telling a single falsehood.

> In reply I am to say that we have noted that Mr. Bevin would be glad to see the arrangements proposed go through for the reasons given in your letter. According to the information available here the inauguration of the flights only now awaits the grant of the necessary operating rights by the Canadian authorities. We have been active in conjunction with the Commonwealth Relations Office and the United Kingdom High Commissioner in Canada in supporting the application of Airwork Ltd. Pending developments there is nothing further that can be done so far as this Ministry is concerned.[4]

Only one week later the Ministry was admitting, 'Airwork have been having great difficulty in obtaining the necessary operating rights from the Canadians'. I also like the sly reference to the Commonwealth Relations Office, just to remind the Foreign Office that this was not its affair. One day after the letter went, the High Commission notified the Ministry of the Canadian response, which was tantamount to a refusal. The

Canadians would not permit the operation unless it was carried out by BOAC or as a sub-contract from BOAC to Airwork; BOAC would have to be responsible for rates, and Airwork would have to conform to bilaterally agreed operating conditions. But neither Airwork nor BOAC was prepared to accept the proposed change in contractual relationship. Airwork had sought the contract on its own initiative and did not wish to give anything away to the corporation, nor in all fairness did BOAC wish to be saddled with the contract. The answers from the Ministry to the High Commission did not concede any of the demands that the Canadians had made. It was time for Airwork to look at alternatives and, as one always does when dealing with obdurate Canadians, it began examining the possibility of operating through the United States, flying to Buffalo in New York state, and then transferring the passengers across the border at Niagara into Canada. But the idea was a non-starter; such a big operation would have been extremely vulnerable to immigration problems and delays both from the United States and Canada. Airwork then tried to satisfy the Canadians by proposing that the Dutch airline, KLM, sponsor the operation, a course of action with which the British Government concurred. But the Canadians still insisted that it be brought under the BOAC umbrella, and went on to be disparaging about KLM. If they were not to be allowed to control the contract by procuring it for themselves and TCA, they saw no reason why the British Government should not wish to do the same by obliging BOAC to take over the contract. When this did not happen, the Canadians indicated they would agree to a partial approval, limited to the end of December and provided that TCA had first approval of the traffic; so finally coming out into the open and admitting that the main objective of their policy had been to force the traffic on to TCA. The IRO would have none of it and cancelled the contract with Airwork. The final letter from this file, from the High Commission in Ottawa and dated 14 January 1949, concludes the story:

> In case the information has not already come your way, we think it worth while to let you know that TCA are now arranging to fly refugees from Germany to Canada (presumably under contract to IRO). At first flights will take place from Munich, but TCA propose to switch their operations to Hamburg in March.
>
> The Canadian authorities are approaching the United Kingdom occupation authorities for permission for these flights.[5]

'Commentator' in *The Aeroplane* got wind of the unsuccessful negotiations and, after castigating the Canadian Government, commented on the time and money that had been wasted, and noted, sadly:

> With every advance in the power of the bureaucrat, the World becomes more inconvenient and galling to citizens of every race and creed, poor and rich alike.[6]

APPENDIX FIVE

GUIDE TO THE BRITISH INDEPENDENT OPERATORS

In its 14 March 1952 issue, *The Aeroplane* summarised, for the first time since the war, the activities of the British independent operators. Here is an abridged version of their compilation.

AIR COURIERS

Formed in 1937, Air Couriers operate from Croydon with three Rapides and one Gemini, mainly on racecourse, newspaper and press photography work. At its base, the company has ARB-approved radio workshops and stores, with full facilities for overhaul, aircraft modification and light-metal fabrication.

AIR ENTERPRISES

Based initially at Gatwick and formed in 1946, Air Enterprises is now operating from Croydon, with a subsidiary base at Renfrew, Glasgow. The company has, since 1949, been operating a summer service to the Isle of Wight under an associate agreement, but Air Enterprises' main work has been that of charter operation, with four Consuls and four Rapides, generally under contract. For instance, the company operates a Consul on permanent charter to the Standard Motor Co. and this aircraft has been specially laid out as a luxury four-seater. Air Enterprises has engineering and maintenance facilities at each of its two bases.

AIR KRUISE

Formed in June 1946 as a small private venture company, Air Kruise has, since 1950, been operating a regular Lympne–Le Touquet summer service in association with BEA. The original and present operating and maintenance base of the company is Lympne, but for a time it operated also from Croydon, and last year took over the tenancy of the Hastings airfield for charter and pleasure work. Air Kruise carried 3,500 passengers on its cross-Channel service during 1951 in its fleet of Rapides.

AIRLINES (JERSEY)

With such a short holiday operating season – amounting to no more than eight weeks out of the fifty-two – independent operators in the Channel Islands do not find business easy, and Jersey Airlines' revenue mileage of about 250,000 with 15,000 passengers carried in its fleet of four Rapides, was good in the circumstances. Formed in 1947, the company's main base is at Jersey Airport, with subsidiary bases at Guernsey, Exeter and St Brieuc. In Jersey the company carries out aircraft overhaul and specialises in radio installation and overhaul.

AIR NAVIGATION AND TRADING

Primarily concerned with aeronautical engineering and contracting at Squires Gate airfield, Blackpool, Air Navigation and Trading also operate a large fleet of aircraft (three Avro 19s, six Ansons, four Rapides, two Dragons) on charter, ambulance and flying club work, both from the main base and from Kingstown Aerodrome, Carlisle.

Among the flights made were several to the Outer Hebrides and Western Isles with replacement trawler crews, and to the Continent with ambulance cases. The company's engineering work includes aircraft conversion and modification, overhauls and prototype development.

AIR TRANSPORT (CHARTER) (CI)

Formed in July 1946, Air Transport (Charter) started operations with its first aircraft, a Dakota, in April 1947, and was the first British operator to use a high-density, thirty-two-seat version of this aircraft.

During the early years the company was based at Jersey Airport. It then ran inter-island services with Rapides between the Channel Islands as well as carrying passengers and cargo on charter in its DC-3s. During 1951 the company began a reorganisation and moved its main operating base to Blackbushe.

In 1951, using its two Dakotas, the company operated Air Ministry contracts and B.E.A. charter, which included flights for the corporation during its engineering strike.

AIRWAYS UNION

Incorporating the original Western Airways – a company started in 1933 by Mr Norman Edgar to operate Bristol Channel ferry services – Airways Union was formed in 1935 and retains its headquarters at Weston-super-Mare. The Weston–Cardiff service is now run by Cambrian Air Services, and Airways Union operate charter services and the flying clubs at Exeter and Plymouth.

AIRWORK

Originally formed by the late Sir Nigel Norman and Mr Alan Muntz in October 1928, Airwork is one of the oldest and most successful of the independent operators. During twenty-three years it has passed through four broad phases: First, at its own airfield, Heston, as a sponsor of private flying; next, in pre-war and war years, as an operator of flying, navigation and radio training centres; then as a repair, maintenance and manufacturing organization for war needs; and, finally, as a large-scale charter operator – but contriving to offer almost every ancillary facility required in aviation.

The development of each of these phases can still be seen in the activities of the firm. Outside repair contracts are carried out in the workshops at Gatwick and at Langley, where experimental work is also done, while normal fleet maintenance is completed at Blackbushe, Airwork's operating base. Though Heston no longer exists as an airfield, Perth airfield is still owned by the firm and training is continuing at five other centres.

Large-scale charter work began in 1946 and Airwork was the first independent operator to order British post-war civil aircraft types with the purchase of six Vikings. Charter work has included the operation of home-leave services for government officials to and from the Sudan and for Service personnel, and the operation of services for oil companies – this apart from the week-to-week demands of the normal charter business.

During 1951, Airwork flew more than 4½ million miles, carrying 58,562 passengers. In addition to its charter fleet of thirteen aircraft – four Hermes, two Bristol Freighters, seven Vikings – Airwork operates no fewer than 256 aircraft, varying from Chipmunks to Ansons and Mosquitos, on behalf of Sudan Airways, Iraq Petroleum, the Air Ministry and the Admiralty.

AQUILA AIRWAYS

The only new independent operator to fly regular services under an associate agreement with BOAC and the only operator in this country to use flyingboats exclusively, Aquila Airways was formed in May 1948.

Initially purchasing five ex-corporation Sunderlands and now with a Solent delivered and three more of these big boats on order, the company has been operating services to Madeira and Lisbon since May 1949, and lately to Las Palmas. It does a limited amount of charter work. During 1951, Aquila's most important charter exercise was the evacuation of the Anglo–Iranian Oil Co.'s staff from Basra. Early this year the appointment of Brigadier-General Critchley to the company's board was announced.

With its operating base at Berth 50, Southampton Docks, Aquila has full maintenance and engineering facilities at Hamble.

BIRKETT AIR SERVICE

One of the oldest of the charter companies operating at present, Birkett Air Service was formed in 1932. It flew then from Heston before moving to Croydon. There the company returned in 1946 to start its post-war press and other charter operations on which Birketts have specialised. The company's brokers are Davies and Newman. Its fleet consists of three Rapides and one Proctor.

CAMBRIAN AIR SERVICES

Formed in 1936 and re-starting operations after the war as a charter operation, Cambrian was one of the first independent concerns to run internal services on an associate agreement with BEA. In May, 1948, the company, in co-operation with Western Airways, re-opened the Cardiff-Weston air ferry which, in the following year and thereafter, Cambrian has operated alone. Other regular services have been flown by the company from Cardiff to Liverpool and the Channel Islands.

Cambrian Air Services' main base is at Cardiff where there are complete maintenance facilities, with a subsidiary base at Haverfordwest, Pembrokeshire. There are six Rapides in the fleet.

CREWSAIR
Operating from Southend Airport, Crewsair was formed in September 1949. In December last year, the company absorbed Trans-World Charter, taking over the latter's fleet of four Vikings. Maintenance is undertaken at Southend by Crewsair (Engineering), which has no financial connection with Crewsair. In the last month of 1951 the company made seven flights, under RAF charter, to Southern Rhodesia. Lep Air Services are the company's brokers.

DERBY AVIATION
Operating from Derby Airport, Burnaston, Derby Aviation was registered in January 1949, and is concerned with light charter and Army co-operation work, flying two Rapides, a Messenger and a Gemini. The company has an ARB-approved overhaul organisation at Burnaston and maintains a subsidiary base at Wolverhampton airport.

EAGLE AVIATION
Formed in April 1948, Eagle Aviation has always worked in the heavy charter field, first with Halifax and Halton aircraft and later with Yorks when it purchased three of these aircraft from BOAC and converted them for freight-passenger work in 1949.

Originally based at Aldermaston, Eagle has been operating from Luton airport since May 1950, with a subsidiary base at Bovingdon airport, Herts. Maintenance is carried out at Luton airport.

EAST ANGLIAN FLYING SERVICES
Apart from normal charter work, East Anglian, formed in July 1946, have been operating associate agreement services with three Rapides from its base at Southend airport to Jersey, via Shoreham, and to Ostend.

FAIRFLIGHT
Now an associate of Surrey Flying Services, Fairflight was registered in August 1949, after taking over from Airflight, both companies then owned by Air Vice-Marshal D.C.T. Bennett. Surrey took over the company in November 1951 and it thus became a subsidiary of Aviation Traders.

The company's main base is at Blackbushe, with subsidiary bases at Stansted and Southend. Overhaul, repair and maintenance is under the control of Aviation Traders at these three bases.

During 1951 Fairflight flew 105,000 revenue miles on freight work, carrying a total of 3,010 tons, and 120,000 revenue miles on general work, carrying 300 passengers. During the five months of the Berlin 'little' airlift in 1951, 350 return flights were made.

FLIGHT REFUELLING

Although Flight Refuelling is not at present engaged in charter work, the name of this company is included in this guide because its fleet is both available for, and obviously suited to, the transport of liquids. The work done during the Berlin Airlift was typical of that which can still be done should the necessity arise. The company is based at Tarrant Rushton Airfield, near Blandford, Dorset.

HUNTING AIR TRANSPORT

One of a number of companies in the Hunting Group, Hunting Air Transport was formed immediately after the war – in September 1945 – and was thus in a good position to take advantage of the post-war air travel boom caused by the shortage of regular transport facilities. Known until a few weeks ago as Hunting Air Travel, HAT started operations with an inevitably assorted series of aircraft, but, with the purchase, in particular, of Vikings, gradually rationalized its fleet to deal with the more stable contract operations which now form the bulk of the company's work.

In August last year, for instance, the company was the first to be awarded a trooping contract, for a period of two years and involving some 220,000 flying hours. HAT has a contract with the War Office for the transport of troops to West Africa, and operations last year included sub-charter work for BEA and Air France, frequent flights to East Africa and a number of special charters for government ministries.

Hunting's base is at Bovingdon Airport, Herts, where the company's associate, Field Aircraft Services, provides all maintenance and engineering requirements for the fleet of eight Vikings and one Dakota.

LANCASHIRE AIRCRAFT CORPORATION

Originally a war-time aircraft repair organisation, Lancashire Aircraft Corporation entered the charter field in January 1946, operating from Blackpool. Leaving its work in engineering to associated companies, Lancashire concentrated on charter flying, expanding rapidly during the following years.

With the purchase of Halton freighters early in 1947, which were based at Bovingdon, the company started on the relatively new business of 'heavy' charter operations, while retaining its original base at Squire's Gate, Blackpool, and moving in also to Yeadon aerodrome, Leeds, and later, to Woolsington airport, Newcastle-upon-Tyne.

Now, with some seventy aircraft, including twenty-three Yorks, six Haltons, fourteen Rapides and eight Consuls, it is, in the matter of fleet size, the biggest of the 'independents' and last summer its board was strengthened by the appointment, as chairman, of David Brown who is chairman of David Brown Corporation.

During 1951 Lancashire flew nearly 1 million miles to places as far apart as Tokyo, Buenos Aires, Montreal and Livingstone. One of Lancashire's bigger jobs was the transport of a ship's Diesel engine from Stavanger, Norway, to Melbourne.

MANX AIR CHARTERS

The only operator based in the Isle of Man, Manx Air Charters was formed in May 1947 and, apart from its normal charter operations, has been flying a Ronaldsway-Carlisle Summer service with Rapides in association with BEA. The company has its own engineering and maintenance facilities.

MORTON AIR SERVICES

Formed in May 1945 as soon as the war in Europe was over, Morton Air Services actually started operations with two Rapides in January of the following year. But the company's history can properly be considered to go back much further, since the managing director was flying on charter services for many years previous to the war. The Rapides of 1946 were supplemented by four Consuls, and MAS was one of the first companies to order Doves, of which it has three.

Since the boom years of 1946 and 1947, Morton Air Services' work has settled down to a useful norm and in 1951 the company, which operates from Croydon, carried some 6,000 passengers. MAS has an associate agreement with BEA for regular summer operations from Croydon and Bristol to Jersey and Guernsey.

Full maintenance facilities are available at the Croydon base and daily maintenance facilities are available at Morton's subsidiary base at Bristol (Whitchurch). At present, the company also keeps one aircraft based at Rangoon, Burma, and another at Karachi, Pakistan.

OLLEY AIR SERVICE

Another of our older independent operators, Olley Air Service was formed in 1934 and so has seen seventeen years of active life – if we count the war period during which Olleys formed part of the Associated Airways Joint Committee. In those pre-war days Olley Air Service – based then, as now, at Croydon – was concerned with a number of other companies operating internal and other services. In the earlier post-war years, the company's capital was largely railway owned.

Since 1946 Captain Olley – who was at one time in charge of Imperial Airways' special charter division – has concentrated mainly on charter, race-meeting and tour work, although the company has an associate agreement with BEA for summer services to the Channel Islands. During 1951 Olley Air Service carried 8,750 passengers.

The company has its own engineering and maintenance facilities at Croydon, and is represented on the Baltic Exchange by Lambert Bros. Air Commerce is a subsidiary company using the Olley aircraft and facilities.

SCOTTISH AVIATION

Formed in 1935, this parent company to Scottish Airlines came into prominence during the war when Prestwick was a vitally important centre for the Atlantic ferry. Scottish

Aviation was then undertaking a great deal of conversion and repair work and the facilities and experience were later applied to civil aircraft conversions for various air line operators, including BEA, and to the design and manufacture of aircraft such as the Prestwick Pioneer. In the earlier days of the peace, Scottish Airlines operated services to Iceland and elsewhere under charter and were directly concerned with air line projects in Greece and Luxembourg.

More settled conditions in international aviation have since caused the operating section of the company to concentrate on charter work, which, for the greater part, is on yearly contracts, but two regular services, Glasgow–Burtonwood–Northolt and Glasgow–Isle of Man, have been operated in associate agreement with BEA. During 1951 Scottish carried 21,084 passengers and 183 tons of freight in its fleet on four Dakotas, one Oxford and two Rapides.

SILVER CITY AIRWAYS

Originally formed for the purpose of flying on the business of its sponsoring companies from England to Australia and South Africa, Silver City Airways has, since those days of 1946 and 1947, provided a different, but very valuable, type of service. Since July 1948 the company has been operating its cross-Channel car-ferry service with Bristol Freighters, first on a charter basis and, later, under an associate agreement with BEA.

During 1951 Silver City carried nearly 13,000 vehicles and 30,000 passengers on the Lympne–le Touquet service in its fleet of eight Freighters. In addition, a large number of export cars were carried on this service for the Rootes Group.

Silver City's maintenance base is at Blackbushe. The operational base is Lympne and subsidiary bases are at Le Touquet, Southampton, Cherbourg, Southend and Ostend.

STARWAYS

With its headquarters at Liverpool Airport, Speke, Starways was formed in 1948. On special press work, newspaper and freight carriage, Army co-operation and general charter, the company flew 200,000 miles in 1951. Starways has full maintenance and repair facilities at Speke for its fleet of two Dakotas, two Ansons and one Rapide.

SURREY FLYING SERVICES

The oldest name among independent companies in this country, Surrey Flying Services was originally formed in 1921 and operated from Croydon until the war. It was restarted as an operating company in October 1951 as a subsidiary of Aviation Traders and in association with Fairflight.

With its main base at Blackbushe and with subsidiary bases at Stansted and Southend, Surrey now operates a fleet of six 'heavies' (two Yorks, three Tudor 5s, one Lincoln) and last year carried 509 tons of freight. During the Berlin 'little' airlift last year, sixty-one return flights were made between Hamburg and Berlin.

Overhauls are carried out at the three bases by Aviation Traders. Personnel employed by Surrey Flying Services and all its associated companies numbers 300.

TRANSAIR

Operating from Croydon airport, Transair was formed in 1947 and now concentrates mainly on newspaper and special mail flights. The company at present operates forty-three newspaper services a week to Paris, Brussels and the Channel Islands and twelve mail flights a week to Paris and Brussels; it flew more than 1 million miles during 1951 with its thirteen aircraft, nine Ansons and four Rapides. Transair has full maintenance facilities at Croydon.

TABLE ONE

Revenue Passengers

To 31 March	BOAC	BEA	BSAA	Independent
1946/47	129,928	71,177	6,937	91,000
1947/48	101,901	511,522	13,772	165,882
1948/49	142,404	577,122	21,005	235,230
1949/50	155,557	751,512		330,096
1950/51	200,514	939,586		165,137
1951/52	250,173	1,135,579		207,683

To 31 March	Independent Associate Agreements	Independent Total Charter	BIATA Charter	Airwork Charter	Military Charter
1946/47		91,000			
1947/48		165,882	133,500	32,382	
1948/49		235,230	179,000	56,230	
1949/50	66,000	264,096	203,000	61,096	
1950/51	55,512	109,625	46,699	58,000	4,926
1951/52	74,426	133,257	21,471	58,000	53,786

(Source: Air Corporations, ATAC, BIATA)

TABLE TWO

BEA	Losses	Deficit Grant	Average number of staff
1 April to 31 March			
1946/47	£2,157,937	£2,122,645	4,254
1947/48	£3,573,989	£3,400,000	7,249
1948/49	£2,763,085	£2,150,000	7,145
1949/50	£1,363,594	£1,535,000	6,479
1950/51	£979,267	£1,000,000	7,048
1951/52	£1,423,611	£1,400,000	7,978

BOAC	Losses (Profit)	Deficit Grant	Average number of staff
1 April to 31 March			
1946/47	£7,258,190	£8,076,844	24,464
1947/48	£7,091,430	£6,300,000	21,844
1948/49	£7,805,974	£5,750,000	21,065
1949/50	£7,791,887	£6,350,000	17,340
1950/51	£4,565,428	£6,000,000	16,000
1951/52	(£274,999)	£1,500,000	16,333

TABLE TWO CONTINUED

BSAA	Losses (Profit)		Average number of staff
1 April to 31 March			
1946/47	(£20,507)		1,031
1947/48	£421,481		1,505
1948/49	£1,133,082		2,088

Imperial Airways	Losses (Profit)	Subsidy	Average number of staff
1 April to 31 March			
1937/38	(£296,824)	£535,160	3,000

AAJC/RAS

1 April to 31 January £359,868

1946/47

(Source: BEA, BOAC Annual report and Accounts up to 1952/53)

ENDNOTES

CHAPTER ONE

[1] The King's Speech at the first session of the new Parliament, 1 August 1945.

[2] Thomson and Hunter, *The Nationalized Transport Industries* (Heinemann, 1973), pp.9–12.

[3] Lord Reith, *Into the Wind* (Hodder & Stoughton, 1949), p.327.

[4] Robert Perkins, MP, a founder and vice-president of the British Air Line Pilots' Association.

[5] Lord Reith, House of Lords debate, 6 November 1945.

[6] Hillman's Airways, Spartan Airlines and United Airways. The group took over British Continental Airways on 1 August 1936. Whitehall Securities was the main backer of British Airways, and also controlled two Scottish airlines, Highland Airways and Northern and Scottish Airways. In August 1937 the two latter airlines merged to form a new company, Scottish Airways, with additional backing from the LMS Railway and David MacBrayne, the Scottish shipowners. The banking house of d'Erlanger had an interest through Hillman's Airways, and Gerald d'Erlanger was on the board of British Airways. Whitehall Securities also owned Saunders–Roe, the Isle of Wight-based aircraft manufacturer.

[7] Derek H. Aldcroft *Britain's Internal Airways, Studies in British Transport History 1870–1970* (David and Charles, 1974), p.218.

[8] 'The basic feature of this type of demand is that the customers are willing to adapt their own requirements to some extent to the requirements of other people if this ensures… a lower price for the individual seat. The operators of inclusive tour services and of group charter flights exploit these characteristics of demand by arranging air services in such a way that they maximize the sale of seats and operate at very high load factors. They have no obligation to ensure that space is available for late-comers: their purpose is to see that load factors are maximized in order to give their customers the lowest possible price.' (Cmnd. 4018, *British Air Transport in the Seventies*, HMSO, 1969, para. 224.)

[9] There is a splendid account of this flight in *The Sky Tramps* by Peter Jackson (Souvenir Press, 1965), pp.16–29.

[10] *The Aeroplane*, 12 September 1934.

[11] Aircraft registration marks are the aviation equivalent of a number plate or licence tag. British aircraft carry registration marks beginning with G (for Great Britain), followed by a hyphen and four capitalised letters; you will find registration marks used throughout the text and captions as aircraft identifiers. Occasionally aircraft carry *names* as well.

[12] Other licences were granted but not taken up, including Southern Airways (a Whitney Straight company) and the Hon. Mrs Bruce's Inner Circle Air Lines.

[13] Ministry of Civil Aviation, *Report on the Progress of Civil Aviation 1939–45*.

[14] Seven companies, all with railway connections, comprised the AAJC: Scottish Airways, Railway Air Services, Isle of Man Air Services, West Coast Air Services, Great Western & Southern Air Lines, Air Commerce and Olley Air Service. Jersey and Guernsey Airways operated outside the AAJC and, with the loss of the Channel Islands, continued to fly as a communications unit.

[15] *Aeronautics*, July 1945.

[16] John Longhurst, *Nationalisation in Practice* (Temple Press, 1950), p.69.

[17] *Ibid.*, p.71.

[18] Second British Commonwealth and Empire Lecture, Journal of the Royal Aeronautical Society, October 1946.

[19] The shipping lines were the Royal Mail, Blue Star, Booth Line, Lamport & Holt and Pacific Steam Navigation.

[20] *The Aeroplane*, 20 August 1943.

[21] Air Booking, Air Commerce, British and Foreign Aviation,★ Channel Air Ferries, Channel Islands Airways,★ Great Western and Southern Air Lines, Guernsey Airways, Highland Airways, Isle of Man Air Services, Jersey Airways, Olley Air Service, Railway Air Services, Scottish Airways, West Coast Air Services, West Coast Airways (Holdings)★ and Western Isles Airways. ★ denotes holding companies.

[22] HMSO, Cmnd. 6605.

[23] Longhurst, p.77.

[24] On 1 September 1945 the two airlines were officially renamed Channel Islands Airways.

CHAPTER 2

[1] Quoted in Michael Bonavia, *The Nationalisation of British Transport* (St Martin's Press, 1987), p.3.

[2] Many stalwart Labour councils owned their own municipal bus companies and were opposed to the idea of handing them over. Furthermore there was to be partial *de facto* nationalisation; the railway companies and electricity companies already owned or participated financially in a number of bus companies and the British Transport Commission subsequently negotiated the purchase of a number of bus groups including the Tilling Group, Scottish Motor Traction and the Red and White Group.

[3] Quoted in *International Aviation*, Vol.3, No.10, 7 December 1945.

[4] Captain E.E. Fresson, *Air Road to the Isles* (David Rendel, 1967), p.227.

[5] *Flight*, 27 December 1945.

[6] *Flight*, 27 June 1946.

[7] *Air Transport*, May 1946.

[8] *Flight*, 4 July 1946.

[9] *The Aeroplane*, 21 March 1947.

[10] *Aeronautics*, 19 August 1949.

[11] *Aeronautics*, January 1949.

[12] Longhurst, pp.109–110.

[13] A.S. Jackson, *Pathfinder Bennett, Airman Extraordinary* (Terence Dalton, 1991), chap.9.

[14] BOAC never used the Tudor in commercial service, but three were delivered and used for crew training.

[15] Third and fourth freedom rights allow an airline to carry passengers and freight between its country of registration and another country. Fifth freedom rights allow that airline to carry passengers and freight between two countries, neither of which is that airline's country of registration. For example, third freedom rights allowed Pan American to carry passengers from the USA to the UK, and fourth freedom rights allowed them to pick up passengers in the UK for travel to the USA. But fifth freedom rights would also allow Pan American to carry passengers from the UK to another country, say Germany.

[16] House of Lords debate, 3 November 1948.

[17] And, it has to be said, of civil aviation. As Colonel Douglas he was an early pioneer, flying for Handley Page in 1919.

[18] Longhurst, p.106.

[19] Sir Miles Thomas, *Out on a Wing* (Michael Joseph, 1964), p.287.

[20] *Ibid.*, p.265.

[21] Derek H. Aldcroft, *The British Economy, Volume 1* (Humanities Press International, 1986), and Alfred F. Havighurst, *Britain in Transition* (The University of Chicago Press, 1979).

[22] Bonavia, p.88.

[23] TNA BT217/662.

[24] TNA, *ibid.*

CHAPTER 3

[1] Longhurst, p.143.

[2] HMSO: Civil Aviation Report, 1946 and 1947.

[3] *Air Transport and Airport Engineering*, November 1947.

[4] TNA T230/3.

[5] Edited by J. Parker van Zandt and published by the Aviation Research Institute, Washington, DC.

[6] *The Aeroplane*, 9 July 1948.

[7] British Midland operated Dakotas from East Midlands and Birmingham up until the end of the 1967 summer season.

[8] *Flight*, 16 May 1946.

[9] Colin Cruddas, *In Cobham's Company* (Cobham plc, 1994), p.82.

[10] *The Aeroplane*, 24 May 1946.

[11] TNA BT217/2172.

[12] W.C.G. Cribbett. An important and influential government official in the history of post-war aviation, he was Deputy Secretary at the Ministry of Civil Aviation 1946–1956, before becoming deputy chairman of BOAC.

[13] TNA BT217/321.

[14] *Ibid.*

[15] *Ibid.*

[16] *Ibid.*

[17] *Aeronautics*, March 1948.

[18] There is a more detailed account in Appendix 4.

[19] *The Aeroplane*, 18 July 1947.

[20] *The Aeroplane*, 4 June 1948.

[21] Air Commodore 'Taffy' Powell, *Ferryman, from Ferry Command to Silver City* (Airlife, 1982), pp.142–143.

[22] *Aeronautics*, September 1947.

[23] *Flight*, 30 January 1948.

[24] *The Aeroplane*, 31 December 1948.

[25] TNA TS52/26.

[26] *The Aeroplane*, 31 December 1948.

[27] TNA AIR 19/781.

[28] Tony Merton Jones, *British Independent Airlines since 1946, Volume 2* (Merseyside Aviation Society and LAAS International, 1976), p.217; *The Aeroplane*, 18 March 1948.

[29] TNA TS52/27.

[30] *The Aeroplane*, 25 February 1949.

[31] In her autobiography, *Nine Lives Plus*, the glamorous Mrs Bruce is somewhat diffident about her life as a bus builder.

CHAPTER 4

[1] Excludes the corporations: BSAA was a substantial contributor, with 2,562 sorties.

[2] Robert Jackson, *The Berlin Airlift* (Patrick Stephens, 1988), p.19.

[3] Sir Frank Roberts, *Dealing with Dictators* (Weidenfeld & Nicolson, 1991), p.133.

[4] Originally the British operation was code-named 'Carter Paterson' after a well-known removals firm, but the name had unfortunate connotations; the Airlift was supposed to be bringing supplies in, not removing them, so in July it was changed to 'Plainfare'.

[5] BEA Report and Accounts 1948/9.

[6] *Propliner*, No.60.

[7] Hammond Innes, *Air Bridge* (Collins, 1951), pp.140–145.

[8] TNA AIR2/10573.

[9] *The Aeroplane*, 4 March 1949.

[10] Jackson, p.142.

[11] TNA AIR2/10573.

[12] *Ibid*.

[13] *Flight* magazine, 28 July 1949.

[14] *The Aeroplane*, 8 July 1949.

CHAPTER 5

[1] Ministry of Civil Aviation, *Report on the Progress of Civil Aviation 1939–45*.

[2] The Tudor was derived from the Avro Lincoln, known originally as the Lancaster IV.

[3] Longhurst, p.159.

[4] Peter Brooks, *The Modern Airliner* (Sunflower University Press, 1982), pp.93–94.

[5] R.E.G. Davies, *A History of the World's Airlines* (Oxford University Press, 1964), p.452.

[6] Brooks, pp.122–23.

[7] *Progress of Civil Aviation*, op. cit.

[8] 'The Status of Civil Aviation in 1946', Royal Aeronautical Society, Second British Commonwealth and Empire Lecture, delivered by Sir Henry Self, 25 September 1946. He also noted that there were forty-one aircraft used for training purposes and four 'employed on development flights'.

[9] *The Aeroplane*, 14 November 1947.

[10] Qantas Empire Airways, which also bought Empire boats, was a joint venture with Imperial Airways.

[11] TNA T230/3.

[12] *Air Transport*, January 1946.

[13] TNA BT217/662.

[14] TNA BT217/1924.

[15] HMSO Cmnd. 7307, 7478.

[16] *Flight*, March 6 1947.

[17] Longhurst, p.95.

[18] Brooks, pp.118–19.

CHAPTER 6

1. *Flight*, 20 June 1946.
2. Longhurst, p.103. Not all Scottish pioneers were so unlucky, however; Captain Eric Starling, former chief pilot with Allied Airways (Gandar Dower), went on to have a successful career as BEA's flight manager in Scotland up until 1968.
3. *Flight*, 27 May 1948.
4. *The Aeroplane*, 28 May 1948.
5. TNA BT245/103.
6. Associated Airways Joint Committee, in practice the railway-owned domestic airlines.
7. The Civil Aviation (Air Transport Advisory Council) Order 1947 gave the ATAC the duty to consider, first, any representations from the public about facilities provided by the corporations and the charges made for them, and secondly, any questions concerning air transport which the minister might refer to it. It was under this second category that associate agreements were recommended.
8. *Flight*, 3 February 1949.
9. Tony Merton Jones's invaluable *British Independent Airlines since 1946* provided the confirmation of those services flown, as opposed to approved.
10. Formed from an amalgamation of Mannin Airways and Ulster Aviation.
11. Z, or Zulu time, is the same as Greenwich Mean Time (GMT).
12. *Flight*, 6 January 1949.
13. Brigadier General Critchley, *Critch!* (Hutchinson, 1961), p.233. General Critchley became blind two years later and writes movingly about how he adjusted to, and overcame, this handicap.
14. TNA AIR 19/781.
15. Quoted in *Flight* magazine, 8 December 1949.
16. *Flight*, 1 September 1949.
17. 'Commentator' in *The Aeroplane*, 3 June 1949.

CHAPTER 7

[1] TNA AIR 19/781 shows that unserviceability of the Hastings frequently accounted for 50 per cent of the aircraft strength.

[2] *The Aeroplane*, 18 November 1949.

[3] TNA BT245/102.

[4] *Ibid*.

[5] TNA AIR 19/781. Although the Melville Committee and Report appear in other files, this is the most comprehensive. Unless otherwise stated, quotations are from this document.

[6] The very modest title conceals the fact that Sir James Barnes was the most senior civil servant at the Air Ministry.

[7] TNA BT245/102.

[8] *The Aeroplane*, 19 January 1951.

[9] TNA BT245/102.

[10] *Ibid*.

[11] TNA FO371/80505.

[12] *The Aeroplane*, 15 June 1951.

[13] Military version of the Vickers Viking.

[14] TNA AIR 20/7419.

CHAPTER 8

[1] Aldcroft, *British Economy*, pp.221–23.

[2] *The Aeroplane*, 7 April 1950.

[3] *Flight*, 18 January 1951.

[4] *The Times*, 19 October 1973.

[5] *The Aeroplane*, 11 November 1949.

[6] House of Commons debate, 13 December 1949, quoted in *Aeronautics*.

[7] *The Aeroplane*, 14 July 1950.

[8] TNA TS 52/27.

[9] Quoted in *The Aeroplane*, 21 January 1965.

[10] *Air-Britain Digest*, winter 1990.

[11] *The Aeroplane*, 15 December 1950.

[12] *The Aeroplane*, 22 December 1950.

[13] Down from 30 per cent in 1930. Derek Aldcroft, *British Transport since 1914* (David & Charles, 1975), p.234.

[14] Roger Elgin and Berry Ritchie, *Fly me, I'm Freddie* (Weidenfeld & Nicolson, 1980), pp.21–23.

[15] *Flight*, 11 May 1951.

[16] *The Aeroplane*, 29 June 1951.

[17] *Aeronautics*, October 1951.

[18] Later British Petroleum (BP).

[19] *The Aeroplane*, 31 August 1951.

[20] *Flight*, 18 January 1952.

[21] Anglo–Iranian managed to persuade the other consortium companies to compensate it for the loss of its Iranian assets!

[22] Quoted in *Flight* magazine, 16 November 1951.

[23] *The Aeroplane*, 9 February 1951.

APPENDIX 1

[1] The sources for this appendix include *Jane's*, *British Civil Aviation* by D.G.T. Harvey, *British Commercial Aircraft* by Paul Ellis, *De Havilland Aircraft since 1909* by A.J. Jackson, *The World's Airliners* by Peter Brooks, the Putnam series *British Civil Aircraft*, John Stroud's articles over the years in *Aeroplane Monthly*.

[2] Sir Robert Wall, *Brabazon* (Redcliffe Press, 1999), p.7.

[3] *Bristol Aircraft* (Putnams).

[4] *Propliner* magazine, issue No.57, 1993.

[5] The Hermes was briefly reintroduced into BOAC service in 1954, for six months, following the grounding of the *Comet* fleet.

[6] *Aeroplane Monthly*, April 1995.

[7] Peter London, *Saunders Roe and Saro aircraft since 1917* (Putnams, 1981), p.212.

APPENDIX 2

[1] Compiled largely from the annual editions of *Aeroplane Directory*, published by Temple Press.

[2] Quoted in *Flight*, 12 July 1962.

APPENDIX 4

[1] *Aeroplane*, 28 May 1948.

[2] TNA, BT217/2172.

[3] TNA, *ibid*.

[4] TNA, *ibid*.

[5] TNA, *ibid*.

[6] *Aeroplane*, 25 March 1949.

BIBLIOGRAPHY

Aldcroft, Derek H., *British Transport* (Leicester University Press, 1971)
Aldcroft, Derek H., *Studies in British Transport History 1870–1970* (David & Charles, 1974)
Aldcroft, Derek H., *British Transport since 1914* (David & Charles, 1975)
Aldcroft, Derek H., *The British Economy Vol. 1, 1920–1951* (Humanities Press, 1986)

Balfour, Christopher, *Spithead Express* (Magna Press, Leatherhead, 1999)
Behrend, George, *Jersey Airlines International* (Jersey Artists, 1968)
Behrend, George, *Channel Silver Wings* (Jersey Artists, 1972)
Bingham, Victor F., *Handley Page Hastings & Hermes* (GMS Enterprises, 1998)
Bonavia, Michael, *The Nationalisation of British Transport* (St Martin's Press, 1987)
Brabazon, (Lord), *Air Transport & Civil Aviation 1944–45* (Todd Publishing, 1945)
Bramson, Alan, *Master Airman (Donald Bennett)* (Airlife, 1985)
Brooks, Peter, *The Modern Airliner* (Sunflower University Press, 1961)
Brooks, Peter, *The World's Airliners* (Putnam, 1962)
Bruce, Mrs Victor, *Nine Lives Plus* (Pelham Books, London, 1977)

Clegg, Peter, *Wings over the Glens* (GMS Enterprises, 1995)
Cluett, Douglas, *Croydon Airport 1928-1939* (London Borough of Sutton, 1980)
Commercial Motor, *Air Transport Manual* (Temple Press, 1934)
Cooper, John C., *Some Historic Phases of British Aviation Policy* (Unknown, 1946)
Corbett, David, *Politics and the Airlines* (George Allen & Unwin, 1965)
Cramp, B.G., *British Midland Airways* (Airlife, 1979)
Critchley, A.C., *Critch!* (Hutchinson, London, 1961)
Cruddas, Colin, *In Cobham's Company* (Cobham plc, 1994)

Davies, R.E.G., *A History of the World's Airlines* (Oxford University Press, 1964)
Davies, R.E.G., *Rebels and Reformers of the Airways* (Smithsonian, Washington, 1987)
Davies, R.E.G., *De Havilland Comet* (Paladwr Press, 1990)
de Havilland, Geoffrey, *Sky Fever* (Airlife, 1979)
Dobson, Alan P., *Peaceful Air Warfare* (Clarendon Press, Oxford, 1991)
Doganis, Rigas, *Flying Off Course* (George Allen & Unwin, 1985)
Doyle, Neville, *From Sea-Eagle to Flamingo* (self published, 1991)
Doyle, Neville, *The Triple Alliance* (Air-Britain (Historians), 2002)
Dyos, H.J., *British Transport:* see also under Aldcroft (Leicester University Press, 1971)

Eastwood, A.B., *Piston Engine Airliner Production List* (The Aviation Hobby Shop, 1996)
Eastwood, A.B., *Turbo Prop Airliner Production List* (The Aviation Hobby Shop, 1996)
Eglin, Roger, *Fly Me, I'm Freddie* (Weidenfeld & Nicolson, London, 1980)
Ellis, Paul, *British Commercial Aircraft* (Jane's Publishing, 1980)

Fresson, E.E., *Air Road to the Isles* (David Rendel, 1967)

Gradidge, J.M.G., *The Douglas DC-3 and its predecessors* (Air-Britain (Historians), 1984)
Grey, C.G., *History of the Air Ministry* (George Allen & Unwin, 1940)

Havighurst, Alfred F., *Britain in Transition, the 20th Century* (University of Chicago Press, 1979)
Hayward, Keith, *Government and British civil aerospace* (Manchester University Press, 1983)
Hedges, David, *The Eagle Years 1948-1968* (The Aviation Hobby Shop, 2002)
Higham, Robin, *Britain's Imperial Air Routes 1918 to 1939* (G.T. Foulis, 1960)
Hooks, Mike, *Croydon Airport* (Chalford, 1997)

Jackson, A.J., *British Civil Aircraft 1919-1972 Vol. 1* (Putnam, 1959)
Jackson, A.J., *British Civil Aircraft 1919-1972 Vol. 2* (Putnam, 1960)
Jackson, A.J., *British Civil Aircraft 1919-1972 Vol. 3* (Putnam, 1960)
Jackson, A.J., *De Havilland Aircraft since 1909* (Putnam, 1962)
Jackson, Peter, *The Sky Tramps* (Souvenir Press, London, 1965)
Jackson, Robert, *The Berlin Airlift* (Patrick Stephens, Wellingborough, 1988)
Jenkins, Gilmour, *The Ministry of Transport and Civil Aviation* (George Allen & Unwin, 1959)
Jones, David, *The Time Shrinkers* (David Rendel, 1971)

Kelf-Cohen, R., *Twenty Years of Nationalisation* (Macmillan, 1969)
Kniveton, Gordon N., *Manx Aviation in War and Peace* (The Manx Experience, 1985)
Kniveton, Gordon N., *Wings of Mann* (The Manx Experience, 1997)

Longhurst, John, *Nationalisation in Practice* (Temple Press, 1950)

Martin, Bernard, *The Viking, Valetta and Varsity* (Air-Britain (Historians), 1975)
Merton Jones, Tony, *British Independent Airlines 1946-1976* (The Aviation Hobby Shop, 2000)
Middleton, D.H., *Airspeed* (Terence Dalton Lavenham, 1982)
Newberry, Peter, *The Vectis Connection* (Waterfront, 2001)

Olley, Gordon, *A Million Miles in the Air* (Hodder and Stoughton, London, 1934)

Payne, L.G.S., *Air Dates* (Heinemann London, 1957)
Penrose, Harald, *British Aviation – Ominous Skies 1935-1939* (HMSO, 1980)

Penrose, Harald, *Wings across the world* (Cassell, London, 1980)

Pereira, Harold B., *Aircraft Badges and Markings* (Adlard Coles, 1955)

Powell, Taffy, *Ferryman, from Ferry Command to Silver City* (Airlife, 1982)

Provan with R.E.G. Davies, John, *Berlin Airlift, the Effort and the Aircraft* (Paladwr Press, 1998)

Pudney, John, *The Seven Skies* (Putnam, 1959)

Raitz, Vladimir, *Flight to the Sun* (with Roger Bray) (Continuum, London and New York, 2001)

Sampson, Anthony, *Empires of the Sky* (Hodder and Stoughton London, 1984)

Sherwood, Tim, *Coming in to Land* (Hounslow Library, Heritage Publications, 1999)

Simons, Graham M., *De Havilland DH89 Dragon Rapide* (Ian Allan, 1986)

Simons, Graham M., *Western Airways* (Redcliffe Press, 1988)

Smith, Myron J., *The Airline Bibliography – Salem College Guide to Sources* (Locust Hill Press, 1988)

Standon, T.G., Tommy, *History of Cambrian Airways* (Airline Publications & Sales Ltd, 1979)

Sterling, Chris, *Commercial Air Transport Books* (Paladwr Press, 1996)

Sterling, Chris, *Commercial Air Transport Books Supplement* (Paladwr Press, 1998)

Stroud, John, *Annals of British & Commonwealth Air Transport* (Putnam, 1962)

Stroud, John, *Railway Air Services* (Ian Allan, 1987)

Taylor, J.W.R., *Civil Aircraft Markings* (Ian Allan (annual publication from 1950))

The Aeroplane, Who's Who in British Aviation (Temple Press, 1947)

The Aeroplane, Directory of British Aviation (*Temple Press* (annual publication))

Thetford, Owen G., *ABC of Airports and Airliners* (Ian Allan, 1948)

Thomas, Miles, *Out on a Wing* (Michael Joseph, 1964)

Tusa, Ann and John, *The Berlin Airlift* (Spellmount, Staplehurst, 1988)

Wall, Robert, *Brabazon, the World's First Jumbo Airliner* (Redcliffe Press, 1999)

Wheatcroft, Stephen, *The Economics of European Air Transport* (Harvard University Press, MA, 1956)

Wheatcroft, Stephen, *Air Transport Policy* (Michael Joseph, 1964)

Wynn, W.E., *Civil Air Transport* (Hutchinson, London, 1946)

ARTICLES AND HMSO

Air Ministry, 'Civil Aviation Statistical and Technical Review 1937' (HMSO, 1938)

Air Ministry, 'Report on the progress of civil aviation' (annual) (HMSO)

ATAC, 'Report of the Air Transport Advisory Council' (annual) (HMSO)

BEA, 'Report and Accounts' (annual) (HMSO)

BIATA, 'Annual Reports British Independent Air Transport Association' (1951/52)

BOAC, 'Report and Accounts' (annual) (HMSO)

Brooks, Peter W., 'The Development of Air Transport' (Transport Economics and Policy, 1967)

Brooks, Peter W., 'Problems of Short-Haul Air Transport' (Royal Aeronautical Society, 1952)

Cadman, Lord, 'Committee of Inquiry into Civil Aviation Cmd. 5685' (HMSO, 1938)

Cribbett, George, 'Some International Aspects of Air Transport' (Royal Aeronautical Society, 1950)

Greig, L.T.H., 'The Economics of Air Line Operation' (Royal Aeronautical Society, 1936)

Humphreys, B.K., 'Nationalisation and the independent airlines' (Journal of Transport History, 1976)

Humphreys, B.K., 'Trooping and British independent airlines' (Journal of Transport History, 1979)

Lyth, Peter J., 'A Multiplicity of Instruments' (Journal of Transport History, 1990)

Merer, J.W.F., 'The Berlin Air Lift' (Royal Aeronautical Society, 1950)

Minister of Civil Aviation, 'British Air Transport March 1945 Cmd. 6605' (HMSO, 1945)

Minister of Civil Aviation, 'British Air Services December 1945 Cmd. 6712' (HMSO, 1945)

Minister of Civil Aviation, 'International Civil Aviation Conference, Chicago Cmd 6614' (HMSO, 1944)

Minister of Civil Aviation, 'Bermuda Agreement between USA/UK Cmd 6747' (HMSO, 1946)

Minister of Civil Aviation, 'Civil Aviation Bill (Bill 99) 2 April 1946' (HMSO, 1946)

Ministry of Civil Aviation, 'Report on the progress of civil aviation 1939-45' (unpublished, 1945)

Ministry of Civil Aviation, 'Civil Aviation Report 1946 and 1947' (HMSO, 1948)

Ministry of Information, 'Merchant Airmen' (HMSO, 1946)

Self, Henry, 'The Status of Civil Aviation in 1946' (Royal Aeronautical Society, 1946)

MAGAZINES

Aeronautical Quarterly (RAeS)
Aeronautics
The Aeroplane
Airline Record (1st and 2nd Edition)
Air Enthusiast
Air Pictorial
Air-Britain Digest
Aircraft
Aircraft Illustrated
Airlift
De Havilland Gazette
Esso World
Fisons World
Flight
Flight International
Institute of Transport Journal
Interavia, Journal of the Royal Aeronautical Society (RAeS)
Journal of Transport Economics and Policy
Journal of Transport History
Modern Transport
Propliner
Shell Aviation News
World Aviation Annual 1948

THE NATIONAL ARCHIVES

Air Ministry, AIR 2/10573, 19/781, 20/7419
Ministry of Civil Aviation, BT 217/321, 217/662, 217/1924, 217/2172, 245/102, 245/103
Foreign Office, FO 371/80505
Treasury, T 220/268, 230/3
Treasury Solicitor, TS 52/26, 52/27

INDEX

If you are interested in purchasing other books published by Tempus,
or in case you have difficulty finding any Tempus books in your local bookshop,
you can also place orders directly through our website

www.tempus-publishing.com